International
IT
Governance

International IT Governance

AN EXECUTIVE GUIDE TO ISO 17799 / ISO 27001

Alan Calder & Steve Watkins

KOGAN
PAGE

London and Philadelphia

Publisher's note

Every possible effort has been made to ensure that the information contained in this book is accurate at the time of going to press, and the publishers and authors cannot accept responsibility for any errors or omissions, however caused. No responsibility for loss or damage occasioned to any person acting, or refraining from action, as a result of the material in this publication can be accepted by the editor, the publisher or any of the authors.

First published in Great Britain and the United States in 2006 by Kogan Page Limited

120 Pentonville Road
London N1 9JN
United Kingdom
www.kogan-page.co.uk

525 South 4th Street, #241
Philadelphia PA 19147
USA

© Alan Calder and Steve Watkins, 2006

The right of Alan Calder and Steve Watkins to be identified as the authors of this work has been asserted by them in accordance with the Copyright, Designs and Patents Act 1988.

ISBN 0 7494 4748 6

British Library Cataloguing-in-Publication Data

A CIP record for this book is available from the British Library.

Library of Congress Cataloging-in-Publication Data

Calder, Alan, 1957-
    International IT governance : an executive guide to ISO 17799/ ISO 27001 / Alan Calder, Steve Watkins. — 1st ed.
        p. cm.
    Includes index.
    ISBN 0-7494-4748-6
    1. Computer security. 2. Data protection. 3. Business enterprises–Computer networks—Security measures. I. Watkins, Steve, 1970- II. Title.
QA76.9.A25C34189 2006
005.8—dc22
                                                        2006007942

Typeset by Digital Publishing Solutions
Printed and bound in the United States by Thomson-Shore, Inc

Contents

How to use this book

This book was designed, and is intended to be used, as a dual analogue and digital resource. The speed of evolution in computing and of the internet means that any book on IT governance and information security starts going out of date fairly quickly. We wanted to be sure that our readers would be able to access information that was as up to date as possible and the reader should therefore assume that the digital companion to this book, the KnowledgeBank, is essential and that it should be used for up-to-date information.

This updated information is available only to people who have purchased a physical, analogue copy of the book and can be accessed by going to www.27001.com, which will provide a link to the KnowledgeBank that supports the book; type the unique user number that is supplied with this book into the KnowledgeBank log-on box. This will enable the reader to access a free six-month subscription to the update services of the website, with a low-cost option to renew the subscription thereafter.

The fact that we were setting up an online component to the book, providing updated security and compliance information, also enabled us to extend the reach of the book. The main website therefore provides extensive information on IT governance practices and procedures, while the book continues to focus on the information security aspect of IT governance. The reader is also now able to access a number of additional services, including a full range of templates (for both forms and procedures) that tie in to the guidance provided in the book, as well as information, alert services and mentoring services that are designed to help readers of the book optimize their IT governance or information security projects. Full information is available on the website.

Acknowledgments

While this book primarily reflects our own experience in, and approach to, information security, it has been immeasurably improved through the contributions of the following, whom we would like hereby to acknowledge and thank: DNV Certification, in the UK, who have reviewed and commented (from the perspective of a certification body) on the core chapters on information security policy, risk assessment and statement of applicability; and Olga Travlos of Xanthos Internet Consultants for her input into the development of the online component of this book.

Introduction

This book on IT governance and information security is a key resource for forward-looking executives and managers in 21st-century organizations of all sizes. There are five reasons for this:

1. The development of IT governance, which recognizes the "information economy"-driven convergence between business management and IT management, makes it essential for executives and managers at all levels in organizations of all sizes to understand how decisions about information technology in the organization should be made and monitored and, in particular, how information security risks are best dealt with.

2. Legislation and regulation is a big issue. In the United States, the Sarbanes–Oxley Act and the COSO frameworks on internal control and risk management give directors of listed companies a clear responsibility to act on IT governance, on the effective management of risk in IT projects and on computer security. Banks and financial sector organizations are subject to the requirements of the Bank of International Settlements (BIS) and the Basel 2 framework, particularly around operational risk—which absolutely includes information and IT risk. Privacy

regulations, including, for instance, GLBA, HIPAA, Senate Bill 1386 and Canada's PIPEDA, and the challenge of delivering IT projects on time, to specification and to budget also affect private and public sector organizations throughout the world.

3. As the intellectual capital value of "information economy" organizations increases, their commercial viability and profitability—as well as their stock price—increasingly depend on the security, confidentiality and integrity of their information and information assets.
4. The dramatic growth and scale of the "information economy" has created new, global threats and vulnerabilities for all networked organizations.
5. The launch of ISO/IEC 27001 makes a single, global standard of information security best practice available. While ISO/IEC 17799 has been in existence for some time (and has recently been updated to contain the latest international best practice), the publication of ISO/IEC 27001 provides an international standard against which any company in the world can seek external certification. Compliance with this standard should enable executives and board members to demonstrate a proper response—to stockholders and customers as well as to regulatory and judicial authorities—to all the challenges identified above.

The information economy

Faced with the emergence and speed of growth in the information economy, organizations have an urgent need to adopt IT governance best practice. The main drivers of the information economy are:

- the globalization of markets, products and resourcing (including "offshoring");
- electronic information and knowledge intensity; and
- the geometric increase in the level of electronic networking and connectivity.

The key characteristics of the global information economy, which affect all organizations, are:

- Unlike the industrial economy, information and knowledge are not depleting resources that have to be rationed and protected.

- Protecting knowledge is less obviously beneficial than previously: sharing knowledge actually drives innovation, and innovation drives competitiveness.
- The effect of geographic location is diminished; virtual organizations operate around the clock in virtual marketplaces that have no geographic boundaries.
- As knowledge shifts to low-tax, low-regulation environments, laws and taxes are increasingly difficult to apply on a solely national basis.
- Knowledge-enhanced products command price premiums.
- Captured, indexed and accessible knowledge has greater intrinsic value than knowledge that goes home at the end of every day.
- Intellectual capital is an increasingly significant part of stockholder value in every organization.

The challenges, demands and risks faced by organizations operating in this information-rich and technologically intensive environment require a proper response. In the corporate governance climate of the early 21st century, with its growing demand for stockholder rights, corporate transparency and board accountability, this response must be a governance one.

What is IT governance?

The OECD, in its *The Principles of Corporate Governance* (1999) defined "corporate governance" as "the system by which business corporations are directed and controlled." Every country in the OECD is evolving—at a different speed—its own corporate governance regime, reflecting its own culture and requirements. Within its overall approach to corporate governance, every organization has to determine how it will govern the information, information assets and information technology on which its business model and business strategy rely. This need has led to the emergence of IT governance as a specific—and pervasively important—component of an organization's total governance posture.

We define IT governance as "the framework for the leadership, organizational structures and business processes, standards and compliance to these standards, which ensures that the organization's information systems support and enable the achievement of its strategies and objectives."

There are five specific drivers for organizations to adopt IT governance strategies:

■ the requirements, for US-listed companies, of Sarbanes–Oxley; for banks and financial institutions, of BIS and Basel 2; and, for businesses everywhere, the requirements of their local corporate governance regimes, all of which have an explicit requirement for boards to manage, on behalf of stockholders, the business risks;

■ the increasing intellectual capital value that the organization has at risk;

■ the need to align technology projects with strategic organizational goals and to ensure that they deliver planned value;

■ the proliferation of (increasingly complex) threats to information and information security, with consequent potential impacts on corporate reputation, revenue and profitability;

■ the increase in the compliance requirements of (increasingly conflicting and punitive) information- and privacy-related regulation.

There are two fundamental components of effective management of risk in information and information technology. The first relates to an organization's strategic deployment of information technology in order to achieve its corporate goals. IT projects often represent significant investments of financial and executive resources. Stockholders' interest in the effectiveness of such deployment should be reflected in the transparency with which they are planned, managed and measured, and the way in which risks are assessed and controlled. The second component is the way in which the risks associated with information assets themselves are managed.

Clearly, well-managed information technology is a business enabler. All directors, executives and managers, at every level in any organization of any size, need to understand how to ensure that their investments in information and information technology enable the business. *Every* deployment of information technology brings with it immediate risks to the organization and, therefore, every director or executive who deploys, or manager who makes any use of, information technology needs to understand these risks and the steps that should be taken to counter them. This book deals with IT governance from the perspective of the director, executive or business manager, rather than from that of the IT specialist. Governance structures, processes and emerging best practice are all dealt with through the KnowledgeBank, while the hard-copy component of this book deals primarily with the strategic and operational aspects of information security.

Information security

The proliferation of increasingly complex, sophisticated and global threats to information security, in combination with the compliance requirements of a flood of computer- and privacy-related regulation around the world, is driving organizations to take a more strategic view of information security. It has become clear that hardware-, software- or vendor-driven solutions to individual information security challenges are, on their own, dangerously inadequate.

While most organizations believe that their information systems are secure, the brutal reality is that they are not. Not only is it extremely difficult for an organization to operate in today's world without effective information security, but such organizations have become threats to their more responsible brethren. The extent and value of electronic data are continuing to grow exponentially. The exposure of businesses and individuals to its misappropriation (particularly in electronic format) or destruction is also growing very quickly. Ultimately, consumer confidence in dealing across the web depends on how secure they believe their personal data to be. Information security, for this reason, matters to any business with any form of web strategy (and any business without a web strategy is unlikely to be around in the long term), from simple business-to-consumer (b2c) or business-to-business (b2b) propositions through enterprise resource planning (ERP) systems to the use of extranets and e-mail. It matters, too, to any organization that depends on computers for its day-to-day existence or that may be subject to the provisions of information privacy and protection regulations.

Newspapers and business or sector magazines are full of stories about hackers, viruses and online fraud. These are just the public tip of the data insecurity iceberg. Little tends to be heard about corporations that suffer profit fluctuations through computer failure, or businesses that fail to survive a major interruption to their data and operating systems. Even less is heard about organizations whose core operations are compromised by the theft or loss of key business data, but who somehow survive it.

Many people do, however, experience the frustration of trying to buy something online, only for the screen to give some variant of the message "server not available." Many more, working with computers in their daily lives, have experienced (once too) many times a local network failure or outage that interrupts their work. With the increasing pervasiveness of computers and as hardware/software computing packages become ever more powerful and complex, so the opportunity for data and data systems to be compromised or corrupted (knowingly or otherwise) will increase.

Information security management systems in the vast majority of organizations are, in real terms, non-existent and, even where systems have been designed and implemented, they are usually inadequate. In simple terms, larger organizations tend to operate their security functions in vertically segregated silos with little or no coordination. This structural weakness means that most organizations have significant vulnerabilities that can be exploited deliberately or that simply open them up to disaster. For instance, while corporate counsel may tackle all the legal issues (non-disclosure agreements, patents, contracts, etc.) they will have little involvement with the data security issues faced on the organizational perimeter. On the organizational perimeter, those dealing with physical security concentrate almost exclusively on physical assets, such as gates or doors, security guards and burglar alarms. They have little appreciation of, or impact upon, the "cyber" perimeter.

The IT managers, responsible for the cyber perimeter, may be good at ensuring that everyone has a password, and that there is internet connectivity, that the organization is able to respond to virus threats, and that key partners, customers and suppliers are able to deal electronically with the organization, but they almost universally lack the training, experience or exposure adequately to address the strategic threat to the information assets of the organization as a whole. There are even organizations where the CIO or IT executives set and implement security policy for the organization on the basis of their own risk assessment, past experiences and interests, with little regard for the real needs or strategic objectives of the organization.

Information security is a complex issue and deals with the confidentiality, integrity and availability of data. IT governance is even more complex and, in information security terms, one has to think in terms of the whole enterprise, the entire organization, which includes all the possible combinations of physical and cyber assets, all the possible combinations of intranets, extranets and internets, and which might include an extended network of business partners, vendors, customers and others. This handbook guides the interested business person through this maze of issues, through the process of implementing internationally recognized best practice in information security, as captured in ISO/IEC 17799:2005, and, finally, achieving certification to ISO/IEC 27001:2005, the first formal international standard for effective information security management.

ISO/IEC 27001, the information security management system (ISMS) standard, is not restricted to a specific sector (e.g. the DOD or the software industry), nor is it restricted to any specific range of products or processes. This book covers many aspects of data security, providing sufficient information for the reader to understand the major data security issues, what to do about them and, above all, what steps and systems are necessary for the achievement of independent certification of the organization's information security management system to ISO/IEC 27001:2005.

This book is of particular benefit to board members, directors, executives, owners and managers of any corporation or organization that depends on information, that uses computers on a regular basis or that has an internet aspect to its strategy. It can equally apply to any organization that relies on the confidentiality, integrity and availability of its data. It is directed at readers who either have no prior understanding of data security or whose understanding is limited in interest, scope or depth. It is not written for technology or security specialists, whose knowledge of specific issues should always be sought by the concerned owner, executive or manager. While it deals with technology issues, it is not a technological book.

Information security is a key component of IT governance. As information technology and information itself become more and more the strategic enablers of organizational activity, so the effective management of both IT and information assets becomes a critical strategic concern for boards of directors. This book will enable directors, executives and business managers in organizations and enterprises of all sizes to ensure that their IT security strategies are coordinated, coherent, comprehensive and cost-effective, and meet their specific organizational or business needs. While this edition of the book is written primarily for US organizations, its lessons are relevant internationally, as computers and data threats are internationally similar. Again, while the book is written primarily with a Microsoft environment in mind (reflecting the penetration of the Microsoft suite of products into corporate environments), its principles apply to all hardware and software environments; ISO/IEC 27001 and ISO/IEC 17799 are, themselves, system-agnostic.

While the hard copy of this book does not contain a whole suite of draft ISO/IEC 27001 process and procedure templates that are designed for implementation by any organization after minimal adaptation, the website (www.27001.com) provides access to a toolkit of such templates. Use of these templates, which are not industry- specific but which do integrate absolutely with the advice in this book, can speed knowledge acquisition and ensure that process development is comprehensive and systematic.

Organizations should, however, always ensure that any processes they implement are appropriate and tailored for their own environment. There are four reasons for this:

- Policies, processes and procedures should always be drafted in the style, and to reflect the culture, of the organization that is going to use them. This will help their acceptance within the organization.
- The processes and procedures that are adopted should reflect the risk assessment carried out by the organization's specialist security adviser. While some risks are common to many organizations, the approach to controlling them should be appropriate to, and cost-effective for, the individual organization and its individual objectives and operating environment.
- It is important that the organization understands, in detail, its policies, processes and procedures. It will have to review them after any significant security incident and at least once a year. The best way to understand them thoroughly is to do the detailed drafting in the first place.
- Most importantly, the threats to an organization's information security are evolving as fast as the information technology that supports it. It is essential that security processes and procedures are completely up to date, that they reflect current risks and that, in particular, current technological advice is taken, to build on the substantial groundwork laid in this book.

This book will certainly provide enough information to make the drafting of detailed procedures quite straightforward. Where it is useful (particularly in generic areas like e-mail controls, protection of personal information, etc.), there are pointers as to how procedures should be drafted. Information is the very lifeblood of most organizations today and its security ought to be approached professionally and thoroughly.

Finally, it should be noted that achieving ISO/IEC 27001 certification does not of itself prove that the organization has a completely secure information system; it is merely an indicator, particularly to third parties, that the objective of achieving complete security is being effectively pursued. Information security is, in the terms of the cliché, a journey not a destination.

1

Why is information security necessary?

An information security management system (ISMS) is necessary because the threats to the availability, integrity and confidentiality of the organization's information are great, and always increasing. Any prudent house-holder whose house was built on the shores of a tidal river would, when facing the risk of floods, take urgent steps to improve the defenses of the house against the water. It would clearly be insufficient just to block up the front gate, because the water will get in everywhere and anywhere it can. In fact, the only prudent action is to block every single possible channel through which floodwaters might enter and then to try to build the walls even higher, in case the floods are even greater than expected.

So it is with the threats to organizational information. All organizations possess information that is either critical or sensitive, ranging from personal data through financial and product information to customer, brand and IP information. In the information economy today, information is widely regarded as the lifeblood of modern business.

Organizations are facing a flood of threats to this information. It is self-evident that organizations should, therefore, take appropriate steps to secure and protect their information assets. This is particularly so because a web of legislation and regulation makes organizations criminally liable, and in some instances makes directors personally accountable, for implementing and maintaining appropriate risk control and information security measures.

"Information security," however, means different things to different people. To vendors of security products, it tends to be limited to the product(s) they sell. To many directors, executives and managers, it tends to mean something they don't understand and that the CIO has to deal with. To many users of IT equipment, it tends to mean unwanted restrictions on what they can do on their corporate PCs. These are all dangerously narrow views.

Nature of information security threats

Information is right at the heart of the modern organization. Its availability, integrity and confidentiality are fundamental to the long-term survival of any 21st-century organization. Unless the organization takes a comprehensive and systematic approach to protecting the availability, integrity and confidentiality of its information, it will be vulnerable to a wide range of possible threats. These threats are not restricted to internet companies, to e-commerce businesses, to organizations that use technology or to organizations that have secret or confidential information. As we saw earlier, they affect all organizations, in all sectors of the economy, both public and private. They are a "clear and present danger," and strategic responsibility for ensuring that the organization has appropriately defended its information assets can no longer be abdicated or palmed off on the CIO.

Information security threats come from both within and without an organization. The situation worsens every year. Random unprovoked attacks by third parties on an organization's information security are at least as great a danger as is deliberate action. Internal threats are equally serious. It is impossible to predict what attack might be made on any given information asset, or when, or how. The speed with which methods of attack evolve, and knowledge about them proliferates, is such that it is completely pointless to take effective action only against specific, identified threats. Only a comprehensive, systematic approach will deliver the level of information security that any organization really needs.

It is worth understanding the risks to which an organization with an inadequate information security system exposes itself. These risks fall into three categories: damage to operations, damage to reputation and legal damage. Damage in any one of these three categories can be measured by its impact on the organization's bottom line, both short- and long-term. While there is no single, comprehensive, global study of information risks or threats on which all countries and authorities rely, there are a number of surveys, reports and studies, in and across different countries and, often, with slightly differing objectives, that, between them, demonstrate the nature, scale, complexity and significance of these information security risks and the extent to which organizations, through their own complacency, or through the vulnerabilities in their hardware and software, are vulnerable to these threats.

Prevalence of information security threats

Ernst & Young (www.ey.com/global/content.nsf/International/Home) have been publishing an annual Information Security Survey since 1993. Their 2004 survey, which interviewed nearly 1,300 executives across 51 countries, is also revealing. Only 20 percent of organizations strongly agreed that information security was a CEO-level priority, and only 24 percent gave their information security departments the highest rating in meeting the needs of the organization.

The executive summary of this survey made two observations:

Since the release of our first survey in 1993, Ernst & Young has examined the various dimensions of information security as practiced by global organizations. Ironically, this year's survey seems to echo the sentiments of previous years, as organizations apparently continue to rely on luck rather than proven information security controls. Perhaps the remarkable thing is how *little* attitudes, practices and actions have changed since 1993— during a period when threats have increased significantly. Two factors lead us to believe matters have deteriorated.

First, the threats are more lethal than they were in 1993. What many organizations are slow to recognize is that what they don't know is hurting them and hurting them badly. While scaremongers focus the public's attention upon the external threats with questionable damage guess-estimates, organizations face greater damage from insiders' misconduct, omissions, oversights, or an organizational culture that violates pre-existing policies and procedures.

Second, there is little visible change in how security is practiced by organizations. In 1994, a respondent told us: "It is apparently going to take a major breach of security before this organization gets its act together." Some ten years later, that sentiment is still quite evident and typifies organizations' reluctance to deal with the significant threats and to invoke well-accepted controls.

The top five incidents identified in the Ernst & Young survey affected more than 50 percent of organizations; hardware failure that brought down critical business systems, the top incident, affected 72 percent of the respondents. Does this mean that they now have tried-and-tested business continuity plans in place? Revealingly, less than 50 percent of the respondents thought that they would be able to continue business operations in the event of a serious disruption. Not being able to continue business operations is a serious threat to the survival of the organization; dealing with the potential impact of this risk is why information security should be a top boardroom priority.

The UK Department of Trade and Industry's (DTI) seventh annual Information Security Breaches Survey (ISBS 2004), managed by PricewaterhouseCoopers, looked at the state of information security across a representative sample of UK organizations. Of all the organizations surveyed, 58 percent recognized that they possessed information that was highly confidential. Amongst large organizations, this rose to 77 percent or higher and, in reality, if the smaller organizations had had a better understanding of their information assets, this figure would probably be reflected across all size bands.

The whole ISBS 2004 report can be found on its own dedicated website, at www.security-survey.gov.uk/. Its main points—which we think are generally true of organizations across the world—are as follows:

■ The percentage of businesses that are highly dependent on electronic information and the systems that process it is now 87 percent, compared with 76 percent two years ago.
■ Over half store highly confidential records on computers.
■ Only half of all wireless networks have security controls in place.
■ Spam is a growing issue (probably, by 2005, representing something like 50 percent of all e-mail).
■ Fewer than 1 in 10 businesses have tested their disaster recovery plans to find out if they would actually work in practice.

■ Two-thirds of businesses had at least one malicious security breach in the last year, an increase from just under half two years earlier.

■ Over a quarter of businesses suffered a significant incident arising from accidental systems failure or data corruption.

■ The average business now has one security incident a month; large businesses have one per week.

■ Organizations were significantly more pessimistic about the future outlook for information security breaches, believing that incidents will happen more often in future and be harder to detect.

■ One-third of large businesses and two-thirds of all companies still have no information security policy.

■ Processes for keeping antivirus software up to date are often weak.

Hackers, crackers, virus writers, fraudsters and the whole menagerie of cyber-criminals are increasingly adept at exploiting the vulnerabilities in organizations' software, hardware, networks and processes. As fraudsters, spam and virus writers and hackers band together to mount joint attacks on businesses everywhere, the need for appropriate defenses can only increase.

However, there is still insufficient awareness and understanding of what can be done to combat the more significant risks, particularly those posed by human actions and those arising from doing business electronically. Only 1 in 10 companies has staff with formal information security qualifications. Often—but not always—information security is *in reality* seen only as an issue for the IT department, which it clearly isn't. Good information security management is about organizations understanding the risks and threats they face and the vulnerabilities in their current computer processing facilities. It is about putting in common-sense procedures to minimize the risks and about educating all the employees about their responsibilities. Most importantly, it is about ensuring that the policy on information security management has the commitment of senior management. It is only when these procedural and management issues are addressed that organizations can decide on what security technologies they need.

The majority of businesses are still spending less that 1 percent of their IT budget on security; the benchmark against which their expenditure should be compared is 5 to 10 percent. That less than half of all businesses ever estimate the return on their information security investment may be part of the problem; certainly, until business takes its IT governance responsibilities seriously, the information security situation will continue to worsen.

Impacts of information security threats

The Big Four consultancy firm KPMG's Information Security Survey 2000, which forms a useful baseline from which to consider the current state of information security, concluded that information security breaches were on the increase, with virus incidents amongst respondent firms increasing from 20 percent to 73 percent, theft of equipment from 23 percent to 46 percent and e-mail intrusion from 2 percent to 29 percent; 78 percent of respondents cited security concerns as the main obstacles to e-commerce. In 55 percent of organizations, ultimate responsibility for information security was not recognized as resting with the board; responsibility had been left with the IT department, and the board apparently had no way of ensuring that appropriate steps had been taken.

PricewaterhouseCoopers carried out, with *CIO* magazine, a worldwide study in 2005, interviewing 8,200 information security executives in 63 countries around the world. PwC observed: "Despite the recent public exposures of phishing scams, identity theft, corporate espionage, intellectual property breaches, and theft of millions of personally identifiable records, only 37% of companies reported that they have a security strategy in place... improvements are far outpaced by the sophistication and volume of threats info security professionals face."

Cybercrime

The Computer Security Institute (CSI), with the participation of the San Francisco Federal Bureau of Investigation's Computer Intrusion Squad, has now conducted nine annual surveys into information security at the CSI member firms. Their membership suggests that their level of information security awareness and commitment are somewhat greater than the average organization's and, therefore, it can be assumed that these results are describing the best actual current performances. The results of the 2004 survey showed that 2004 total financial losses to criminal abuse, across the 269 respondents who participated, was $141 million. While the biggest loss arose from virus attacks ($55 million) and denial-of-service attack ($26 million), $11 million of these losses was from theft of proprietary information against $8 million for financial fraud and $7 million in laptop thefts. It was clear that nearly half of those who took part in the overall survey were unable (because they had no method of tracking) or unwilling (because of the possible reputational damage) to provide estimates of their financial losses from the successful attacks they had experienced. Equally clear is the fact that incidents of cybercrime originate equally from outside and inside the attacked computer systems.

PricewaterhouseCoopers' European Economic Crime Survey 2001 questioned 3,400 organizations in both the public and private sectors. Forty-three percent of them are reported to have said that cybercrime would be the biggest and most dangerous form of criminal activity in the future.

Europol, the European police agency, observed in its 2003 report on EU organized crime: "The establishment of worldwide financial markets, economic globalization, and the creation of the EU common market have provided good opportunities for organized crime groups." In section 4.4, the report observes that "organized crime groups are clearly among the major beneficiaries of technological progress... crucially, the development of cyberspace [has] provided great opportunities and a vast arena in which organized crime groups can operate... High technology crime will continue to represent one of the major areas of crime in the future, paralleling the development of e-commerce and internet banking."

Finally, the magazine *Information Security* carried out an online survey of 2,545 information security practitioners in a broad spectrum of public and private organizations in North America, Europe and the Far East. Although this was carried out in July and August 2001, its findings are still very relevant:

■ A virus, worm, Trojan or some other form of malware had affected 90 percent of the organizations—even though 80 percent of them had antivirus software in place.

■ The number of organizations hit by web server attacks doubled in number between 2000 and 2001.

■ Insider security incidents occurred more often than outsider ones, but security professionals were more concerned about securing the external perimeter of the organization than dealing with the internal issues.

These internal security incidents included installation of unauthorized software at 78 percent of the participant organizations, use of company computing resources for illegal or illicit communications or activities (such as porn site surfing or e-mail harassment) and the use of company computing resources for personal profit (gambling, unsolicited e-mail or spam, personal e-commerce businesses, etc.).

In conclusion, it is worth reviewing the CSI's comment on its own surveys: "Over its seven-year lifespan, the survey has told a compelling story. A sense of the 'facts on the ground' has emerged. There is much more illegal and unauthorized activity occurring in cyberspace than corporations admit to their clients, stockholders and business partners or report to law enforcement. Incidents are widespread, costly and commonplace." Could there be a clearer statement of the need for effective IT governance in organizations?

Cyberwar

Cybercrime is a serious issue. It may be a lesser danger to organizations than the effects of what is called "cyberwar." On 12 September 2001, the US General Accounting Office (GAO) reported that 24 US federal bodies, from the Treasury to the Pentagon, had computer systems "riddled with weaknesses." It said that hackers could read or tamper with critical information. On 18 September, the Nimda worm infected and shut down 100,000 computers worldwide within 24 hours. It is believed that every significant terrorist or criminal organization has cyber-capabilities and has become very sophisticated in its ability to plan and execute attacks using the most recent technology.

More than 400 million computers are linked to the internet; many of them are vulnerable to indiscriminate cyber-attack. The critical infrastructure of the first world is subject to the threat of cyber-assaults, ranging from defacing websites to undermining critical national computer systems.

In February 2003, the White House published the *National Strategy to Secure Cyberspace*, in which the president recognized that securing cyberspace would be an extraordinarily difficult task, requiring the combined and coordinated effort of the whole of society and that, without such an effort, an infrastructure that is "essential to our economy, security and way of life" could be disrupted to the extent that society would be debilitated. The requirement that US federal agencies comply with the Federal Information Security Management Act is a logical outcome of this concern.

Future risks

There are a number of trends that lie behind these increases in threats to computer-based information security, which when taken together suggest that things will continue to get worse, not better:

■ The use of distributed computing is increasing. Computing power has migrated from centralized mainframe computers and data processing centers to a distributed network of desktop, laptop and microcomputers, and this makes information security much more difficult to ensure.

■ There is a strong trend toward mobile computing. The use of laptop computers, personal digital assistants (PDAs), mobile phones, digital cameras, portable projectors and MP3 players has made working from home and while traveling relatively straightforward, with the result that network perimeters have become increasingly porous. This means that the number of remote access points to networks, and the number of easily accessible endpoint devices, has increased dramatically, and this has increased the opportunities for those who wish to break into networks and steal or corrupt information.

■ There has been a dramatic growth in the use of the internet for business communication, and the development of wireless, voice over IP (VoIP) and broadband technologies will drive this even further. The internet provides an effective, immediate and powerful method for organizations to communicate on all sorts of issues. This exposes all these organizations to the security risks that go with connection to the internet:

— The internet is really just a backbone connection that enables every computer in the world to connect to every other computer. This gives criminals a direct means of reaching any and every organization that is connected to the internet.

— The internet is inherently a public space. It is accessible by anyone from anywhere and consists of the millions of connections, some permanent and some temporary, that come about because of this. It has no built-in security and no built-in protection for confidential or private information.

— The internet (together with cellular telephony) is also, in effect, a worldwide medium for criminals and hackers to communicate with one another, to share the latest tricks and techniques and to work together on interesting projects.

— Better hacker tools are available every day, on hacker websites that, themselves, proliferate. These tools are improved regularly and, increasingly, less and less technologically proficient criminals—and computer-literate terrorists—are thus enabled to cause more and more damage to target networks and systems.

— Increasingly, hackers, virus writers and spam operators are cooperating to find ways of spreading more spam: not just because it's fun, but because there's a lot of money to be made out of the direct e-mail marketing of dodgy products. "Phishing" and other internet fraud activity will continue evolving and will become an ever bigger problem.

■ This is leading, inevitably, to an increase in "blended" threats, which can only be countered with a combination of technologies and processes.

■ Increasingly sophisticated technology defenses, particularly around user authorization and authentication, will drive an increase in "social engineering"-derived hacker attacks.

■ Widespread computer literacy. While most people today have computer skills, the next generation is growing up with a level of familiarity with computers that will enable them to develop and deploy an entirely new range of threats. Instant messaging is an example of a new technology that is better than e-mail, because it is faster and more immediate, with many more security vulnerabilities than e-mail. We will see many more such technologies emerging.

■ Wireless technology—whether WiFi or Bluetooth—makes information and the internet available cheaply and easily from virtually anywhere, thereby potentially reducing the perceived value and importance of information and, certainly, exposing confidential and sensitive information more and more to casual access.

■ The falling price of computers has brought computing within most people's reach. The result is that most people now have enough computer experience to pose a threat to an organization, if they are prepared to apply themselves just a little bit to take advantage of the opportunities identified above.

What do these trends, and all these statistics from so many organizations in so many countries (and information security professionals would argue that, as most organizations don't yet know that their defenses have already been breached, the statistics are only the tip of the iceberg), mean in real terms to individual organizations?

In simple, brutal terms, they must mean that:

- No organization is immune.
- Every organization, at some time, will suffer one or more of the disruptions, abuses or attacks identified in these pages.
- Businesses will be disrupted. Downtime in business critical systems (such as ERP systems) can be catastrophic for an organization. However quickly service is restored, there will be an unwanted and unnecessary cost in doing so. At other times, lost data may have to be painstakingly reconstructed and, sometimes, it will be lost for ever.
- Privacy will be violated. Organizations have to protect the personal information of employees and customers. If this privacy is violated, there may be legal action and penalties.
- Organizations will suffer direct financial loss. Protection in particular of commercial information and customers' credit card details is essential. Loss or theft of commercial information, ranging from business plans and customer contracts to intellectual property and product designs, and industrial know-how can all cause long-term financial damage to the victim organization. Computer fraud, conducted by staff with or without third party involvement, has an immediate direct financial impact.
- Reputations will be damaged. Organizations that are unable to protect the privacy of information about staff and customers, and which consequently attract penalties and fines, will find their corporate credibility and business relationships severely damaged and their expensively developed brand and brand image dented.

The statistics are compelling. The threats are evident. No organization can afford to ignore the need for information security. The fact that the risks are so widespread and the sources of danger so diverse means that it is insufficient simply to implement an antivirus policy, or a business continuity policy, or any other stand-alone solution. A conclusion of the CBI Cybercrime Survey 2001 was that "deployment of technologies such as firewalls may provide false levels of comfort unless organizations have performed a formal risk analysis and configured firewalls and security mechanisms to reflect their overall risk strategy." Nothing has changed.

The only sensible option is to carry out a thorough assessment of the risks facing the organization and then to adopt a comprehensive and systematic approach to information security that cost-effectively tackles those risks.

Legislation

Certainly, organizations can legally no longer ignore the issue. There are a number of US statutes that are relevant to information security, including the Sarbanes–Oxley Act, GLBA, HIPAA, FISMA, OPPA, Senate Bill 1386, CAN-SPAM, and so on. EU Safe Harbor regulations and the needs of, for instance, SAS 70 audits all impact how executives should think about information security.

HIPAA and GLBA are perhaps the most high-profile of these recently passed laws; they require organizations to implement data security measures to prevent unauthorized or unlawful processing (which includes storing) and accidental loss or damage to data pertaining to living individuals.

There can be no doubt that the implications of this are that directors of listed businesses, of public sector organizations and of companies throughout their supply chains must be able to identify the steps that they have taken to protect the confidentiality, integrity and availability of the organization's information assets. In all of these instances, the existence of a risk-based information security management policy, implemented through an information security management system (ISMS), is clear evidence that the organization has taken the necessary and appropriate steps.

Benefits of an information security management system

The benefits of adopting an externally certifiable information security management system are, therefore, clear:

- The board and executives of the organization will be able to demonstrate that they are complying with the requirements of SOX and applicable statutes and regulations and/or complying with current international best practice in risk management with regards to information assets and security.
- The organization will be able to demonstrate, in the context of the array of relevant legislation, that is has taken appropriate action to comply with the laws.
- The organization will be able systematically to protect itself from the dangers and potential costs of computer misuse, cybercrime and the impacts of cyberwar.

∎ The organization will be able to improve its credibility with staff, customers and partner organizations and this can have direct financial benefits through, for instance, improved sales.

∎ The organization will be able to make informed, practical decisions about what security technologies and solutions to deploy and thus to increase the value for money it gets from information security, to manage and control the costs of information security and to measure and improve its return on its information security investments.

2

Sarbanes–Oxley and regulatory compliance

Sarbanes–Oxley

The Sarbanes–Oxley Act of 2002 (SOX), introduced in the United States in the aftermath of Enron, has important IT governance implications for listed US companies, their foreign subsidiaries and foreign companies that have US listings. It applies to all Securities and Exchange Commission (SEC)-registered corporations, irrespective of where their trading activities are geographically based. Compliance is mandatory and this, combined with significant potential sanctions for individual directors, is driving SOX compliance requirements through the supply chain.

While the Act lays down detailed requirements for the governance of listed corporations, the three highest-profile and most critical sections—which were implemented in phases—are 302, 404 and 409 (see Table 2.1).

The SEC, which is responsible for implementation of SOX, has relevant information available at www.sec.gov/spotlight/sarbanes-oxley.htm, and the Sarbanes–Oxley website itself is at www.sarbanes-oxley.com.

Table 2.1

	Section		
	302	404	409
Requirement	– Quarterly certification of financial reports – Disclosure of all known control deficiencies – Disclose acts of fraud	– Management's annual certification of internal controls – Independent accountant must attest report – Quarterly reviews of updates/changes	– Monitor operational risks – Material event reporting – 'Real-time' implications – four business days allowed for report to be filed
Responsibility	– CEO – CFO	– Management – Independent accountant/auditor	– Management – Independent accountant/ auditor

Internal controls and audit

Under SOX, management is required to certify the company's financial reports, and both management and an independent accountant are required to certify the organization's internal controls. In almost every organization, financial reporting depends on the IT infrastructure, whether it is for the rendering of an invoice, the effective operation of an ERP system, or an integrated, organization-wide management information and control system. Unless appropriate internal controls are built into this infrastructure, management will not be able to make the required certification.

The SEC has mandated US corporations to use a recognized internal control framework that has been established by an organization that developed the framework through a due process, including inviting public comment. One widely used framework is known as the COSO framework or, to give it its own title, the "Internal Control—Integrated Framework," which contains the recommendations of the Committee of Sponsoring Organizations of Treadway Commission (www.coso.org). The sponsoring organizations included the AICPA, the Institute of Internal Auditors, the Institute of Management Accountants and the American Accounting Association. The PCAOB (Public Company Accounting Oversight Board, at www.pcaobus.org, created under SOX to oversee the activity of the auditors of public companies in the United States) expects the majority of public companies to adopt the COSO framework, and its Auditing Standard No 2, dealing with audit of internal control over financial reporting, assumes that the COSO framework (or one substantially like it) will have been adopted.

Auditing Standard No 2 contains, at paragraph 15, a key statement that links SOX compliance and ISO/IEC 27001: "Not all controls relevant to financial reporting are accounting controls. Accordingly, all controls that could materially affect financial reporting, including controls that focus primarily on the effectiveness and efficiency of operations or compliance with laws and regulations and also have a material effect on the reliability of financial reporting, are a part of internal control over financial reporting."

COSO identifies two broad groups of IT systems control activities: general controls and application controls. General controls are those controls that ensure that the financial information from a company's application systems can be relied upon. General controls exist most commonly as part of an information security management system (such as that identified in ISO/IEC 27001 or ISO/IEC 17799). Application controls are embedded in the software to detect or prevent unauthorized transactions. Such controls can be used to ensure the completeness, accuracy, validity and authorization of transactions.

Paragraph 50 of Auditing Standard No 2 identifies the need for what we call an IT governance framework in maintaining the internal control environment: "information technology general controls over program development, program changes, computer operations, and access to programs and data help ensure that specific controls over the processing of transactions are operating effectively."

Auditing Standard No 2 goes on, at paragraph 52, to evaluate the effectiveness of company-level controls at the outset of the audit engagement, on the basis that it is the company-level controls that have such a "pervasive impact on controls at the process, transaction or application level." These company-level controls include consistent policies and procedure and codes of conduct—all of which are at the heart of ISO/IEC 17799. The auditing standard specifically cross-references the existing *Consideration of Internal Control in a Financial Statement Audit*, issued by the AICPA in 1990, because it sets out clearly the effect of information technology on internal control over financial reporting.

Enterprise risk management

Enterprise risk management (ERM) has emerged over the last few years as a fundamentally new way for organizations to approach risk. This is driven partly by the extensive overlap between the risk management requirements of SOX, Basel 2 and corporate governance regimes elsewhere in the world, as well as ongoing changes in the global information economy. Organizations face new and complex risks in a rapidly changing business, technological and regulatory environment. They cannot afford not to identify and control against all areas of risk—including those that might remain unidentified or unforeseen, such as currency fluctuations, human resource issues in foreign countries, changing or disappearing distribution channels, corporate governance and regulatory pressures, and the range of risks associated with technology, information and intellectual assets.

An enterprise risk management process should ensure that a uniform approach to risk identification, measurement and treatment is taken across the organization.

COSO ERM framework

COSO, whose internal control framework has become the de facto standard for companies complying with SOX, started work on developing a separate risk management framework in 2001. This framework, the "Enterprise Risk Management—Integrated Framework," was designed to provide a common framework, "key principles and concepts, a common language, and clear direction and guidance."[1] This framework expands on the internal control framework, providing a broader and more robust focus on enterprise risk management; because it incorporates the internal control framework, organizations could (as COSO suggests) move toward implementing an ERM framework to satisfy their internal control needs as well as their broader business risk management needs.

COSO defines ERM as "a process, effected by an entity's board of directors, management and other personnel, applied in strategy setting and across the enterprise, designed to identify potential events that may affect the entity, and manage risk to be within its risk appetite, to provide reasonable assurance regarding the achievement of entity objectives." It's a definition broad enough to encompass the Basel 2 definition of operational risk as well as that in SOX. It is about achieving the organization's business strategy, and it deals with strategic, operational, reporting and compliance goals or objectives.

The COSO ERM framework has eight components:

- internal environment;
- objective setting;
- event identification;
- risk assessment;
- risk response;
- control activities;
- information and communication;
- monitoring.

An effective ERM framework will be one in which all eight components are present and functioning effectively in each of the four categories of objectives. Of course, the components will not function identically in every organization, and implementations will be less formal and structured in smaller organizations than in larger ones. The COSO ERM framework comes with detailed implementation guidance, and any organization considering adoption of such a framework should acquire and study both the ERM framework and the "Application techniques." There are a number of general points that relate to IT governance.

ERM involves analysis and treatment of all business risks—those that are transferable/insurable as well as a wide array of traditionally non-insurable risks. The ERM implementation process is an inherently collaborative one that requires teamwork among many disciplines within an organization. Depending on the business sector, it will require, for instance, risk management, credit management, treasury and accounting input, as well as operational management, marketing, R&D and legal counsel. It is better to have someone specifically charged with leading the ERM process, and this person should have the full support of the CEO, the board and the management.

Regulatory compliance

Organizations have traditionally responded to regulatory compliance requirements on a law-by-law or department-by-department basis. That was, last century, a perfectly adequate response. There were relatively few laws, compliance requirements were generally firmly established and well understood, and the jurisdictions within which businesses operated were well defined.

Over the last decade, all that has changed. Rapid globalization, increasingly pervasive information technology, the evolving business risk and threat environment, and today's governance expectations have, between them, created a fast-growing and complex body of laws and regulations— such as HIPAA, SOX and GLBA—that all impact the organization's IT systems. While global companies are in the forefront of finding effective compliance solutions, every organization, however small and in whatever industry, is faced with the same broad range of regulatory requirements.

These regulatory requirements focus on the confidentiality, integrity and availability of electronically held information, and primarily—but not exclusively—on personal data. Many of the new laws—such as SB 1386 and OPPA—appear to overlap and, not only is there very little established legal guidance as to what constitutes compliance, new laws and regulatory requirements continue to emerge. Increasingly, these laws (such as SB 1386) have a geographic reach that extends to organizations based and operating outside the apparent jurisdiction of the legislative or regulatory body. Similarly, US organizations can find themselves subject to the requirements of foreign regulations, such as the EU Safe Harbor regulations or Canada's PIPEDA. In the public sector, FISMA sets out very clear information security requirements for all government bodies in the United States.

In the face of new, blended, complex and evolving threats to their data, organizations have business and regulatory obligations to protect and maintain the data and to make the data available when required. They have to do this in an uncertain compliance environment where the rewards for success don't grab headlines, but the penalties for failure do. Fines, reputation and brand damage and, in some circumstances, jail time for directors are outcomes that every business wants to avoid, and wants to avoid as systematically and cost-effectively as possible.

In most instances, there is not yet a body of tested case law and proven compliance methodologies to which organizations can turn in order to calibrate their efforts. There are no technology products that, of themselves, can render an organization compliant with any of the data security regulations, because all data security controls consist of a combination of technology, procedure and human behavior. In other words, installing a firewall will not protect an organization if there are no procedures for correctly configuring and maintaining it, and if users habitually bypass it (through, for instance, Instant Messenger, internet browsing or the deployment of rogue wireless access points).

The adoption of an externally validated, best-practice approach for information security—one that provides a single, coherent framework that enables simultaneous compliance with multiple regulatory requirements—is, therefore, a solution to which organizations are increasingly turning.

While the relevant statutes and compliance requirements are covered in more detail in Chapter 27, the key planning issue at this point is the requirement that the ISMS be designed in such a way that it helps the organization meet its regulatory compliance requirements.

IT governance

Public corporations are increasingly expected to take proactive steps to identify and meet their compliance requirements. Continued pressure, from governments, institutional stockholders and the general public, will ensure that directors have little "wiggle room"; non-compliance is likely to have a terminal impact on the careers of those directors who think that it is a viable option. The guidance laid out in the PCAOB's Auditing Standard No 2 points inexorably at the need for organizations to create and implement IT governance frameworks.

The IT governance portal at www.itgovernance.co.uk reflects clearly the principles that have been set out above, as well as the broader belief that organizations should integrate their IT strategies and their business strategies, because it is mission-critical for most organizations efficiently to share information with customers, partners, suppliers and a wide range of stakeholders. As organizations recognize that IT management should have a fundamental input to the development of business objectives and business strategies, so IT is increasingly being seen as a critical enabler of business processes. At the same time, many of the management issues around IT are changing from concerns about financial controls and other threats and vulnerabilities that also need to be controlled to responding to the challenges and opportunities made possible by IT.

The most practical and effective way for directors to handle their IT governance obligations and, specifically, their information security risks, and to be seen to do so systematically and comprehensively, is to adopt and implement an information security policy and information security management system that is capable of being independently certified as complying with ISO/IEC 27001:2005. The standard provides the only independently developed framework for the management of information security. While compliance with the standard does not of itself confer immunity from legal obligations, it does point clearly to management's implementation of best practice, of effective IT governance, and can, therefore, help to develop competitive advantage in an organization and be available as part of a potential legal defense against any of the threats identified above.

Note

1 Executive summary, "Enterprise Risk Management— Integrated Framework," COSO, September 2004.

3

Information security standards

Benefits of certification

There are a number of direct, practical reasons for implementing an information security policy and information security management system (ISMS) that is capable of being independently certified (sometimes called "registration") as compliant with ISO/IEC 27001:2005. A certificate tells existing and potential customers that the organization has defined and put in place effective information security processes, thus helping create a trusting relationship. ISO/IEC 27001 certification will cost a fraction of the cost associated with an SAS 70 audit (typically upwards of $100,000) and demonstrates the existence of a best-practice-based information security infrastructure. The certification process also helps the organization focus on continuously improving its information security processes. Of course, above all, certification, and the regular external review on which ongoing certification depends, ensures that the organization keeps its information security system up to the mark and, therefore, that it continues to assure its ability to operate.

Most information systems are not designed from the outset to be secure. Technical security measures are limited in their ability to protect an information system. Management systems and procedural controls are essential components of any really secure information system and, to be effective, need careful planning and attention to detail.

ISO/IEC 27001 provides the specification for an information security management system and, in the related code of practice, ISO/IEC 17799, it draws on the knowledge of a group of experienced information security practitioners in a wide range of significant organizations across more than 40 countries to set out best practice in information security. An ISO/IEC 27001-compliant system will provide a systematic approach to identifying and combating the entire range of potential risks to the organization's information assets, the variety and impact of which were described in Chapter 1. It will also provide corporate directors with both a systematic way of meeting their responsibilities under Sarbanes–Oxley and the wide range of interlocking data protection and privacy legislation to which they are subject, and demonstrable evidence that they have done so to a consistent standard.

History of ISO/IEC 27001 and ISO/IEC 17799

ISO/IEC 17799 is also known, in the UK, as BS 7799 Part 1. BS 7799 was originally the outcome of a joint initiative by the DTI in the UK and leading UK private sector businesses. The working party, which started work in 1992, produced the first version of BS 7799 in February 1995. This was, originally, a code of practice for IT security management. Organizations that developed ISMSs that complied with this code of practice were able to have them independently inspected but there was no formal certification scheme in place and, therefore, formal certification was not possible.

BS 7799 underwent a significant review in 1998. Feedback was collated and, in April 1999, a revised standard was launched. The original code of practice was significantly revised and retained as Part 1 of the standard, and a new Part 2 was added. Part 1 was issued as a single-part standard, titled "Information Technology—Code of Practice for Information Security Management" and replaced BS 7799-1:1999, which was then withdrawn. It provided guidance on best practice in information security management. It therefore took the form of guidance and recommendations. Its foreword clearly stated that it was not to be treated as a specification. It became internationalized as ISO/IEC 17799 in December 2000. It was substantially revised and updated in the course of 2005, and a new version, ISO/IEC 17799:2005, was published in July 2005.

Part 2, titled "Specification for Information Security Management Systems," formed the standard against which an organization's security management system was to be assessed and certified. BS 7799 Part 2 underwent further reviews in 2002 and 2005, and a number of significant changes were made at each point. Significantly, BS 7799-2:2005 was internationalized as ISO/IEC 27001:2005 and published as such in October 2005. It "forms the basis for an assessment of the Information Security Management System (ISMS) of the whole, or part, of an organization. It may be used as the basis for a formal certification scheme." It is, in other words, the specific document against which an ISMS will be assessed.

Use of the standard

As a general rule, organizations implementing the standard need to pay close attention to the wording of the standard itself, and to be aware of any revisions to it. Non-compliance with any revisions will jeopardize any existing certification. The standard itself is what any ISMS will be assessed against; where there is any conflict between advice provided in this or any other guide to implementation of ISO/IEC 27001 and the standard itself, it is the wording in the standard that should be heeded. An external auditor will be assessing the ISMS against the published standard, not against the advice provided by this book or any third party. It is critical, therefore, that those responsible for the ISMS should be able to refer explicitly to its clauses and intent and should be able to defend any implementation steps they have taken against the standard itself. An appropriate first step is, therefore, to obtain and read a copy of both the international standards, which are available from national standards bodies and from the website www.27001.com.

ISO/IEC 17799

In 1998, when the original BS 7799 was revised for the first time, prior to becoming BS 7799 Part 1, references to UK legislation were removed and the text was made more general. It was also made consistent with OECD guidelines on privacy, information security and cryptography. Its best-practice controls were made capable of implementation in a variety of legal and cultural environments.

The reason for developing an international standard on information security management was described by BSI-DISC, on their website, as follows:

> many organizations have expressed the need to have a common standard on best practice for information security management. They would like to be able to implement information security controls to meet their own business requirements as well as a set of controls for their business relationships with other organizations. These organizations see the need to share the benefits of common best practice at a true international level to ensure that they can protect their business processes and activities to satisfy these business needs.

In other words, the ISO/IEC 17799:2000 Code of Practice was intended to provide a framework for international best practice in information security management and systems interoperability. It also provides guidance, to which an external auditor will look, on how to implement a certifiable ISMS. It does *not*, as the standard is currently written, provide the basis for an international certification scheme. The guidance that this book provides in implementing an ISMS will, therefore, start with the requirements of ISO/IEC 27001:2005 and then look to ISO/IEC 17799:2005 for guidance as to the range of actions that should be considered. In this book, "Part 2" (where it is used) or "the standard" refers to ISO/IEC 27001:2005 and "17799" refers to ISO/IEC 17799:2005.

It is particularly important to note that, while 17799 provides international best practice in information security, it is subject to changes in the information security environment. It had been written, and rewritten, over a number of years prior to its date of original publication and subsequent revisions. The speed with which information technology has evolved, and at which it goes on evolving, already means that some of the specific guidance in 17799 may be inadequate to deal with newly identified threats and vulnerabilities and the most current responses to them. It is likely that a new version of the standard will be published within the next three years, and any organization investigating certification should be aware of developments on this front. This book may therefore go beyond the current requirements of the standard in a number of areas, mostly to do with the internet and web commerce. Any ISMS should, equally, go beyond the specific requirements of the standard where the situation—and the risk assessment—requires it.

It is equally important to note that, just as both parts of the standard have to be revised and updated as they cease to be comprehensive in terms of today's information security threats, so the hard-copy component of this book will quickly cease to be completely up to date. The IT Governance online KnowledgeBank, to which this book provides initial free access, will continue to publish up-to-date information and guidance (and much more) on all the issues covered here. It will be a valuable resource for any organization implementing, or maintaining, an ISMS but will not replace the need to take completely up-to-date advice, particularly on issues to do with the internet and web commerce.

This book sets out how to implement an ISMS that is capable of certification to ISO/IEC 27001:2005. It will do so broadly within the context of the Microsoft suite of products, as these are the products most widely used in those parts of the world likely to be interested in certification. The implementation steps set out in this book, however, apply in all software and hardware environments. The standard itself was specifically written to be technology-independent.

This book will refer very explicitly to ISO/IEC 27001 and to ISO/IEC 17799 in order to comment on the implementation steps necessary to reflect the recommendations of ISO/IEC 17799 and to comply with the standard. However, the reader must obtain current copies of both documents and use them alongside this book and the KnowledgeBank in order to optimize an information security project and gain the full value of this book.

PDCA and process approach

The 2002 version of the standard for the first time promoted the adoption of a "process approach" for the design and deployment of an ISMS. This approach, widely know as the "Plan–Do–Check–Act" (PDCA) model, is familiar to quality and business managers everywhere. The introduction to ISO/IEC 27001 describes this model and sets out how to apply it in an information security environment. This approach should be thoroughly understood before work starts and should inform every step. This book has been constructed to reflect the PDCA cycle.

The 2002 version of the standard was designed for better alignment, or integration, with related management systems (e.g. ISO 9000) within the organization; this was a development long advocated by the authors, and has been maintained into ISO/IEC 27001:2005.

A note on numbering

ISO/IEC 27001 adopts a logical numbering methodology for its clauses and sub-clauses, as does ISO/IEC 17799:2005. The two standards are not completely aligned, although Annex A to ISO/IEC 27001 uses exactly the same numbering system as ISO/IEC 17799, to ensure that the specification and guidance on controls remain in line, which at least makes life easier for the manager. In order to reduce confusion, we have tried to avoid using or referring to ISO/IEC 17799's numbering system but sometimes it has been unavoidable.

Structured approach to implementation

The standard sets out, in clause 4.2.1, the required, structured approach to the establishment of an ISMS. There are eight steps to this, the "Plan" stage of the project:

1. Define the scope of the ISMS.
2. Define the information security policy.
3. Define a systematic approach to risk assessment.
4. Carry out a risk assessment to identify, within the context of the policy and ISMS scope, the important information assets of the organization and the risks to them.
5. Assess the risks.
6. Identify and evaluate options for the treatment of these risks.
7. Select, for each approach, the control objectives and controls to be implemented.
8. Prepare a statement of applicability.

Once these steps have been carried out, it is possible to begin implementation (the "Do" stage) of the system. The standard defines the ISMS as "part of the overall management system, based on a business risk approach, to establish, implement, operate, monitor, review, maintain and improve information security." The implementation process will go through its own five steps:

1. formulation of the risk treatment plan and its documentation, including planned processes and detailed procedures;
2. implementation of the risk treatment plan and planned controls;
3. appropriate training for affected staff, as well as awareness programs;
4. managing operations and resources in line with the ISMS;
5. implementation of procedures that enable prompt detection of, and response to, security incidents.

The "Check" stage has, essentially, only one step: monitoring, reviewing, testing and audit. However, monitoring, reviewing, testing and audit is an ongoing process that has to cover the whole system, and a certification body should want to see evidence of at least one set of tests and audits on the ISMS having been completed prior to a certification visit.

Testing and audit outcomes should be reviewed by management, as should the ISMS in the light of the changing risk environment, technology or other circumstances; improvements to the ISMS should be identified, documented and implemented. This is known as the "Act" stage.

Thereafter, it will be subject to ongoing review, further testing and continuous improvement.

A "mini-PDCA" approach should also be applied to each control.

This book takes a sequential approach to the establishment and implementation of an ISMS. In reality, once they realize the scale of the information risks they face, many organizations will want to tackle a number of the necessary tasks in parallel. Certainly, most organizations will come to ISO/IEC 27001 with some information security structures already in place.

Certification bodies, however, will usually assess the ISMS on the basis that its establishment has followed the stages set out here. There is good reason for this. The risk assessment is the critical step; controls implemented before an initial risk assessment has been carried out may be deficient or inappropriate. It is quite possible that some of the controls implemented prior to completion of a proper risk assessment might be overly robust, and not therefore cost-effective, and certainly not reflecting the standard or the guidance of ISO/IEC 17799; certification might be just as difficult to achieve with overly robust controls as with weak ones.

Therefore, if component tasks of establishing the ISMS are being carried out in parallel, or the organization already has elements of an ISMS in place, it will be critically important that the risk assessment is completely objective and thorough and that its findings are allowed to override any controls that have been implemented beforehand.

Implementation issues

Clause 4.2.2 of the standard requires the organization effectively to implement the control objectives and controls selected as a result of the process required under clause 4.2.1 and discussed later in this book in Chapters 4, 5 and 6. The steps identified below are key to effective implementation, and the board should commit itself to tackling them.

Implementation of an ISMS will have significant impacts on the way people work. Effective leadership, change management and internal communication are essential components of any successful ISO/IEC 27001 system roll-out. An overview of key issues that will contribute to a successful implementation are set out below and followed up where appropriate with more specific information and analysis in later chapters. The authors recommend that the implementation project itself produces and maintains a project-level risk log, with one of the highest potential impacts being assigned to the risk associated with senior management understanding *and* commitment.

Quality system integration

Many organizations that tackle ISO/IEC 27001 already have an ISO 9000:2000-certificated quality assurance system in place. The standard is designed to encourage integration of quality and other management systems. The ISMS should be integrated with the quality assurance system to the greatest extent possible. In particular, clauses 4.3 (documentation), 4.3.2 (document control) and 4.3.3 (records) of the standard can (and should) be met by applying any existing documentation control requirements of an ISO 9000 management system. Procedures within the ISMS have to be numbered and documents have to be controlled. The assumption of this book is that the ISO 9000 approach will be adopted by any organization that implements an ISMS, and that the specific requirements of the above clauses in the standard will also be considered.

Effectively, therefore, what one is doing is *extending* an existing management system to include information security management, not bringing in a whole new system. This is an important message that should underpin the change management and communication plans; the smaller the perceived mountain, the more quickly will an organization set out to climb it.

In circumstances where the organization does not already have an existing ISO 9000-certified management system and wishes guidance on the documentation, document control and records issues of ISO/IEC 27001, it should obtain and use the guidance in any current manual on the implementation of ISO 9000. Note that the ISO/IEC 27001 specifications for document control (4.3.2) and record control (4.3.3) mirror those contained in ISO 9000:2000, where they are numbered 4.2.3 and 4.2.4 respectively.

It is also important that the assessment and certification body chosen by the organization understands and accepts this approach. If it does not, get a new one; the task of having the existing system reassessed (and only at the next planned surveillance date) is much smaller than the task of creating and implementing a wholly new and parallel ISMS.

Documentation

As set out above, the organization should adopt, for its ISO/IEC 27001 management system, at least the same documentation principles that are required for ISO 9000. A properly managed ISMS will be fully documented. Clause 4.3.1 of the standard describes the minimum documentation that should be included in the ISMS to meet the requirement that the organization maintain sufficient records to demonstrate compliance with the requirements of the standard. The types of documents that are required include:

▪ The information security policy, the scope of the ISMS, the risk assessment, the control objectives, and the statement of applicability (developed as described in Chapters 5 and 6).

▪ Evidence of the actions undertaken by the organization and its management to specify the scope of the ISMS (the minutes of board and steering committee meetings, as well as any specialist reports).

▪ A description of the management framework (steering committee, etc.). This could usefully be related to an organizational structure chart.

▪ The risk treatment plan and the underpinning, documented procedures (which should include responsibilities and required actions) that implement the specified controls. A procedure describes who has to do what, under what conditions, or by when, and how. These procedures (there would probably be one for each of the implemented controls) would be part of the policy manual, which itself could be on paper or electronic.

▪ The procedures (which should include responsibilities and required actions) that govern the management and review of the ISMS. These would also be part of the policy manual. These would be developed in line with the guidance contained in this chapter.

The policy manual should be a controlled document, available to all staff. It can be done in paper form but is most effective on an intranet. Intranets can be inexpensively developed. An intranet ensures that the current version of any procedure is immediately available to all members of staff without inconvenience. A structured numbering system should be adopted that ensures ease of navigation of the manual and ensures that document issue is controlled, that replacement pages and changes are tracked and that the manual is complete. Staff should obviously be trained in how to use the manual; this is usually best done as part of the staff induction process.

Clearly, there will be a number of security system documents that, themselves, need to be subject to security measures. These will include documents such as the risk assessment, the risk treatment plan and the statement of applicability, which contain important insights into how security is managed and which should therefore be classified and restricted and treated in accordance with the information classification system described in Chapter 8. Access should be limited to people with specified ISMS roles, such as the information security adviser.

ISO/IEC 27001 clearly recognizes that there is no such thing as a "one size fits all" approach. Instead, it recommends that the extent of the ISMS documentation should reflect the complexity of the organization and its security requirements.

Leadership

This, like all key business initiatives, has to be provided from the top. Clause 5.1 of the standard specifically requires that this commitment be evidenced. Ideally, the CEO should be the driving force behind the program, and its achievement should be a clearly stated goal of the current business plan. The CEO needs completely to understand the strategic issues around IT governance and information security and the value to the enterprise of successful certification. The CEO has to be able to articulate them and to deal with objections and issues arising. Above all, he or she has to be sufficiently in command of this part of the business development to be able to keep the overall plan on track against its strategic goals. The organization's board of directors should give as much attention to monitoring progress against the ISO/IEC 27001 implementation plan as they do to monitoring all the other key business goals. If the CEO and board are not behind this project there is little point in proceeding; certification will not happen without clear evidence of such a commitment. This principle, of leadership from the top, is of course essential to all major change projects.

The standard will not allow any certification body to certify an ISMS without getting firm evidence of the commitment of senior management. The ISMS simply will not be adequate and the risks to the organization will not have been properly recognized or fully addressed, and the strategic business goals are unlikely to have been considered.

Change management

There have been many books written about change management programs and initiatives. Many such programs fail to deliver the benefits that have been used to justify the expense of commencing and seeing them through. Successful implementation of an ISMS does not require a detailed change management program, particularly not one devised and driven by consultants. What it does require is complete clarity amongst upper management, those charged with driving the project forward and those whose work practices will be affected as to why the change is necessary, what the end result must look like and why this result is essential.

The design and implementation of the ISMS should be driven by a project team that is drawn from those parts of the organization most likely to be affected by its implementation as well as a very small number of departmental experts, including HR/personnel. The balance is important; a properly functioning ISMS depends on everyone in the business understanding and applying its controls and, if the project team is made up of a preponderance of non-technical people, it is more likely to produce something that everyone in the business understands. The team certainly should include at least one experienced project manager, who will be responsible for tracking and reporting progress against the planned objectives. The project team should report directly to the CEO and have the appropriate delegated authority to implement the board-approved plan. Clause 5.1.e requires the provision of adequate resources to establish the ISMS, and this is the first step to doing so.

There needs to be an outline timetable and top-level identification of responsibilities and the critical path to completion. This should be prepared by the project team and, once it has been critically tested by the CEO and upper management, approved by the board. This plan should be capable of appearing on two sides of paper and should provide sufficient scope for those who will have to implement it to find appropriate solutions to the many operational challenges that there will be.

A key preliminary step in any successful change program is to identify and isolate, or convert, potential opposition. Where an ISMS roll-out is concerned, there is sometimes internal resistance from the IT department. There are a number of possible reasons for this, including the desire of the head of IT not to lose control of IT security, the IT department's desire to maintain its mystique and the fear that its existing controls might be found to be inadequate. This is not surprising. ISO/IEC 27001 does require the organization's board and senior management to take control of its ISMS and the whole organization to get behind and understand key aspects of security policy. The resistance of the IT department must be expected and overcome at the outset. There are circumstances where this can lead to a change in IT staff, either forced or unforced, and the organization should expect this and prepare appropriate contingency plans.

Training will be an important facilitator of the change program. The project team will need initial training in the principles of ISO/IEC 27001, the methodology of change and project management and the principles of internal communication. Staff throughout the business will need specific training in those aspects of security policy that will affect their day-to-day work. The IT manager and IT staff will all need competency in information security and, if this needs to be enhanced by training, this should be delivered by an organization that recognizes and understands the technical aspects of ISO/IEC 27001 training.

Communication

Underlying any successful change management program, and especially necessary for the successful roll-out of an ISMS, is a well-designed and effectively implemented internal communications plan. Compliance with clause 5.1.d suggests that key components of this plan must include:

■ Top-down communication of the vision—why the ISMS is necessary, what the legal responsibilities are, what the business will look like when the program is complete and what benefits it will bring to everyone in the organization.
■ Regular cascade briefings to all staff on progress against implementation objectives. These briefings should quickly become part of the existing organizational briefing cycle, so that ISO/IEC 27001 progress becomes

part of the normal business process—"just another thing that we're doing."

■ A mechanism for ensuring that key constituencies and individuals within the business are consulted and involved in the development of key components of the system. This ensures that they buy in to the outcome and to its implementation.

■ A mechanism for ensuring regular and immediate feedback from people in the organization or in affected third party organizations so that their direct experience of the initial system as it is implemented is used in the evolution of the final version.

■ These face-to-face communications should be underpinned with an effective information-sharing system. Most usually, this will be part of the corporate intranet, on which regular progress reports as well as detailed information on specific aspects of the ISMS are posted. E-mail alerts can tell staff to access the intranet for new information whenever it is posted, and the site can encourage feedback by means of a "write to the CEO" function.

Reviews

Clause 4.2.3 of the standard requires the effectiveness of the implementation of the identified controls to be verified by reviews carried out in accordance with the standard's Appendix B.4.5. This will be discussed in some detail in Chapter 28. The records of the management body (to be discussed in Chapter 4), which is responsible for implementing the ISMS, should record that these reviews were carried out on particular dates, what the results of the reviews were and what actions, if any, were required as a result.

Continual improvement and metrics

Clause 7 of the standard, "ISMS Improvement," was already embedded in specific components of the 1999 version. It is now overt and part of the PDCA approach. The corrective action requirements of clause 7.2 are met by an effective ISMS audit plan (Chapter 27), competent review of nonconformities (part of the IS manager's responsibility) and related documentation. Prevention is always better than correction and, as discussed later in that chapter, the IS manager should have a specific responsibility in terms of preventive action planning and implementation.

The combination of effective corrective and preventive plans, together with a formal review process and strong internal audit structure, within the context of an ISMS developed in line with the recommendations of this book, will enable an organization to demonstrate its approach to continual improvement.

A long-term approach to continuous improvement must include measuring the effectiveness of the ISMS and of the processes and controls that have been adopted. Clearly, information security as an organizational function needs to be measured against performance targets in just the same way as are other parts of the organization. In order to develop a useful set of metrics, an organization will have to identify what to measure, how to measure it and when to measure it.

Clause 4.2.2.d of the standard was newly introduced in 2005 and is a mark of the growing requirement for an ISMS to include methods of measuring the effectiveness of controls and groups of controls, and for specifying how these measures are to be used to ensure that control effectiveness is maintained. The fact that a new standard, to deal with ISMS measurements, is being developed should come as a surprise to no one. The requirement for greater measurement appears in the revisions to 4.2.3.a ("execute monitoring and review procedures and other controls to detect security events") and 4.2.3.c ("measure the effectiveness of controls"), the requirement in 7.2.f to review "results from effectiveness measurements," and the requirement in 7.3.e to review output that includes a review of the "improvement to how the effectiveness of controls is being measured."

Some of the areas that should be considered for measurement include the effectiveness and value-adding capability of the incident handling process, the effectiveness and cost savings provided by staff training, the improvement in efficiency generated by access controls and external contracts, the extent to which the current scope is meaningful and relevant in the changing business place, and so on.

A new standard on ISMS metrics and measurements is currently in the early stages of development within the ISO/IEC JTC1 SC 27 working group, but is unlikely to be available before 2007, even as a draft. In the meantime, the www.27001.com website will provide users of this book with access to emerging best practice in ISMS metrics and measurements.

4

Organizing information security

It is both practical and sensible to consider the organization's information security management structure at an early stage in the implementation process. This does, in fact, need to be thought through at the same time as the information security policy is being drawn up, as set out in Chapter 5. An effective information security management structure also enables the risk assessment (to be discussed in Chapter 6) to be effectively carried out.

This is the second detailed control specified in the standard, in clause A.6.1, "Internal Organization." Detailed controls are selected in response to the risk analysis (see Chapter 6); the organization will need to start putting its information security management structure in place from the commencement of its ISO/IEC 27001 project. The standard clearly states that the objective of clause A.6.1 is to "manage information security within the organization" and, in A.6.1.1, it specifies that a management framework must be established to initiate and control the implementation of the ISMS. This requirement incorporates the management information security forum identified in the earlier version of the standard. At A.6.1.2 it specifies that (where appropriate to the size of the organization) there might also need to be a cross-functional forum of people from within the organization to coordinate the implementation of controls. ISO/IEC 17799 explains, at 6.1.1 and 6.1.2, what best practice expects of the management structure and from the coordination activity.

Internal organization

ISO/IEC 17799 says that upper management should "actively support security within the organization through clear direction, demonstrated commitment, explicit assignment and acknowledgement of information security responsibilities." In practical terms, this means that the board and executive should charter a forum or steering group to ensure that there is clear direction and visible management support for security initiatives within the organization. It could be part of an existing executive body, which might be appropriate in a smaller organization where the members of the top management team will also, broadly, be the members of the information security forum. More usually, it will be a separate cross-functional body, adequately resourced for its responsibility, reporting to a member of the top management team. In this book, we will usually refer to this management group as "the forum." The effectiveness of this forum will be fundamental to both the effectiveness of the ISMS and compliance with clauses 5.1 and 5.2 of the standard.

Once the ISMS has been fully established, the forum should meet at least twice a year and preferably quarterly. All its activities should be formally documented, together with its decisions and the reasons for them. Copies of all material presented at the meetings should be retained, and subsequent meetings should track actions agreed, report on progress for each of them and document these steps. This group should be responsible for:

- Identifying information security goals that meet the organization's requirements; ensuring that there are adequate resources for achieving them; and ensuring that the ISMS is properly integrated into the organization's processes.
- The review and approval of the organization's information security policy, setting the scope of the ISMS, ensuring that information security objectives and plans are established, agreeing the ISMS itself and agreeing how roles and responsibilities should be allocated within the organization in respect of the policy. This should include appointing, or

agreeing the appointment of, the manager responsible for information security within the organization, together with the key responsibilities of the role.

■ Ensuring that sufficient resources are provided to develop, implement, operate and maintain the ISMS.

■ Monitoring changes in exposure of key organizational information assets to major threats, deciding (within the context of any existing organizational risk treatment framework) acceptable levels of risk and ensuring that awareness of these threats is developed as well as ensuring that the importance of complying with the ISMS is adequately communicated to the organization.

■ Ensuring that procedures and controls are implemented that are capable of promptly detecting and responding to incidents, as well as the review and oversight of information security incidents, and receiving reports from the information security manager on the status and progress of specific implementations, security threats, results of reviews, audits, etc. and ensuring adequate steps are taken to implement any findings.

■ The approval of major initiatives (such as any individual initiative associated with the implementation of ISO/IEC 27001) to improve information security within the organization.

■ Establishing means of ensuring compliance with the policy and reviewing these measures periodically.

■ Ensuring that information security requirements meet the business objectives.

■ Ensuring that control implementation is coordinated across the organization.

■ Ensuring that adequate steps are taken, on an ongoing basis, to improve the ISMS.

Management review

The standard introduces, at clause 6, a requirement for an upper management review of the ISMS, and this should take place at predetermined intervals, agreed by the board, usually annual. The review process is similar to that required by ISO 9000, and the standard sets out the minimum inputs and outputs expected of such a review, which, ideally, should be carried out by the forum. The inputs are all discussed at appropriate points in this book, and the information security manager should be made responsible for gathering together the input and communicating, to all concerned, the outputs (decisions) of the review.

Information security manager

ISO/IEC 17799 expects one senior executive to be made responsible for all security-related activities. There is a potential conflict between this expectation and the requirement in the standard (control A.10.1.3) for segregation of duties, and the organization should pay particular attention to the standard when finalizing its arrangements. This person could be appointed before the forum is set up, and his or her brief could include the formation of the forum. The benefit in this route is one of speed and, potentially, of simplicity. The senior executive who has been charged with the responsibility of ensuring implementation of the ISMS could simply select and appoint an appropriate executive and the information security manager (while each organization will apply a title appropriate to its own culture, this book will for consistency use this title throughout) and a project team, who could then take things forward. The selection and training of the members of a forum are potentially more time consuming, and the period during which they are learning their roles will precede the point at which they are competent to select and appoint an appropriate manager. The organization may not wish to pursue this slower route.

While the information security manager does not need to be the same person who is appointed as the organization's information security expert (the skill sets required for the managerial role, particularly in a larger organization, are likely to be different from those required for the security expert's role), this person will still need adequate training in information security matters, and the discussion below, headed "Specialist information security advice," should be read in conjunction with this section. Obviously, the person selected for the executive role will need to be an effective manager, with well-developed communications and project management skills.

This manager should be charged with a number of defined and key activities. Depending on the culture and structure of the organization, these could include:

■ establishing and chartering the management information security forum (unless the organization chooses to establish the forum first and then ask the forum to select the manager);

- developing, with the forum, the security policy, its objectives and strategy;
- defining, with the forum, the scope of the ISMS;
- briefing the forum on current threats, vulnerabilities and steps taken to counter them;
- carrying out the initial risk assessment;
- identifying changed risks and ensuring that appropriate action is taken;
- ensuring that the risk is managed by agreeing with the executive board, and the forum, the organization's approach to risk management, the risk treatment plan and the level of assurance that will be necessary;
- selecting control objectives and controls that, when implemented, will meet the objectives;
- preparing the Statement of Applicability;
- recording and handling security incidents, including establishing their causes and determining appropriate corrective and/or preventive action;
- reporting to the forum on progress with implementing the ISMS, and on incidents, issues, security matters and current threats;
- carrying out reviews;
- monitoring compliance with the standard;
- preventive action, including all the requirements identified in clause 7.3 of the standard. There should be a documented procedure that identifies the IS manager's responsibility for preventive action and that sets out how the risk treatment plan should be managed and what additional monitoring and information-gathering may be necessary for this responsibility to be effectively discharged.

The cross-functional management forum

ISO/IEC 17799 also explains in some more detail what is best practice around the ISO/IEC 27001 (A.6.1.2) requirements for information security coordination. This is particularly relevant for larger organizations, where security activity needs to be coordinated across a number of divisions, companies or sites, each of which may have its own information security manager or adviser. This cross-functional forum should, practically speaking, be integrated into the management information security forum. ISO/IEC 17799 identifies the range of activities that might be carried out by this cross-functional forum as:

- agreeing, across the organization, specific roles and responsibilities in respect of information security;
- agreeing the specific methodologies and processes that are to be used in implementation of the information security policy;
- agreeing and supporting cross-organizational information security initiatives;
- ensuring that the corporate planning process includes information security considerations;
- assessing the adequacy and coordinating the implementation of specific controls for new systems, products or services;
- reviewing information security incidents;
- ensuring that the whole organization is aware of the way in which information security is tackled.

There is a lot of overlap between the possible functions of the management forum and the cross-functional group. An external certification auditor will want to know how the two key functions, coherent management of information security and coordination of information security-related activity, have been tackled. One route, clearly, is for each forum to have very clearly differentiated functions and for the reporting lines between the two to be drawn very unambiguously.

Usefully, in all but the largest organizations, these two forums can be combined. Practically, this is sensible, as otherwise the structural issues of relating the two forums and of clarifying what issues are dealt with at which level can create unnecessary bureaucracy. Where two separate groups are set up, the first to operate more at the strategic level and the second more at the implementation level, the time of the information security and functional specialists will be stretched as they will need to contribute to both. The managerial benefits of combining the two groups are so significant that this book will proceed on the basis that this is the appropriate route and our use of the term "forum" will henceforth refer to this combined group.

The detailed work (much of what is set out in ISO/IEC 17799's proposals for the activities of the coordination forum) of the management forum is then best dealt with by asking the manager responsible for information security to draw up, outside the formal meetings, proposals as to how each of the issues should be dealt with. These proposals should then be tabled, discussed and agreed by the forum. All meetings of this forum should be documented, as should actions agreed and progress against them.

ISO/IEC 27001 project group

Ideally, the forum should be set up at the outset of the project and chaired by the senior executive or VP who is designated as responsible for the implementation of the ISMS. The forum should, initially, be the project team that sees implementation through to successful conclusion and whose on-going role clearly evolves from this initial responsibility. This intention should be clearly documented in the project plan and in the first minutes of the forum and/or terms of reference for the group.

Members

Members of the forum should be selected from across the organization. Members need to be in executive or similarly senior positions within the organization. Key functions that should be represented are quality/process management, human resources, training, IT and facilities management; they may all have to change their working practices significantly as a result of the decision to implement an ISMS. Apart from the executive responsible for information security and the trained information security expert, the most critical representation will be from sales, operations and administration. These tend to be the functions in which the majority of the organization's personnel are employed and the ones that will be most affected by the implementation of an ISMS. Ideally, the people invited to represent these functions should be amongst the most senior and widely respected individuals within them.

As discussed earlier in this book, the change process that ISO/IEC 27001 implementation will require has a cultural impact. It is critical that those most able to represent and articulate the needs and concerns of the key parts of the organization are included on the working party. Without their involvement, there is unlikely to be the "buy-in" necessary for the ISMS to be effectively developed and implemented.

Clause 5.2.2 of the standard requires the organization to ensure that all personnel are competent to perform the tasks assigned to them in the ISMS. This will require the organization to determine the competences required, first of the forum members and, later, of those charged with implementation. This chapter has pointed at the range of competences that may be required, and final decisions should be documented. See also the discussion on training in Chapter 9.

As soon as the members of the implementation team have been chosen, and once their mission and role have been explained to them, it will be necessary to give them some initial exposure to the standard and to information security. There are a number of ways that this can be done. One is to send them on a training course. However, the training courses that exist, at the date of writing of this book, tend to be focused more on the needs of the project manager responsible for implementing an ISMS or on information security specialists; they tend not to be suitable as a general introduction to the subject for people who will not need to become too deeply involved in many of the details of the ISMS. Another, obviously, is to give them each a copy of this book; the first six chapters of the book are probably the ones that will be most useful for the non-specialist members of the implementation team.

It is equally critical that all members of the working party understand clearly that their role is to put together and implement an ISMS that meets the corporate requirement. The chief executive needs to set this requirement clearly in front of the working party. There will undoubtedly be divergences of opinion between members of the team at many points during the implementation process and on a wide variety of issues. This should make for a stronger ISMS, as what emerges will be more likely to meet all the requirements of the organization. However, if the process is not effectively managed, this working party could also be the graveyard of the information security strategy.

When healthy disagreement degenerates to competition and open warfare, there will be little or no progress; if what emerges from the process is simply the view of one faction or another, it will not be successfully implemented. Equally, it is possible for the working party to become bogged down in procedural issues or to be ultra-cautious in how it tackles the implementation challenge. While the danger of the project dragging on can be dealt with by setting a very clear date by which implementation must be complete (even to the point of writing it into the individual performance objectives of all the members of the team) it can still fail because the working party simply doesn't work effectively. Clearly, therefore, the most important choice to be made in respect of both the implementation working party and the management forum into which it will evolve is that of its chair.

Chair

The choice of chair for this group is usually critical to its success, both as a group and in terms of how the rest of the organization views and responds to it. The chair needs, therefore, to be someone who is capable of commanding the respect of all members of the working party. He or she needs to be wholly committed to achieving the goal of a certified ISMS within the board-agreed timetable. He or she needs to be pragmatic and prepared to "think outside the box" in identifying solutions to organizational problems that are affecting implementation. This person should not be from any one of the organization's support functions as this will usually brand the project as an unimportant one. It should, on no account, be led by an IT person, as the implementation of an ISMS simply cannot afford to be seen as only an IT project. He or she should, preferably, have a broad managerial responsibility within the organization as well as experience in implementing cross-organizational change projects. Ideally, he or she will be the chief executive or other senior executive who has been charged with implementation of the corporate security policy. In smaller organizations, this person might also be the executive responsible for information security; in larger organizations, where this is likely to be a full-time role, the manager responsible for information security should properly report to the chair of the forum. The need for segregation of duties needs also to be considered.

Not only is the structure outlined here the most effective method for delivery of the ISMS, but it is also very clear evidence of commitment from the very top of the organization to its implementation. The external ISO/IEC 27001 auditor should be suitably impressed.

Records

Meetings should be scheduled ahead of time, to ensure that everyone who will be needed can diarize them and be present. The frequency of meetings during the implementation phase will reflect the urgency and complexity of the implementation plan. In practical terms, meetings held fortnightly for the first few months of the implementation timetable can contribute to building momentum in it. After that, they can drop to monthly events. Once implementation is complete, the forum might meet on a quarterly basis or when there are significant changes or business issues to consider. The forum should decide how often it needs to meet, set out its reasons and record the decision.

Meetings do not, of course, require physical attendance. They can take place by videoconference or by teleconference. What matters is that all members are able to take part, that they have adequate notice of the meeting and that the meetings are properly managed and documented.

Normal meeting principles should be established and maintained. All meetings should have an agenda and an attendance record, and action points/key decisions should be minuted, with information about who is responsible for what actions and within what timescales. Minutes should be retained as part of the quality records, and the external auditor is likely to want to review them. In practical terms, the quality function within the organization is usually best placed to provide the secretariat to this group.

While the external auditor will be particularly interested in what has been done about action points identified in the minutes, forum meetings can easily degenerate into long reviews of the minutes and actions arising from the previous meeting. Pragmatically, if the minutes are scheduled on the agenda to be dealt with at the end of the meeting, right before any other business, meetings will be quicker and the organization will make substantially faster progress with the overall implementation. The chair should, prior to the meeting, have ensured that action points have been dealt with; this enables them to be reported on very quickly when the appropriate point on the agenda is reached.

As a matter of principle, one of the authors insists on starting meetings at the scheduled time, irrespective of how many people are in the room, and refuses to sum up progress so far for late arrivals. In the long (and sometimes the short) run, everyone learns to arrive on time.

Allocation of information security responsibilities

ISO/IEC 27001, at control A.6.1.3, requires that "responsibilities for the protection of individual assets and for carrying out specific security processes shall be clearly defined." While the information security policy may provide general guidance as to who is responsible for which information security asset, this guidance is likely to be very broad, particularly if the policy model suggested in this book is adopted. It will not necessarily be clear to individual employees, from the policy statement, what their specific responsibilities will be. In any case, the organization will need to define clearly who is responsible for which security process and/or information asset and may have to look at geographic or site responsibilities as well.

For instance, while the need for an information security manager is clear, it is nevertheless usual to identify individual owners of information security assets throughout the organization and confirm to them in detail and in writing their responsibilities in respect of these assets. This is an incredibly effective way of ensuring that the security of individual information assets is properly maintained on a day-to-day basis. Clause 6.1.3 of ISO/IEC 17799 provides more information on this issue but does not add anything to what we have said here.

There are generic responsibilities for members of particular groups of staff. The responsibilities of the members of the forum have been discussed, as have those of the information security manager. Those mentioned below could provide the basis for defining individual responsibilities within the organization and should be drawn more specifically to reflect the organizational structure and systems.

IT departments should be responsible for the overall security of the system(s) for which they are responsible. This includes threat identification, assessing risks, managing projects, reviews and reporting on activity. Server room security should be another of their responsibilities.

Local administrators will have specific responsibilities for user registration and deletion, system monitoring, preparing security procedures, managing change control with defined boundaries, handling data back-up, designing application security, implementing internal controls and testing contingency and fall-back plans.

System managers should be responsible, at the system level, for threat identification, assessing risks, implementing selected security controls, securely configuring the system(s), setting up the user ID and password system, setting up system security monitoring, implementing change control, setting up all necessary security procedures and maintaining and testing business continuity plans.

Network managers should be responsible (at the individual domain or independent network level) for network perimeter threat identification, assessing risks, implementing selected network security controls (including firewalls), securely (designing and) configuring the network, setting up security monitoring, implementing change control, setting up security procedures and maintaining and testing network recovery plans.

Site managers should be responsible, in respect of the physical site for which they are the nominated manager, for threat identification, assessing risks, implementing selected physical controls (including perimeter controls), fire detection and response, utility services and their back-up, delivery and dispatch controls, and maintaining and testing the site's business continuity plan. For the purposes of the ISMS, every site from which the organization operates should have at least one site manager. Where the site is a large and complex one, perhaps including a number of organizations, or divisions of organizations, then a number of site managers may be required.

A method of coordinating their activity will then be necessary. Clearly, the site manager responsibility would normally be combined with a number of other line management responsibilities.

IT users throughout the organization should be required to be aware of and follow the organization's security policy and procedures, maintain the clear desk policy and other physical security procedures, follow the password and access control procedures, back up PC data (particularly important for notebook and PDA users) and report security incidents.

Third parties should be required to comply with their contractual responsibilities and to be aware of the host organization's security procedures and practices.

The identification of these individual responsibilities will be done throughout the process of pulling together the detailed information security procedures; it is important for the forum members and the information security manager to be aware from the outset that this will be a key component of the drafting process for every procedure. It would be as well to adopt, at the outset, a standard template for the drafting of processes or procedures that includes headings such as "purpose," "process/procedure owner," "individuals/roles identified as having responsibilities under this document," "date for review (if any)." These are in addition to the parameters required to effect suitable document control and confidentiality/availability status. There may be other items worth adding to such a template; the purpose is to ensure that all the key components are systematically included in each new document.

Approval process for information processing facilities

Control A.6.1.4 of ISO/IEC 27001 requires the organization to establish an authorization process for new information processing facilities. This is a wide-ranging requirement that impacts, particularly in the normal office networked environment, on virtually any addition or change to virtually any component of the system. An "information processing facility" could be a new software system, a new data centre, a new workstation or server, a new piece of software or even a new software utility.

Modern computer systems and, particularly, networked environments change quickly as software is improved and business requirements—often at the individual user level—evolve. ISO/IEC 17799 recognizes that this is an issue for personal information processing facilities that are being used at home or outside the workplace for processing business information, just as it is an issue in the workplace.

It is critical that the organization designs and adopts an authorization process that recognizes these environments and that provides appropriate flexibility to the business and its employees while simultaneously assuring its information security.

Such an authorization process should identify those changes that can be made without needing individual review and evaluation and set out a procedure that will enable them to be documented and made quickly and easily. Other facilities or changes might need minimal review and yet others might pose the level of risk that would require a full evaluation before they are authorized. At various stages in this book, controls around such changes will be considered; the principle that the authorization process needs to be appropriate to the risk needs to be established at the outset.

At the simplest level, any new equipment must be chosen to meet defined security and business requirements. Business unit manager authorization should be obtained to demonstrate that business requirements are met. IT department approval is required as evidence that the equipment complies with the organization's technical requirements, and the security manager's approval is required to indicate that it will comply with, and not cause breaches to, existing security controls and procedures. These authorizations should be documented (signed and dated by an authorized person). The organization should design a simple "new equipment" approval form that deals with this; the form might be combined with the capital expenditure requests, for simplicity.

Product selection and the Common Criteria

The implementation of an ISMS will require the forum and information security adviser to source, assess and implement a range of information technology security equipment of which they have no previous experience. It will be insufficient simply to rely on the experience of the current IT management or the information provided by the vendor that most recently pitched its wares to the IT or procurement people inside the organization.

One method of assessing the suitability of information security products to identify those that will most adequately meet the security requirements of the organization is to use the Common Criteria. The Common Criteria for Information Technology Security Evaluation (ITSEC) define general concepts and principles of IT security evaluation and present a general model of evaluation that describes IT security objectives, selects and defines IT security requirements, and assists in writing high-level specifications for products and systems. Their origins go back over 10 years and across North America and Europe, and are now an international standard (ISO 27).

The Common Criteria (CC), in effect, provide a common standard against which security products can be evaluated and certified. In North America, the National Institute of Standards and Technology (NIST) and the National Security Agency (NSA) are jointly responsible for the US involvement in the CC scheme and for the US version of it, the Common Criteria Evaluation and Validation Scheme (CCEVS). It publishes, on its website (http:// niap.nist.gov/cc-scheme), a list of validated products that have been independently assessed and have met the CC standards. It should be noted that, as these assessments are not done free, few of the newest products, or those designed by new businesses, appear in the directories. However, CC does offer a method of assessing products against standards.

Specialist information security advice

ISO/IEC 17799:2005 dropped the specific requirement for an organization to deploy a specialist information security adviser. It does, however, recognize that an organization needs to have specialist advice available, and what was a separate control prior to this revision has now been included in control 6.1.1, discussed above. The organization may need advice from in-house or specialist external security advisers. While ISO/IEC 17799 no longer provides detailed guidance on this issue, our view is that, while not all organizations will wish to employ their own specialist internal adviser and may prefer that a non-specialist internal adviser is given the security management responsibility, this person should have access to external advice that provides specialist input that covers any areas in which the in-house person is deficient. It is particularly important that, in the areas of security technology and information technology generally, specialist advice is retained and is easily available. The speed with which technology, vulnerabilities, threats and defenses are evolving is so fast that it is difficult for any single individual to keep completely on top of them all.

While there is a discussion in Chapter 9 of this book about information security education and training, particularly for the users of information security facilities, it is at this point appropriate to look at the qualifications that might be appropriate for an in-house specialist adviser or that one might expect to be evidenced by an external specialist.

One option is for the organization to employ someone who appears to be qualified by experience to provide the required specialist information and security advice. It can be difficult for an inexperienced recruiter to identify someone who is really adequately experienced for this role. As correct selection of this person is critical to the early success of the ISO/IEC 27001 project, it is worth taking a structured approach to resolving the issue.

It is recommended that any organization pursuing ISO/IEC 27001 specifies from the outset that its information security adviser be appropriately qualified and that, if someone who does not have a formal qualification but claims to be qualified through experience is recruited for the role, he or she be required (as a condition of continuing in employment beyond the initial probationary period) to demonstrate this competence by acquiring an appropriate qualification.

The key areas in which the information security adviser should be able to demonstrate competence are:

▪ information security management concepts (confidentiality, integrity, availability, vulnerability, threats, risks and countermeasures, etc.);
▪ current legislation and regulations that impact information security management in North America;
▪ current national and international standards, frameworks and organizations that facilitate the management of information security;
▪ the current business and technical environments in which information security management takes place (security products, malicious software ("malware"), relevant technology, etc.);
▪ the categorization, operation and effectiveness of a variety of safeguards.

Globally, there are now about 30 different vendor-neutral information security certificates, including those sponsored by the International Information Systems Security Certification Consortium [(ISC)^2]. There are also a growing number of training courses that relate specifically to these two core information security standards. There is a further discussion of training in Chapter 9, and information about current information security certificates is available from the KnowledgeBank on the IT Governance website.

It is also now possible to obtain a distance learning, postgraduate qualification in information security management from the UK's Open University. This course, numbered M886, is designed to help employees understand, create and manage both strategic and operational aspects of information security, and it uses the UK version of this book as its core textbook. We believe that this course is unique.

The organization should, in appointing its information security adviser, pay as much attention to the quality of the individual as to his or her qualifications and formal experience. The nature of information security threats is always changing, and the technology and context within which an organization is maintaining its information are in constant flux. The information security adviser needs to be able to respond to new threats and find and protect vulnerabilities in new technologies that the organization wants to deploy to improve its competitive advantage. This requires a flexibility of thought allied to a depth of experience and a structured, balanced—and open-minded—approach to all the information security issues that the organization will encounter. Of course, high-quality people need appropriate compensation packages; this will be money well spent.

It is imperative that the organization has a method of remaining current with changing issues in the information security environment. The starting point should be NIST's Computer Security Resource Center (CSRC), whose website is at http://csrc.nist.gov. This site is an excellent information center resource for information security professionals; in particular, it carries substantial quantities of technical and security information on most issues that will be of interest in setting up a certifiable ISMS.

There are a number of sources of regular information on information security issues. There are two other specific information security magazines worth investigating and whose subscription cost offers (we believe) clear value for money. These are: 1) *SC Magazine*—available online and offline, with editions for the US, UK and Asia Pacific, with a website at www.scmagazine.com; and 2) *Information Security*—available worldwide and published by TruSecure Corporation, whose website is www.infosecuritymag.com. There are also online services and information security websites. Ernst & Young have a very comprehensive independent security portal at www.esecurityonline.com; this is a good source of independent information and has a wide range of white papers on security issues. It also contains substantial information on security products. An online service worth exploring is *Security Wire Digest*, published twice a week by TruSecure's *Information Security* magazine and distributed by e-mail. Their contact details are as above and there is an online registration process to receive this e-mail.

Each of these sources of information should supplement regular visits to the Microsoft website as well as those of providers of any other chosen and installed corporate software, including particularly the providers of the chosen firewall and antivirus software. These sites will usually be the first places that identify specific threats to their software and propose solutions. The information security specialist should follow all these information sources on a regular basis and act immediately a new threat or vulnerability is identified. Sometimes, the newspapers can identify threats as fast as any other organization; no source of information should be ignored!

Contact with authorities and with special interest groups

ISO/IEC 27001 requires, at controls A.6.1.6 and A.6.1.7, that "appropriate contacts" will be maintained with "relevant authorities" (law enforcement bodies, fire departments, and supervisory or regulatory bodies, ISPs and telecommunications operators) and with "special interest groups and other specialist security forums and professional associations (e.g. sources of specialist advice)." Neither the standard nor ISO/IEC 17799 sets out what would constitute "appropriate contacts"; the latter does, however, set out clearly the purpose in maintaining contacts with authorities and is to enable the organization to take appropriate action quickly, or to obtain appropriate advice, should events (security incidents) require it.

To an extent, this will be considered further in Chapter 26, which deals with business continuity management. For the purposes of this chapter, though, the organization's information security adviser (who is expected, by the standard, to be consulted and involved in all information security incidents) should systematically develop, over the first month in the role, a series of contacts with the local police and, through them, with the nearest police specialist "cybercrime" unit, with the organization's contracted providers of information and telecommunications services and, in particular, with those members of their staff who are responsible for dealing with information security issues, and with local or national networks of information security specialists.

Independent review of information security

Finally, this section of the standard requires the organization to have its implementation of its information security policy independently reviewed. ISO/IEC 17799 makes it clear that this does not mean bringing in outside auditors to review the ISMS ahead of bringing in outside third party certification auditors to certify it.

It does, however, recognize (as does a quality management system) that an organization ought to have its implementation of any key system or process reviewed by someone other than the person responsible for implementing it. This is a standard principle of an ISO 9000-certificated management system, and any organization that has such a management system in place can simply graft an extra responsibility on to those who have the existing ones. Clause 6.1.8 of ISO/IEC 17799 explicitly says that reviews can be carried out by an existing internal audit function.

An internal audit function that only has experience in financial audit will not, however, be adequately trained to carry out a quality audit. Equally, an audit function that already deals with internal audit of another management system will not be automatically capable of competently conducting an ISO/IEC 27001 audit.

All third party certification services providers will offer training courses for internal audit teams and it would be appropriate to use the company that is going to deliver the organization's ISO/IEC 27001 certification for this training. Quality system auditing is a necessary basis for ISMS auditing, but is not sufficient. At the very least, the internal auditor should attend a course that is run by a certification body and that is designed to inform and assist delegates who need a clear introduction to principles and objectives of ISO/IEC 27001 and information security management.

Summary

The organization should put in place, from the outset, the management framework required by the standard and make it responsible for implementation of the board's information security policy. Initial training of the key people, particularly the specialist information security adviser, is important and worth investing the time and money in before starting the process of implementation. Once the groundwork is laid, progress can be quick.

5

Information security policy and scope

Once the management structure has been thought through, the initial ISMS establishment issues have been completely understood and the initial training of the key personnel who will be involved in the development of the policy has been completed, the next step in the Plan phase can commence.

Information security policy

The first step in the establishment of an ISMS is the definition of the information security policy. This requirement is set out in clause 4.2.1 of the standard (and control A.5.1). It is not always, however, as straightforward as it seems. It may be an iterative process (particularly in complex organizations dealing with complex information security issues and/or multiple domains) and the final form of security policy that is adopted may therefore have to reflect the final risk assessment that has been carried out and the statement of applicability that emerges from that.

Clause 4.2.1 sets out clearly the components of the ISMS policy. Its scope, and the policy itself, must take into account the characteristics of the business, its organization, location, assets and technology. The policy must include a framework for setting its objectives and establish the overall sense of direction. It must take into account all relevant business, legal, regulatory and contractual security requirements. It must establish the strategic context (for both organization and risk management) within which the ISMS will be established. It must establish criteria for the evaluation of risk and the structure of the risk assessment. Of course, top management must approve it.

The security policy will also have to be regularly reviewed and updated in the light of changing circumstances, environment and experience. As a minimum, if there is no earlier reason for the executive board to review its policy, it should be reviewed annually and the board should agree that the policy remains appropriate (or otherwise) to its needs in the light of any changes to the corporate context, to the risk assessment criteria or in the identified risks. There may be components of the policy that ought to be reviewed very regularly, even monthly, and these should be identified through the risk assessment.

Initially, the information security policy is a short statement (we think organizations should aim for a maximum of two pages) that is designed to set out clearly the strategic aims and control objectives that will guide the development of the ISMS. The policy may go through a number of stages of development, particularly in the light of the risk assessment, but the final version must satisfy clause 5.1.1 of the standard and appropriately reflect the good practice that is set out in clause 5 of ISO/IEC 17799, and the guidance in the introduction to ISO/IEC 17799 should have been read and taken into account. Proof that the policy has been approved by management, published and communicated internally, and that it is reviewed regularly (usually annually, as a minimum), with any changes similarly published and communicated, will enable the organization to satisfy control A.5.1 of the standard, "Security Policy."

The key questions that the initial policy statement must succinctly answer are:

- Who?
- Where?
- What?
- Why?

Usually, the executive who has been charged with leading the implementation of the ISMS will be charged with drafting a security policy and formal paper that proposes how these questions should be answered. This paper should seek to be as objective as possible in working through the possible answers to these four questions so that the executive board can identify and focus on those issues that require clarification or where difficult decisions may be necessary.

A copy of that section of the minutes (preferably initialed by the chair as a correct copy) of the board meeting in which the security policy was debated and adopted should be filed with the security policy documentation. It can be a controlled document and it does, for audit purposes, provide useful and immediate evidence of the process by which the policy was adopted, and of any amendments to it. This, together with the proposal that was put to the board, is the first part of the evidence that clause 4.3 (documentation requirements) of the standard requires to demonstrate that the actions set out in clause 4.2 did take place.

The policy itself should then be issued as a controlled document and made available to all who fall within its scope; as a minimum, members of the senior management team should receive individual copies and copies should be posted on all internal noticeboards, both the physical and electronic ones. These copies of the policy document should, of course, be clearly marked as controlled copies, to ensure that they are updated to reflect any changes that take place. Copies handed out, as part of training or awareness seminars, should be marked as uncontrolled copies.

Who?

"The board and management" have to be completely behind and committed to the ISMS; therefore, the policy statement must be issued under their authority and there should be clear evidence, in the form of written minutes, that the policy was debated and agreed, both by the board as a whole and by the management steering group. Any revisions to the policy should also be debated and agreed by both the board and the steering group. From a practical point of view, it is worth keeping the policy statement as simple, as comprehensive and as broad as possible so as to allow management adequate freedom to respond to changing corporate and security circumstances in implementing it without needing to return to the board and the forum for the policy itself to be freshly agreed.

It will also require participation by all employees in the organization and may require participation from customers, suppliers, stockholders and other third parties. This is part of the context of the ISMS referred to earlier. In thinking through the security policy, the board and the forum will need to consider how it will impact on these constituents and/or audiences and the benefits and disadvantages that the corporation will experience as a result of this.

Where? (Scope of the policy)

Those parts of the organization to which the policy is going to apply need to be clearly identified. This may be done on the basis of corporate, divisional or management structure, or on the basis of geographic location. A virtual organization, or a dispersed, multi-site operation, may have different security issues than one located on a single site. In practical terms, a security policy that encompasses all of the activities within a specific entity for which a specific board of directors or management team is responsible is more easily implemented than one that is to be applied to only part of the entity. It is important to ensure that the board of directors that is implementing the policy does actually have adequate control over the operations specified within the policy and that it will be able to give a clear mandate to the executive management team to implement it within that entity. Chapter 6's "Identify the boundaries" should also be read at this point, particularly as the ISMS is required to be considered within the overall organizational context.

It is critical, if there are aspects of the organization's activities or systems that are to be excluded from the requirements of the security policy, that these are clearly identified—and explained—at this stage. Multi-site or virtual organizations will need to consider carefully the different security requirements of their different sites and the management implications of them. There should be clear boundaries ("defined in terms of the characteristics of the organization, its location, assets and technology") within which the security policy and ISMS will apply. Any exclusions should be openly debated by the board and the steering group and the minutes should set out how and why the decision was taken. It is possible that, in fact, divisions of the organization, components of the information system or specific assets will not be able to be excluded from the scope either because they are already so integral to it or because their exclusion might have the effect of undermining the information security objectives themselves. It must, therefore, be clear that any exclusions do not in any way undermine the security of the organization to be assessed.

Auditors will be assessing how management applies its policy across the whole of the organization that is defined as being within the scope of the policy and should be expected to test to their limits the boundaries of the stated scope to ensure that all interdependencies and points of weakness have been identified and adequately dealt with.

In reality, as stated earlier, the process of designing and implementing an effective ISMS may be made simpler by including the entire organization for which the board has responsibility.

There is an argument, in large, complex organizations, for a phased approach to implementation. Where it really is possible to define adequately a subsidiary part of the organization, such that its information security needs can be independently assessed, it may be possible to gain substantial experience in designing and implementing an ISMS, as well as a track record of success and the momentum that accompanies it, such that a subsequent roll-out to the rest of the organization can be carried through successfully and smoothly. These considerations apply to any large, complex project, and the appropriate answer depends very much on individual organizational circumstances.

It would certainly be a mistake to define the scope too narrowly. While it may appear, on the surface, that this is a route to a quick and easy certification, it is in fact a route to a worthless certificate. Any external party, assessing the nature of an organization's ISMS, will want to be sure that all the critical functions that may affect its relationship are included and a limited scope will not do this. We are aware that some certification organizations are prepared to consider scopes that cover less than a complete business unit and, in our opinion, they are doing a disservice to their clients as well as to the integrity of the ISO/IEC 27001 certification scheme. Do not be tempted to use such certification bodies.

The overall issue of scoping is certainly one where experienced, professional support can be helpful in assessing the best way forward.

What?

The statement that the board and management "are committed to preserving the confidentiality, integrity and availability of information" is at the heart of a security policy and an ISMS. It is important to define precisely the key terms used in the policy, and we recommend that the definitions contained in ISO/IEC 27001 and, where necessary, in ISO/IEC 17799 are used. The introduction to ISO/IEC 17799 defines information very widely:

> Information [can be] printed or written on paper, stored electronically, transmitted by post or using electronic means, shown on films, [or] spoken in conversation.

In other words, appropriate protection is required for *all* forms of information:

> Confidentiality [is defined in clause 3.1 of the standard as] ensuring that information is accessible only to those authorized to have access.
>
> Integrity [is defined as] safeguarding the accuracy and completeness of information and processing methods by protecting against unauthorized modification.
>
> Availability [is defined as] ensuring that authorized users have access to information and associated assets when required.

Availability is particularly important to corporations engaged in e-commerce. Any corporation that depends for its very existence on the availability of its website, but that fails to take adequate steps to ensure that the site is up, running and running properly at all times, is likely to fail as a business much more quickly than a traditional bricks-and-mortar corporation that is unable to open its shop doors for a few days.

Board, executive management team and staff of the organization should all understand that these are the definitions of these words and they should be prominently described and set out in the early briefings to staff and in internal communications. Auditors from certification bodies are likely to check (probably randomly) that staff understand what these words mean and, while they will not look for staff to remember verbatim these definitions, will want staff to demonstrate practical understanding of how the pursuit of these aspects of information security is likely to impact their own work. This level of understanding is required, as a minimum, so that each member of staff is able to recognize and react appropriately to a security incident. Information security incident management is covered in Chapter 25, and staff's role in this in Chapter 9, "Human resources security."

As part of defining the "what," the organization will also need to define which physical and intellectual assets are to be covered by the policy; the kinds of technology employed and the basis on which the organization operates will also strongly influence the scope of the ISMS.

There is also the point at which the organization needs to determine its criteria for accepting risks and identify the levels of risk it will accept. It is a truism to point out that there is a relationship between the levels of risk and reward in any business. Most corporations, particularly those subject to SOX, will want to be very clear about which risks they will accept and which they won't, the extent to which they will accept risks and how they wish to control them. Management needs to specify its approach, in general and in particular, so that the corporation can be managed within that context. Risk assessment is discussed further in Chapter 6.

Why?

Information security, says the introduction to ISO/IEC 17799, is "the protection of information from a wide range of threats in order to ensure business continuity, minimize business damage and maximize return on investments and business opportunities" and is also "essential to maintain competitive edge, cash-flow, profitability, legal compliance and commercial image."

The initial staff communication process should set out clearly the nature of the threats faced by the organization and the possible costs, in both financial and non-financial terms, of information security breaches. The information provided in this book can be used for that purpose but, wherever possible, local and/or industry-specific information should be sought and used, as this gives immediacy and currency to the possible threats. Illustrations of the possible consequences to the organization itself should be developed in order to help all those involved to appreciate fully the need for the ISMS.

The "where" and the "what" answers above form the basis of the statement of the scope of the ISMS. There is a further, and more detailed, discussion of some of the issues related to scoping the policy in the next chapter, in the context of risk assessments. There should be a single document that sets out clearly the organization(s) that fall within the scope of the policy, which locations, which assets and which technologies. This statement of scope is an essential initial document, which not only helps focus the development of the ISMS but also makes clear to all concerned the seriousness of their responsibilities. It may be sensible, at this stage, to divide the organization into separate security domains. A "domain" is a discrete logical or physical area of an organization or network that is the subject of security controls designed to protect it from outside access. A domain should be capable of representation on a diagrammatic map. An organization or a network may be made up of one or a number of domains.

A policy statement

The initial policy statement might, therefore, read as follows:

> The board and management of organization Y, which operates in sector Z (or is in the business of Z, etc.), located in [ ], are committed to preserving the confidentiality, integrity and availability of all the physical and electronic information assets throughout their organization in order to maintain its competitive edge, cash-flow, profitability, legal and contractual compliance and commercial image. Information and information security requirements will continue to be aligned with organizational goals and the ISMS is intended to be a mechanism for information sharing. All employees of the organization are required to comply with this policy and with the ISMS that implements this policy. Certain third parties, as defined in the ISMS, will also be required to comply with it. This policy will be reviewed when necessary and at least annually.

In addition, the policy should contain a statement about the following:

■ Establishment of a top-level management steering group to support the ISMS framework and periodically review the security policy.
■ A description of the approach to risk management, the criteria against which risk will be evaluated, and the structure of the risk assessment.
■ Specific regulatory compliance requirements should be briefly identified, such as contingency and business continuity plans, the need for data back-up, avoidance of viruses, access control to systems, security incident reporting, and any specific requirements of, for instance, GLBA, HIPAA and other relevant legislation.
■ There should be a clear statement of the requirement that information security continue to be aligned to business goals and that the ISMS be subject to continuous improvement.

- All staff will receive security awareness training and specialized staff will receive more specialized training.
- The commitment to comply with, and achieve certification to, ISO/IEC 27001 could be formally stated.

This statement is sufficiently general to cover all the key components of information security for organization Y for the foreseeable future, but sufficiently precise and clear to be effective as a policy statement. It should clearly be approved by the management information security forum and signed by the most senior person in the organization (chairman, president, chief executive, director-general, etc.). A template for an information security policy is available through the website.

The security policy statement can be expanded, in the light of the risk assessment, to take into account the further guidance of clause 5.1.1 of ISO/IEC 17799. The policy statement proposed here does, however, meet the requirements of clause 4.2.1 of the standard.

Costs and monitoring progress

Any sensible board or management team will, at this stage, also require an estimate of the costs and resources involved in implementing the ISMS, an assessment and quantification of the potential benefits and an outline implementation plan that describes, at the top level, who will be responsible for doing what and by when. Such a document should be prepared and presented to the board along with the proposed security policy. This document should set out clearly the proposed dates at which the board will be invited to review progress toward final implementation so that it can ensure that its policy is being properly implemented.

As all organizations have their own preferred formats for doing this, this book does not set out how to do it. It only argues that review dates should be realistically spaced and that the plans it approves should allow executive management sufficient flexibility in implementing a policy that will have to be designed in the light of facts that are not known at the point at which the policy is adopted.

It is suggested that the key points at which progress might be reviewed are:

1. After completion of a draft Statement of Applicability (SoA). Any costs incurred prior to this should be minimal but, until the SoA defines what needs to be done, it will not be possible to budget effectively for the implementation.
2. After implementation of the initial suite of procedures that apply the identified controls.
3. After completion of the first cycle of system audits and reviews in accordance with control A.15.2 of the standard and prior to the initial visit by the certification body.
4. Annually, as part of the regular review of the ISMS, to ensure that the budget is being correctly applied and that any new technology issues, threats or vulnerabilities have been taken care of.

It is assumed that the organization will already have well-developed procedures for dealing with projects that are missing key review dates and in which there is overspending or underperformance. The book's website provides guidance on effective project governance, and this hard copy will not, therefore, make any proposals about what action should be taken to rectify any shortfalls, but will make the observation that early and vigorous action by the board to ensure that there is compliance with its requirement to design and implement an information security policy and management system will go a long way to proving to the organization the seriousness of the endeavor and, thus, to bring about its achievement.

6

The risk assessment and Statement of Applicability

Establishing security requirements

ISO/IEC 17799:2005 identifies three sources for establishing the organization's information security requirements: the risks that the organization faces (discussed further below); the risks arising from the compliance and contractual requirements imposed on the organization in each of the jurisdictions in which it operates (compliance requirements in particular discussed in Chapter 27); and the "particular set of principles, objectives and business requirements for information processing that an organization has developed to support its operations," which should largely fall out of the IT architecture the organization has established.

Where an organization's risk assessment and Statement of Applicability (SoA) were developed prior to release of ISO/IEC 17799:2005 and the publication in 2005 of ISO/IEC 27001, the organization should consider revising its risk assessment and will certainly need to revise its SoA to conform with the revised standards.

Risks, impacts and risk management

All organizations face risks of one sort or another on a daily basis. Risk management is a discipline that exists to deal with non-speculative risks, those risks from which only a loss can occur. In other words, speculative risks, those from which either a profit or a loss can occur, are the subject of the organization's business strategy whereas non-speculative risks, which can reduce the value of the assets with which the organization undertakes its speculative activity, are (usually) the subject of a risk management plan (in the standard, a "risk treatment plan"). These are sometimes called permanent and "pure" risks, in order to differentiate them from the crisis and speculative types.

Risk management plans usually have four, linked, objectives. These are:

1. to eliminate risks;
2. to reduce those that can't be eliminated to "acceptable" levels; and then either
3. to live with them, exercising carefully the controls that keep them "acceptable"; or
4. to transfer them, by means of insurance, to some other organization.

Pure, permanent risks are usually identifiable in economic terms; they have a financially measurable potential impact upon the assets of the organization. Risk management strategies are usually therefore based on an assessment of the economic benefits that the organization can derive from an investment in a particular control; in other words, for every control that the organization might implement, the calculation would be that the cost of implementation would be outweighed, preferably significantly, by the economic benefits that derive from, or economic losses that are avoided as a result of, its implementation. The organization should define its criteria for accepting risks (for example, it might say that it will accept any risk whose economic impact is less than the cost of controlling it) and for controlling risks (for example, it might say that any risk that has both a high likelihood and a high impact must be controlled to an identified level, or threshold).

The issue of the Treadway Commission's "Enterprise Risk Management—Integrated Framework" and the requirements (for financial sector organizations) of the Basel 2 accord have raised risk management and, in particular, operational risk management to a core function in most large organizations.

This book is not about risk management as a function, and appropriate training should be sought by anyone who is going to carry out such an activity. However, it is against this background, and that of the "ERM—Integrated Framework," that the requirements of IT governance and ISO/IEC 27001 should be considered. The standard requires a risk assessment to be undertaken. This is the foundation of the ISMS, and this requirement came center stage in the 1999 revision of BS 7799. It is even stronger in ISO/IEC 27001. Clause 4.2.1.c of the standard (Define a systematic approach to risk assessment) says an appropriate risk assessment, suited to the ISMS and the identified business, legal and regulatory requirements, *shall* be undertaken. The risk assessment should identify the threats to assets, vulnerabilities and impacts on the organization and should determine the degree of risk.

ISO/IEC 17799:2005 provides substantial guidance on risk assessment but no detailed guidance on how the assessment is to be conducted, because every organization is encouraged to choose the approach that is most applicable for its industry, complexity and risk environment. In its introduction, ISO/IEC 17799:2005 describes risk assessment in terms compatible with our introduction to it and refers the reader looking for more guidance to ISO 13335-3, which contains examples of risk assessment methodologies. This guide, while possibly helpful, is not mandatory. The UK standards body, BSI, has also published a third part to its version of the information security standard, BS 7799-3:2006, which deals with risk assessment and which is likely to form the basis of ISO/IEC 27004 when it is published.

ISO/IEC 17799 adopts (from ISO Guide 73:2002) definitions of risk, risk analysis, risk assessment, risk evaluation, risk management and risk treatment. We recommend that these definitions are, for the sake of consistency, adopted by any organization tackling risk management, and this book will proceed on that basis.

ISO/IEC 17799:2005 is clear, in its introduction, that risk assessment is a "systematic study of assets, threats, vulnerabilities and impacts to assess the probability and consequences of risks" or, in our terms, the systematic and methodical consideration of: 1) the business harm likely to result from a range of business failures; and 2) the realistic likelihood of such failures occurring. The insertion into ISO/IEC 17799:2005 of a new clause 4, dealing with risk assessments, indicates the importance of this issue and the expectation that every control decision that an organization makes will explicitly reflect a risk assessment.

The risk assessment must be a formal process. In other words, the process must be planned and the input data, their analysis and the results should all be recorded. "Formal" does not mean that risk assessment tools must be used although, in many situations, they may improve the process and add significant value. The complexity of the risk assessment will depend on the complexity of the organization and of the risks under review. The techniques employed to carry it out should be consistent with this complexity and the level of assurance required by the board.

Who conducts the risk assessment?

It is entirely up to the individual organization to choose who is to undertake this risk assessment, and how. There are two issues to consider before deciding who. The first is that the standard expects that periodic reviews of security risks and related controls will be carried out—taking account of new threats and vulnerabilities, assessing the impact of changes in the business, its goals or processes, technology and/or its external environment (such as legislation, regulation or society) and simply to confirm that controls remain effective and appropriate. Periodic review is a fundamental requirement of any risk assessment or risk management strategy.

The second is that it is an assumption of the standard (stated in the foreword) "that the execution of its provisions is entrusted to appropriately qualified and experienced people." The need for such a person was covered in some detail in Chapter 4. It is essential that the risk assessment is conducted by an appropriately qualified and experienced person. This is logical; the key step on which the entire ISMS will be built needs, itself, to be solid. The ISO/IEC 27001 auditor will, therefore, want to see documentary evidence of the formal qualifications and experience of this person.

A number of organizations will already have a risk management function, staffed by people with training that enables them to carry out risk assessments. The role of the risk management department is, usually, systematically to identify, evaluate and control potential losses to the organization that may result from things that haven't happened yet. The skills and methodology of this department may, or may not, meet the requirements of the standard. Either way, there are potentially significant benefits for such an organization if its information security risk assessments can be carried out by the same function that handles all risk assessments. The benefits lie not just in cost-effectiveness but in the fact that such a risk management, or risk control department, will have an existing and ongoing understanding of the business, its goals and environment and an appreciation of all the risks faced by the business in the pursuit of its objectives and, equally, should be able to assess how all the different risks, and the steps taken to counter them, are related and coordinated.

Many organizations, however, do not already have an internal risk management function. There are two possible ways to tackle the issue of risk assessment. The first is to hire an external consultant (or firm of consultants) to do it. The second is to train someone internally to do it. The second is preferable in most cases, as the risk assessment "shall be reviewed at appropriately defined intervals as required" and having the expertise in-house enables this to be done cost-effectively. Chapter 4 discussed how to recruit and/or train a specialist information security adviser and, if information security risks are the only ones being considered, then this would be the appropriate person to undertake the risk assessment.

In circumstances where the organization has existing arrangements with external suppliers for risk assessment services, or is in the process of setting up a risk management function or capability (in the context of responding to the COSO ERM framework, perhaps), then it should from the outset investigate ways in which its risk assessment processes can be integrated.

It is more difficult for a smaller business to retain specialist information security expertise in-house than for a larger one; the internal risk assessment role needs to be maintained over time and the person concerned needs to continue being trained and involved in risk assessment issues, both inside and outside the organization. The disadvantage of hiring external risk assessors, apart from the level of cost, is that the organization does not necessarily get continuity of involvement from a firm of assessors. The advantage of the external hire, apart from it being a variable cost, is that the external assessor should be up to date on relevant issues and should be wholly objective. A possible middle route is to contract on a multi-year basis with an appropriately trained individual or consultancy firm to provide this service personally as and when it is required. However the organization chooses to acquire this resource, it is crucial that he or she is in place and able to be fully involved in the risk analysis and assessment process that the rest of this chapter describes.

There are software tools that have been designed to assist in risk assessment, but the use of them is not mandatory. It is essential, though, that the risk assessment should be done methodically, systematically and comprehensively. An appropriate software tool, designed with ISO/IEC 27001 in mind and kept up to date in terms of changing information security issues, can be effective in this process.

Security in any system should be commensurate with its risks. However, determining which security controls are appropriate and cost-effective can be a complex and subjective process. One of the prime functions of security risk analysis is to put this process on to a more objective basis. Most forms of risk analysis involve the use of risk analysis tools, specific to ISO/IEC 27001, that are designed to ensure that the scope of the exercise is comprehensive and the process rigorous, and that the full collection of assets and the entire range of risks are identified and appropriately dealt with. The KnowledgeBank contains a current list of, and report on, ISO/IEC 27001 risk analysis tools. It is recommended that every approach to risk assessment be made using the same tool that the organization intends to use in the future for its periodic reassessments of risk.

There are a number of different approaches to risk analysis. However, these essentially break down into two: quantitative and qualitative.

Quantitative risk analysis

This approach looks at two issues; the probability of an event occurring and the likely loss should it occur. A single figure is produced from these two elements, by simply multiplying the potential loss (measured in monetary terms) by its probability (measured as a percentage). This is sometimes called the "annual loss expectancy (ALE)" or the "estimated annual cost (EAC)." Clearly, the higher the number that an event or risk has, the more serious it is for the organization. It is then possible to rank events in order of risk (ALE) and to make decisions based upon this.

The problems with this type of risk analysis are usually associated with the unreliability and inaccuracy of the data. Probability is usually subjectively assessed and is rarely precise. In some cases, this approach can promote or reflect complacency about the real significance of particular risks. The monetary value of the potential loss is also often subjectively assessed and, when the two components are multiplied together, the answer is equally subjective.

In addition, controls and countermeasures often have to tackle a number of potential events, and the events themselves are frequently interrelated. A detailed ranking in order of ALE can make it difficult to identify these interrelationships and lead to poor decisions about controls, and this approach is not, therefore, recommended.

Nevertheless, we recognize that a number of organizations have successfully adopted quantitative risk analysis.

Qualitative risk analysis

This is by far the most widely used approach to risk analysis and is the approach expected by clause 4.2.1.d (Identify the risks) of the standard. Numeric probability data are not required and only estimated potential loss is used. Most qualitative risk analysis methodologies make use of a number of interrelated elements, and they are best laid out in tabular form in a corporate asset and risk log, so that, for each asset, its owner(s), threat(s), vulnerabilities and impact(s) are identified.

Assets within the scope (4.2.1.d1)

The first step is to identify all the information assets (and "assets" includes information systems—refer to the information security policy for this definition) within the scope (4.2.1.a) of the ISMS and, at the same time, to document which individual and/or department "owns" the asset.

Threats (4.2.1.d2)

These are things that can go wrong or that can "attack" the identified assets. They can be either external or internal. Examples might include fire or fraud; many such potential threats are described in Chapter 1. Threats are always present for every system or asset—because it is valuable to its owner, it will be valuable to someone else. You could assume, if you can't identify a threat to an asset, that it is not really an asset.

Vulnerabilities (4.2.1.d3)

These leave a system open to attack by something that is classified as a threat or allow an attack to have some success or greater impact. For example, for the external threat of "fire," a vulnerability could be the presence of inflammable materials (e.g. paper) in the server room. In the language of the standard, a vulnerability can be exploited by a threat.

Impacts (4.2.1.d4)

The successful exploitation of a vulnerability by a threat will have an impact on the asset's availability, confidentiality or integrity. These impacts should all be identified and, wherever possible, assigned a monetary value.

Risk assessment (4.2.1.e)

The risks then have to be assessed, to identify the potential business harm that might result from each of the identified risks. There should then be an assessment of the likelihood of the failure. This enables one to identify the level of risk (and, pragmatically, a low–medium–high classification is usually adequate) and this enables one to conclude, for each risk, whether it is acceptable or some form of control is required.

Controls (4.2.1.f)

These are the countermeasures for vulnerabilities. Apart from knowingly accepting risks that fall within the criteria of acceptability, or transferring the risk (through contract or insurance) to others, there are four types:

- Deterrent controls reduce the likelihood of a deliberate attack.
- Preventative controls protect vulnerabilities and make an attack unsuccessful or reduce its impact.
- Corrective controls reduce the effect of an attack.
- Detective controls discover attacks and trigger preventative or corrective controls.

It is essential that any controls that are implemented are cost-effective. The principle is that the cost of implementing and maintaining a control should be no greater than the cost of the impact. It is not possible to provide total security against every single risk, but it is possible to provide effective security against most risks, but these can change and so the process of reviewing and assessing risks and controls is an essential, ongoing one.

The process for assessing risk builds on the scoping document discussed in the previous chapter and should be focused on critical systems and information assets (at least initially—organizations can, if they wish, deal with non-critical systems and assets at a later date) and can be broken down into a number of clearly defined steps:

1. Identify the boundaries of what is to be protected.
2. Identify all the systems necessary for the reception, storage, manipulation and transmission of information within those boundaries and the information assets within those systems.
3. Identify the relationships between these systems, the information assets and the organizational objectives and tasks.

4. Identify the systems and information assets that are critical to the achievement of organizational objectives and tasks and, if possible, rank them in order of priority.
5. Identify the potential threats to those critical systems and assets.
6. Identify the potential vulnerabilities of those critical systems and assets.

Clearly, the next step will be to identify the impacts and then the risks that relate to each of the assets. However, we will first explore each of the steps above in more detail.

Identify the boundaries

It is essential to decide the boundary within which protection is to be provided. The business environment and internet are each so huge and diverse that it is necessary to draw a boundary between what is within the organization and what is without. In simple terms, boundaries are physically or logically identifiable. Boundaries have to be identified in terms of the organization, or part of the organization, that is to be protected, which networks and which data, and at which geographic locations.

The first step is to identify which organization is within the scope of the ISMS. Scope was first tackled in Chapter 5. The organization that is within the scope must be capable of physical and/or logical separation from third parties and from other organizations within a larger group. While this does not exclude third party contractors, it does make it practically very difficult (although not necessarily impossible) to put an ISMS in place within an organization that shares significant network and/or information assets or geographic locations. A division of a larger organization that, for instance, shares a group head office and head office functions with other divisions could not practically implement a meaningful ISMS. Usually, the smallest organizational entity that is capable of implementing an ISMS is one that is self-contained. It will have its own board of directors or management team, its own functional support, its own premises and its own IT network.

It is nevertheless possible for divisions of larger organizations to pursue certification independently; the critical factor is the extent to which they can be practically differentiated from other divisions of the same parent organization.

For larger organizations, with a multiplicity of systems and extensive geographic spread, it is as a general rule often simpler to tackle ISO/IEC 27001 and, in particular, risk assessment on the basis of smaller business units that meet the general description set out above. Larger organizations that have a single business culture and largely common systems throughout are probably better off creating a single ISMS.

Once the organizational scope is identified, it is necessary to list the physical premises that the chosen organization occupies and to identify its network and information assets. The implementation team should list these, but should only do it at this point at the highest possible level.

Identify the assets

The key information assets will usually be either information systems or bodies of information. A system consists of a number of components. A single data asset (such as a file, whether electronic or paper) is a component of a system. At this stage, we are concerned only with the systems, although at a subsequent point it will be necessary to analyse vulnerabilities down to the individual data asset level.

These systems will include a number of IT systems (e.g. client relationship management system, payroll system, e-mail system, resource planning system, accounting system, etc.), the telecommunications systems and the paperwork filing systems. The implementation team should list the key systems throughout the organization; there are software tools that can be used to ensure that all the data assets and all the IT systems have been identified, and these are discussed later.

Telecommunications systems might include mobile phones as well as desk-based systems; personal digital assistants are as important a component of the IT system as are the remote access points and subcontracted services. The human resources filing system is as important as that used in the chief executive or chairman's office. All the systems need to be identified and, if in the process of doing this there are found to be significant sharings of assets or information sharings that were not identified earlier, then the scope of the ISMS may need to be revisited.

Every asset has an owner and, for the risk assessment to be useful, it is necessary to identify (by position, rather than name) the individual who owns—and who is therefore directly accountable for—each information asset.

Identify relationships between assets and objectives

The key objectives should be identified in the organization's business plan. If, of course, they are not, then this is a good opportunity for senior executives to identify and agree the key objectives of the organization and to map the tasks necessary to deliver them. Objectives are often expressed as being to do with increasing market share, or increasing profitability, or increasing margin. These, however, are really the outcomes of pursuing headline objectives such as "sell more of product x to customer type y." There will be a hierarchy of objectives that reflects the value that the organization places on the outcomes that their achievement will deliver. There will also be a number of underlying objectives, which are really business requirements (the activities that are considered important for the ongoing effective operation of the organization). "Comply with the law" is likely to be such an objective and will be common to most organizations. Organizational business plan objectives should, like all objectives, be SMART (specific, measurable, achievable, realistic and time-bound). The key objectives should be clearly documented and this, or an excerpt from the business plan in which they are identified, should form part of the quality records.

Once the key objectives are clearly identified, then those systems that are most important to their delivery can also be identified. This is best done by the whole implementation team, in a single session (which, depending on the size of the organization, may take one or more days) with lots of flip charts. The starting point, after agreeing the scope of the planned ISMS, should be to brainstorm a list of all the systems used within the business, whether digital or not. This phase is described in the section above, which deals with identification of systems. Once this is done, the team can move on to review and understand the business objectives and then get started on identifying the relationships between systems and objectives.

The objective is to reach a conclusion that reflects all members' experience and knowledge, that they all believe identifies all the systems and in which all the business objectives have their critical system dependencies identified. It is possible that some objectives will have more than one system, and these interdependencies should also all be noted. Note that external consultants could only achieve this objective through a facilitated workshop or an extensive series of one-on-one interviews. It is important that the whole range of experience, perception and prejudice is involved in the process at this time, as otherwise it is likely that key dependencies may be missed or misconstrued.

It usually makes sense, in this same session, to move straight on to ranking the systems in order of critical priority to the business. This tends to be the best way to take full advantage of the momentum generated in the first session and ensures that the fullest possible analysis of the priorities is carried out. Meaningful prioritization will depend, of course, on the effectiveness of the earlier analysis and ranking of business objectives.

The resulting report, a schedule that shows prioritized, critical systems as dependencies of key organizational objectives, should be reviewed and agreed by the senior management team of the organization. It is critical that there is the fullest possible agreement on this, as this will be a key building block of the ISMS. The whole process set out above should be fully documented and kept with the quality records.

It is worthwhile, in tackling this (and the tasks below), to adopt an approach that is pragmatic, questioning and transparent. By this, we mean that a risk assessment should be done/driven by human beings—it is a subjective exercise in an environment where returns are derived from taking risks—and that it is preferable to be "approximately correct, rather than precisely wrong." All individual inputs will reflect individual prejudice; the process of gathering input should question this input to establish what is known—and what unknown—in the individual assessment.

Identify potential threats and vulnerabilities

For each of the systems on the schedule, it is now necessary to identify the possible vulnerabilities, the potential threats and their likely impacts on the key business systems. There is a high number of threats, and the range of possible vulnerabilities is also substantial. The input of the trained information security expert is, at this point, invaluable. Threats tend to be external to the systems (but not necessarily to the organization). They include hostile outsiders such as hackers, non-hostile outsiders such as suppliers or cleaning contractors, and insiders, both the disaffected and the committed but careless or even just the poorly trained. Vulnerabilities are security weaknesses in the existing systems, which can either be exploited by threats or allow damage, accidental or otherwise, to information assets.

Essentially, threats for each of the systems should be considered under the headings of threats to confidentiality, to integrity and to availability. Some threats will fall under one heading only, others under more than one. It is important to have carried out this analysis systematically and comprehensively, to ensure that no threats are ignored or missed. The quality of the controls that the organization eventually implements will reflect the quality of this particular exercise.

A number of external threats might be classified under all three headings. A hacker might be able to steal confidential data and then disrupt the information system so that data are no longer available or, if they are, they are corrupted. A virus can affect not only the integrity and availability of data but also, because it could mail out a copy of an address book, confidentiality as well. A business interruption, such as a fire in the server room or a filing cabinet, is likely to affect the availability and integrity of information.

Similarly, what is likely to be a threat to one system is not necessarily a threat to another. For example, a fire in the server room is a threat to a number of systems based there, but is unlikely to be a threat to an organization's mobile phone network.

The standard, at clause 5.1.f, requires management to determine the acceptable level of risk, and this was previously discussed in Chapter 5 and earlier in this chapter.

Identify impacts and their probabilities

At the same time as identifying all the possible threats, their potential impacts on the organization should be considered. This will require thinking through the repercussions of any particular threat, and its consequent cost, throughout the organization. While no organization will want to spend substantial sums protecting itself against minor threats, however pervasive they are, it is important to ensure that the threat is properly classified. For instance, something that on the face of it might appear to be a minor threat may have major repercussions.

An example might be cleaning contractors who inadvertently pick up (a minor threat, being the unintentional error of a third party) the only copy of an extremely confidential document off an executive's desk (a minor vulnerability, the forgetfulness of an executive) in the ordinary course of cleaning and dispose of it. At this point, only the availability of the data has been affected, and the repercussions might be minor, as it may be possible—if embarrassing and time-consuming—to recreate the document. However, once an industrial espionage operative, rummaging through the waste sacks of the organization, finds the document and makes it available to the organization's competitors, the confidentiality of the information will have been compromised and the cost to the organization of the security breach starts increasing dramatically.

A telephone system that crashes, losing all stored voicemail, could have a critical impact on any organization that relies on voicemail for sharing critical information; such an organization needs to have thought through how it will manage the security of these data.

Inevitably, the exercise to identify threats and vulnerabilities to the systems cannot be carried out without also identifying vulnerabilities in systems, and impacts on the organization, that are not necessarily threats to the availability, confidentiality or integrity of its information, but to which there is nevertheless a significant cost. An example is in digital telephone systems, which enable direct-line users to access their voicemail externally and to redirect calls. The evident threat to data confidentiality is that unauthorized users could access information stored in voicemail. If voicemails can be deleted externally, then there is the threat that unauthorized users might make information unavailable. In addition, an unauthorized user could be able to use the organization's telephone number to forward calls to his or her own number anywhere else in the world or even to dial from the extension to anywhere else in the world. One example of such a breach cost an organization $50,000 in a single weekend of fraudulent activity. There was no threat, here, to information security; there was, however, a vulnerability in the system that was externally exploited at the expense, and to the potential reputational damage, of the organization. There is a paper on the NIST website (http://csrc.nist.gov) that deals with PABX security, and it might be worth reviewing.

Broadly speaking, impacts will fall into one (or more) of four damage categories: damage to the organization's competitive position, its finances, its reputation or its legal liability. The project team should analyze each impact into its applicable damage categories.

The next step is to assess the extent of the possible loss for each potential impact. One object of this exercise is to prioritize treatment (controls) and to do so in the context of the acceptable risk threshold; it therefore makes sense to categorize possible loss rather than attempt to calculate it exactly. The categories of business loss (for a large organization) might be:

None   Losses are between nil and $1,000
Minor   Losses would be lower than $10,000
Medium   Losses would be lower than $100,000
High   Losses would be lower than $1 million
Very high Losses would be lower than $10 million
Extreme   Disastrous—the financial viability of the organization is threatened

The financial equivalents provided above should be adjusted, under the board's guidance, to levels appropriate to the size of the organization and its current risk treatment framework. In assessing the potential costs, all identifiable costs—direct, indirect and consequential—including the costs of being out of business should be taken into account. The "better to be approximately correct than precisely wrong approach" should continue to be deployed in this exercise.

The penultimate step is to assess the probability of each impact occurring and to plot this assessment on to a risk level matrix for each impact. The probabilities that might be used are:

Negligible	Unlikely
Very low	Likely to occur less frequently than once per year
Low	Likely to occur once every year
Medium	Likely to occur every six months
High	Likely to occur every month
Very high	Likely to occur a number of times during a month
Extreme	Likely to occur at least daily

The final step in this exercise is to transfer the risk level assessment for each impact to the asset and risk log. We suggest that three levels of risk are usually adequate: low, moderate and high. Where the likely impact is low and the probability is also low, then the risk level could be considered low; where the impact is at least high and the probability is also at least high, then the risk level would be high; anything between these two measures would be classed as moderate. However, every organization has to decide for itself what it wants to set as the thresholds for categorizing each potential impact, and from time to time it may be helpful to have four or more risk levels in order to prioritize action better.

Selection of controls and Statement of Applicability

The standard, at clause 4.2.1.g, requires the organization to select appropriate control objectives and controls from those specified in ISO/IEC 27001 Annex A, and requires this selection to be justified. However, it clearly invites organizations to approach this exhaustively and says, quite clearly, that additional controls may also be selected. ISO/IEC 27001 auditors are likely to challenge implemented controls that are in excess of those required by the risk assessment on the basis that this may indicate inadequate controls applied elsewhere. ISO/IEC 17799 provides good practice on each of the listed controls. There are, however, some areas in which organizations may need to go further than is specified in ISO/IEC 17799, and the extent to which this may be necessary is driven by the extent to which technology and threats have evolved since the finalization of ISO/IEC 17799:2005.

Controls are selected in the light of a control objective. A control objective is a statement of an organization's intent to control some part of its processes or assets and what it intends to achieve through application of the control. The selection of controls should be cost-effective, which means that the cost of their implementation (in cash and resource deployment) should not exceed the potential impact (assessed in line with our discussion above) of the risks (including safety, personal information, legal and regulatory obligations, image and reputation) they are designed to reduce.

It is important that, when considering controls, the likely security incidents that need to be detected should be considered and planned for. Clause 4.2.2.g of the standard requires the implementation of controls that will enable "prompt detection of and response to security incidents." In effect, the process of selecting individual controls from those listed in Annex A should include consideration of what evidence will be required:

- to demonstrate that the control has been implemented and is working effectively; and
- that each risk has, thereby, been reduced to an acceptable level, as required by clause 4.2.1 of the standard. In other words, controls must be constructed in such a manner that any error, or failure during its execution, is capable of prompt detection and that planned corrective action, whether automated or manual, is effective in reducing the risk of whatever may happen next to an acceptable level.

The ISO/IEC 27001 Annex A has 11 major clauses, each of which has a number of subsections. There are, in total, 133 sub-clauses, each of which has a four-character alphanumeric clause number. Each of these is a control under ISO/IEC 27001 and each of them needs to be considered and a decision made as to whether or not it is applicable. As the controls are selected, the Statement of Applicability (SoA) can start to be drawn up. This SoA, specified in clause 4.2.1.h of the standard, is documentation of the decisions reached against the previous requirement and also an explanation or justification of why any controls that are listed in Annex A have not been selected. This document needs to be reviewed on a defined, regular basis and will be one of the first documents that the external auditor will want to see. It is also the document that is used to demonstrate to third parties the degree of security that has been implemented and is referred to, with its issue status, in the certificate of compliance issued by third party certification bodies.

The Statement of Applicability could adopt the format set out below, in which the wording provided in the standard is repeated with appropriate variations to reflect the actual decisions made by the management steering group and its reasoning. The Statement of Applicability can also refer to other documents, where these form the basis for any specific decisions recorded in it. There are different ways of expressing the way in which different controls are applied, some of which are in the example below. The Statement of Applicability should be signed by the owner of the security domain for which it has been drawn up. This document is, for the external certification auditor, key evidence of the steps taken between risk assessment and implementation of appropriate controls.

Introduction

This is the Statement of Applicability, as specified in clause 4.2.1.h to ISO/IEC 27001:2005 ("the Standard"), for ABC Inc. It was adopted by the Management Steering Group on [date] and will be reviewed in the light of significant information security incidents and at least annually. It reflects a risk assessment carried out on [date]. Controls are addressed in the same order and using the same numbering as in Annex A of the Standard and this statement explains which controls have been adopted, and identifies those that have not been adopted and sets out the reasons for these decisions.

Statement of Applicability

A.5.1.1   Information Security Policy
ABC Inc approved an Information Security Policy that conforms to the guidance of ISO/IEC 17799:2005 on [date] and has published and communicated it to all employees and relevant external parties.

A.6.1.1   Management commitment to information security
ABC Inc has established an Information Security Steering Group, which reports to the CEO, and which includes representatives from all the key parts of the organization. This group approved—and is responsible for regular reviews to—the Information Security

	Policy and is responsible for assigning and/or resourcing security roles within the organization, and for driving and reviewing implementation across the organization of the ISMS and any individual initiatives, including information security training and awareness. An external information security adviser has been contracted to provide specialist advice as well as ongoing expertise to the steering committee.
A.6.1.2	The steering group provides a cross-functional forum within which representatives from key parts of the organization are able to coordinate implementation of the complete range of information security controls. A separate forum for information security coordination has not been created as it is considered more effective for this to be handled through the management steering group.
A.9.2.1	Equipment siting and protection In each situation where there is a possibility that sensitive information might be overseen, a risk assessment is carried out and the appropriate controls, as identified in this section, are applied.
A.10.8.4	Physical media in transit This control has not been adopted, as ABC's physical media never leave its premises.

This book will now explore each of the controls specified under Annex A, looking to the good practice set out in ISO/IEC 17799, and at how best to implement them. The book will tackle the controls in the order laid out in the standard; the organization should, however, tackle and implement controls in the order of priority identified through the risk assessment and risk treatment plan. The controls that are most critical for the organization will be those that relate to the threats and vulnerabilities that it has identified, through the risk assessment process, as being most serious to its most critical systems.

Gap analysis

The reality is that most organizations that embark on ISO/IEC 27001 already have a number of information security measures in place; ISO/IEC 27001 necessitates ensuring that those controls that are in place are adequate and appropriate and that additional required controls are implemented as quickly as possible. In other words, an analysis of the gap between what is in place and what will be required must be carried out. This gap analysis can be conducted either bottom-up or top-down. A bottom-up analysis will start by gathering information on all the controls currently in place inside the organization and then assess whether or not they are adequate against the requirements of the organization's Statement of Applicability and the standard. A top-down approach starts with the controls identified in the Statement of Applicability and assesses the extent to which they have already been implemented. The authors' preferred approach is the top-down one, as this will most quickly identify the critical loopholes in the existing security systems as well as the controls that are unnecessary and can be eliminated or limited.

There are software-based gap analysis tools that help the organization take a structured and systematic approach to gap analysis. In some cases these tools are integrated into the risk assessment tool and, in others, they are free-standing. Both options have their advantages. Again, there is information in the KnowledgeBank about current gap analysis tools.

The Statement of Applicability will be complete once all the identified risks have been assessed and the applicability of all the identified controls has been considered and documented. Usually, the Statement is started before any controls are implemented and completed as the final control is put in place.

Risk assessment tools

There is an increasing number of software tools available that can, to one extent or another, automate the risk assessment process and generate the Statement of Applicability. In theory, such a tool ought to encourage the user to perform a thorough and comprehensive security audit on the organization's information systems, and ought not to produce too much paperwork as a result. Tool availability is likely to change as the standard is more widely taken up, and any organization interested in pursuing this route should therefore do up-to-date research on what is available before making a short-list. The KnowedgeBank contains information on currently available tools.

The organization will need to compare tools before making a selection and should concentrate, in the comparison process, on the extent to which the tool really does easily and effectively automate the risk assessment and Statement of Applicability development process, the amount of additional paperwork it generates, the flexibility it offers for dealing with changing circumstances and frequent, smaller-scale risk assessments, and the meaningfulness of the results it generates. Of course, normal due diligence should also be done into the status of the supplier and manufacturer of the product to ensure that it is properly supported and likely to continue to be. References might also be sought from happy customers.

Risk assessments can be, and often are, done without using such tools. A thorough risk assessment of any significant business will be very time-consuming. If an off-the-shelf software risk assessment tool is not deployed, the organization will almost certainly need to use a database to gather to-gether details of all the assets within the scope of the policy, as well as the full range of threats and vulnerabilities. "Time-consuming" means several months and, for larger organizations, even longer. The use of a software tool will depend on the culture of the organization and the preferences of the information security adviser and manager. Practically speaking, once the organization has decided to purchase such a tool, it becomes dependent on that tool and on the staff members who are trained to use it; in considering the appropriate route forward, consideration should be given to the likeli-hood of being able to recruit staff who have broad risk assessment experience and can adapt to the organization's environment as against the likelihood of recruiting and retaining staff who have specific experience with one risk assessment tool.

If the organization decides to purchase such a tool, the steering group should document the reasons for its choice and selection; whoever is to use it will, of course, have to be trained in its use. Evidence of this training and level of proficiency achieved should be retained on the personnel file of the individuals concerned.

Risk treatment plan

Clause 4.2.2.a of the standard requires the organization to "formulate a risk treatment plan that identifies the appropriate management action, responsibilities and priorities for managing information security risks." This then refers to clause 5, a substantial clause dealing in detail with management responsibility. Clearly, the risk treatment plan needs to be documented. It should be set within the context of the organization's information security policy and it should clearly identify the organization's approach to risk and its criteria for accepting risk, as discussed earlier in this chapter. The risk assessment process must be formally defined and responsibility for carrying it out, reviewing it and renewing it formally allocated. At the heart of this plan is a detailed schedule, which shows, for each identified risk, how the organization has decided to treat it, what controls are already in place, what additional controls are considered necessary, and the time-frame for implementing them. The acceptable level of risk needs to be identified for each risk, as well as the risk treatment option that will bring the risk within an acceptable level.

The risk treatment plan links the risk assessment (expressed in the corporate information asset and risk log) to the identification and design of appropriate controls, as described in the Statement of Applicability, such that the board-defined approach to risk is implemented, tested and improved. This plan should also ensure that there is adequate funding and resources for implementation of the selected controls and should set out clearly what these are.

The risk treatment plan should also identify the individual competence and broader training and awareness requirements necessary for its execution and continuous improvement.

We see the risk treatment plan as the key document that links all four phases of the PDCA cycle for the ISMS. It is a high-level, documented identification of who is responsible for delivering which risk management objectives, of how this is to be done, with what resources, and how this is to be assessed and improved; but at its core is the detailed schedule describing who is responsible for taking what action, in respect of each risk, to bring it within acceptable levels.

7

External parties

Control A.6.2 of the standard deals with external party access to the organizational information assets. The control objective is to maintain the security of those of the organization's information processing facilities and information assets that are "accessed, processed, communicated to or managed by" external parties.

Identification of risks related to external parties

A.6.2.1 specifically requires the organization to identify and assess the risks associated with allowing external parties—particularly those involved in outsourcing arrangements—to access its information processing facilities and to implement appropriate controls. A.4.2.2 covers controls to secure customer dealing and clause A.6.2.3 requires the organization to incorporate its arrangements involving external party access into agreements that contain all the necessary security requirements.

ISO/IEC 17799 expands on these requirements. It says that, where there is a proper business reason for an external party to be given access to the organization's systems or security domain, a risk assessment should be carried out to determine the security implications and control requirements. The controls should then be agreed with the external party and incorporated into a contract, with any relevant penalties for breach clearly defined.

The list of potential external parties is long: service providers (e.g. ISPs, ASPs, utilities, managed security services), customers, outsourcing suppliers, consultants and auditors, software or hardware developers or suppliers, (outsourced) support staff such as cleaners and caterers, and the wide range of temporary personnel, including student placements. All these types of external parties need to be considered and there needs to be a consistent and systematic method of ensuring that appropriate agreements are concluded with them.

There will be many occasions on which an organization trading normally will need to grant such external party access to its information processing facilities. It is therefore sensible to design a standard procedure for carrying out these risk assessments and to implement it from the outset. The procedure can be restricted to a single, standard form and carried out by the organization's security manager (who should, of course, be the person who has received training in risk assessments, as described in Chapter 6). The elements of such an internal form, which should be adapted to the needs of an individual organization, are set out below, and our guidance should be expanded to include the suggestions in ISO/IEC 17799, clause 6.2.1.

Risk assessment

This risk assessment is carried out in accordance with the requirements of clause [number] of the ISMS of ABC Inc. It is subject to review in accordance with the risk assessment review requirements of the ISMS.

Date:

External party: [Name]

[Address]

Information facility or asset to be accessed:

Type of access (physical, logical, on-site or off-site) required:

Value, sensitivity and criticality of the information involved [see below]:

Duration/frequency of access required:

Which external personnel will handle the data?

Business reason for providing access:

Risks of providing access:

Existing controls (list them) adequate Y/N?
Third party controls (list them) adequate Y/N?
New controls required—specify:
Risk assessment carried out by:
Review date:

These forms should be signed, dated and subject to the documentation control methodology adopted by the organization. It would also be logical for these forms to be subject to a sequential numeric control, to ensure that none of them is lost or mislaid. The party should not be given access until completion of the risk assessment and signature of the consequent agreement. Of course, the organization's risk assessment might conclude that a particular category of external party is going to need access to such a large extent that it is not feasible to carry out a risk assessment for each individual. For instance, customers, auditors, temporary staff and consultants are categories of external party for whom the organization could, on the basis of a standard risk assessment, identify a standard access policy and agreement that will enable them to proceed quickly and painlessly. Similarly, for customers (discussed later), there could be a standard access policy that they accept by default on entering the website.

Types of access

Broadly speaking, there are two types of access that external parties may need to be given. The risks associated with each type are different and, therefore, they need to be considered differently. The types of access that are to be considered are: 1) physical access, to offices, computer rooms, filing cabinets, etc.; 2) logical access, to databases, networks, information systems, voicemail systems, etc.

In considering the type of access that is required, the value, to the organization, of the information to which the external party is going to have access must be estimated as this is a key component in assessing the level of risk and therefore the type of control required. It is not necessary to estimate, for every occurrence, the monetary value of the information; this can be time-consuming and the answer not necessarily useful. It is more sensible to adopt a set of standard value indicators, linked to the information classification (which will be discussed in more detail in Chapter 8) such as "low," "medium" and "high," and to use these to drive the level of control that is implemented in respect of any access. It is important to remember that, for almost any service that is outsourced, the organization will be transferring the responsibility to design, implement and maintain controls that ensure compliance with all applicable legislation but that accountability for compliance—and the penalties and reputational damage, both corporate and personal, that follow non-compliance—still sit with the organization itself. In other words, it is not possible to outsource being compliant; this single fact necessitates a clear focus on contractual requirements in outsourcing contracts and this, in turn, depends on experienced professional advice from an appropriately qualified law firm. Where the supplier of outsourced services has a different geographic and jurisdictional location from the organization, and particularly where it may be supplying services across more than one area, the risk assessment and control development in the contracting process have to be particularly systematic and rigorous.

It is important also to consider the other types of access that might be available to the external party simply as a consequence of the access that has been granted. For instance, a technician who has access to the organization's premises may, as a result, be in a position where he or she can observe what takes place in the premises or what is on computer screens within the environment. The technician may also have access to information about how the organization prices its offering and how it writes its contracts—simply by virtue of his or her employer having entered into a commercial agreement. All this information may be valuable; it is necessary to have thought through the various implications and, having carried out the risk assessment, to impose appropriate controls.

Reasons for access

There are a number of reasons why the staff of external parties may need to be granted access, often remotely—i.e. logical access—to the organization's information processing facilities and/or assets:

■ Hardware and software support personnel may need access to system-level or application-level functionality.
■ Software development personnel may need access to system-level or application-level functionality or even to source code.

■ Trading or joint venture partners may need access if the organization exchanges information, shares databases or otherwise shares information with them.

■ Providers of outsourced services—in any number of service areas, from payroll, through manufacturing to customer support services—may need access to confidential and protected information both to prepare tenders or bids and, if they are successful, to manage the service itself.

■ Software vendors, including e-learning suppliers, may need to install specific software packages on the organization's network.

■ Professional advisers may need specific information about the organization to support their activity on its behalf—including potentially the manager of the branch of the financial institution at which the organization has banking facilities, who may have access to extremely valuable information about the organization's trading situation.

The reason that external access is such a risk to any organization is that there is no real way of knowing the adequacy of the ISMS in that external organization. If the external party has inadequate security controls (for example, its virus control or personnel recruitment controls), or controls that are adequate for the external party but inadequate for the host organization, then the simple act of allowing the external party access will create an immediate vulnerability in an otherwise strong host organizational ISMS. Any access to the organization's network that originates beyond the secure perimeter is capable of being a threat; the organization needs to find ways of allowing the external party access that is, for business reasons, necessary, without creating the security vulnerability that comes along with it.

One reason why ISO/IEC 27001 is being widely taken up is that, for customers of any certificated organization, an ISO/IEC 27001 certificate is evidence that the organization has in place adequate controls. It is also, increasingly, a standard pre-contract or tender stage checklist item for many organizations: they expect external parties who are tendering to supply outsource services to demonstrate their compliance with ISO/IEC 17799. It is not, however, complete evidence, and the cautious organization will carry out a more detailed risk assessment in the light of the value to it of the information to which it is going to give access. For instance, the organization could decide that it will automatically give any external parties that have an ISO/IEC 27001-certified ISMS access to information that has low- or medium-level values and that it might require additional information and controls in respect of high-value information. The external party organization's Statement of Applicability would be used to establish what level of security it has implemented and this will inform the host organization's risk assessment.

Outsourcing

Outsourcing (which is not necessarily the same as "offshoring") is a strategic issue for any organization. There are many aspects to such a decision and other books deal with them in some detail. This section deals with information security risks in relation to outsourcing and should be read in conjunction with Chapter 12's section on third party service delivery management.

The need to address security issues that arise from a strategic decision to outsource a service to a particular service provider is part of the standard's control A.6.2. The security consequences of outsourcing the management and control of some or all of its information systems, networks and/or desktop environments need to be systematically assessed. Examples of outsourcing contracts that might be covered by this specification are those for the supply and management of a desktop computer network (including servers, firewall, etc.), customer support services, internet service provision, network service provision, facilities maintenance, etc.

Clearly, a risk assessment should be carried out prior to finalizing a decision to outsource any service, and the cost of implementing whatever controls may be necessary should be considered in the cost–benefit assessment.

An outsourcing contract covers a far more significant business relationship than a simple external party service contract does. In effect, when an organization outsources a significant part of its business, it is also outsourcing a significant part of its risks and vulnerabilities and, simultaneously, its information security capability. It is critical, therefore, that it take appropriate, contractual and managerial steps to protect its information. A specialist legal adviser should draft the contract that the organization will use for this relationship. Clearly, all the controls described above, in respect of external party contracts, should form part of this outsourcing contract, within a section specifically identified, for ease of reference, as dealing with information security issues.

In addition, the following should also be addressed as part of the negotiating and drafting process:

- what steps the outsourcing provider will take to meet its own legal obligations—e.g. data protection legislation;
- what arrangements it will put in place to ensure that all parties, including staff and subcontractors working for the outsourcing provider, are aware of their information security responsibilities in respect of the host organization;
- how the integrity and confidentiality of both the host organization's and the outsourcing provider's assets will be maintained and tested; this is best dealt with through a detailed security management plan that sets out in appropriate detail what steps will be taken, and by whom, to ensure that this happens;
- what physical and logical controls will be used to restrict and limit to authorized users access to the organization's sensitive information (physical controls are discussed in Chapter 10, logical controls in Chapter 18);
- business continuity arrangements (discussed in detail in Chapter 26);
- what levels of physical security are to be provided for outsourced equipment, and additional equipment necessary to deliver the outsourcing contract (Chapter 11, extended to the outsourcing provider's premises);
- the right to audit the outsourcing provider's implementation of the contract.

On-site contractors

External party organizations that need physical access to the organization or that need to be co-located on site may also give rise to specific security risks. Examples of on-site contractors would include:

- hardware and software maintenance and support personnel;
- cleaning, catering and security staff, and staff working in the growing range of outsourced services;
- temporary and casual staff, including internships and other short-term appointments;
- consultants and professional advisers, including lawyers, accountants, auditors, etc.

In general, anyone who is not on a permanent contract of employment falls within the category of "on-site contractor." It certainly includes everyone who is employed by any professional adviser, including auditors, merchant banks, marketing agencies, etc. It is particularly important to handle the employees of IT contracting suppliers properly and to ensure that controls that would be applied to permanent employees of the ISO/IEC 27001-compliant organization are not bypassed or undermined by the employment of subcontractors.

A risk assessment should be carried out, as documented in the ISMS, for all these organizations, and appropriate controls identified that will reflect the risk assessed. These controls will fall into two broad groups. The first group is of those that will be required, contractually, of the external party, and the second will be of those that are implemented by the organization in order to safeguard its assets.

It would not be unusual to require, contractually, all organizations whose personnel are operating on-site to ensure that those personnel abide by the ISMS of the contractor with specific reference (by listing or naming them) to those controls that are most pertinent to its activity. This is similar to the requirement that might be imposed for external party staff to comply with the host organization's health and safety at work or environmental management rules. For instance, a provider of temporary staff might be required (if the risk assessment identified this as appropriate) under its contract with the organization to carry out a certain level of résumé and reference check for those staff that it supplies and to enforce on them an appropriate non-disclosure agreement. Simultaneously, the contractor might decide that temporary personnel from this supplier should not be granted access to information or network resources of a particular type, even though a permanent member of staff in a similar role might have such access.

In other words, each risk assessment needs to be carried out in detail, the risks properly assessed and appropriate controls implemented to counter the identified risks. Where external party organizations are concerned, the contract specifies precisely what is required and what the consequences of non-compliance will be. It is an effective way in which an organization can control the risk that is inherent in allowing any external party access to its information assets. Organizations that rely heavily on the use of external party contractors should design and implement a process that will simplify the work required to ensure that they will comply with requirements but that does not lose any of its necessary rigor. An effective way to do this is always to restrict the number of organizations with which there are contracts and to require them to undertake all the vetting, with significant penalties for failure.

External parties should not be granted access until the risk assessment has been carried out and the appropriate contract agreed and signed.

Addressing security when dealing with customers

Control A.6.2.2 deals specifically with customers who are able to access organizational information assets. It was introduced as a consequence of the 2005 revision to ISO/IEC 17799. It reflects the importance of e-commerce customer interactions in information security planning and addresses what should be done prior to giving customers access to organizational information (which is likely to be subject to data protection and privacy regulation) or assets (which include confidential information and intellectual property).

The risks that must be considered arise from four factors: software vulnerabilities; customer self-selection; the customer's direct, unsupervised access to the organization's information systems; and the opportunity for the customer to load and manipulate data on those systems. Control A.10.9, electronic commerce services (see Chapter 16), addresses many of the technical issues; this section is intended to address specific customer access and legal issues.

An organization must, before allowing customers access to any of its information systems (whether through its website, an extranet or otherwise), consider:

■ How it will protect its assets (hardware, software and information) from attack by a customer, ensure that information integrity and confidentiality are protected and identify any breaches that have occurred. This control depends on a combination of technological and logical controls, such as firewalls, routers, demilitarized zones and user access controls.

■ What information and access requirements will be generated by specific products and services or by the needs and desires of customers, so as to ensure that the site is designed in such a way as to provide the required information easily and completely and thereby avoid encouraging customers to deviate from the options made available to them.

■ Access, based on a "what is not expressly allowed is forbidden" policy, to ensure that appropriate access IDs and passwords are allocated, with a clear method of defining access rights and user privileges and a method for revoking any individual's access rights, so that no individual is enabled to do anything other than what the organization allows him or her to do.

■ The incident management procedure (see Chapter 25) must have a strand that is explicitly linked to customer access and possible security events.

■ The way in which the organization will address the myriad federal, state and other legal and regulatory issues, from jurisdiction through data and privacy protection, intellectual property rights, copyright, service provision and liabilities (organization and customers), through to the right to revoke any individual's access. One method of dealing with all these issues is to have them detailed in an access agreement that a customer must accept before accessing the organization's website.

Of course, there will also be security issues in customer sales agreements, particularly where intellectual property and information are concerned, and these should also be addressed in a customer agreement that is consistent with whatever is deployed on the website. Expert legal advice should be taken before finalizing any such agreement.

Addressing security in third party agreements

The information security manager or the corporate counsel (or whoever has the accountability in the organization and has the appropriate level of responsibility for the issue of legal agreements) should have standard agreements available that are capable of customization to reflect the terms of an agreement with any third party about how the controls identified in the risk assessment are to be implemented.

The guidance below, and in clause 6.2.3 of ISO/IEC 17799, focuses almost entirely on contracts with service suppliers; customers can, however, also access organizational information assets and, therefore, they need to be subject to appropriate contracts; these were covered in the previous section.

There are, broadly, two levels of access to the organization's information systems and assets that need to be considered. The first relates to the risks arising from limited access to corporate information (such as in a consultancy agreement, a corporate investigation, merger and acquisition activity, etc.), the second to the closer, more extensive and longer-term exposures that accompany, for instance, an outsourcing contract.

The first set of risks are usually effectively covered by a non-disclosure agreement (NDA) that comprehensively covers issues such as intellectual property, ownership of data assets, confidentiality, non-disclosure, etc. The second set of risks needs a far more substantial contract, entered into after a detailed planning period that might be driven by an information security checklist to establish the extent to which the third party is capable of meeting the organization's information security requirements.

The standard third party agreement, or contract template, should be drafted by the organization's counsel; most legal firms will have someone who specializes in information security and this person's involvement should be sought. Just as appropriate expertise is required of the person conducting a risk assessment, so should it be required of the person drafting the legal contracts. The fact that the lawyer is a lawyer is inadequate, just as prior experience in drafting a non-disclosure agreement may also be inadequate. The legal protection that one is seeking is very important and the organization should ensure that its legal expertise comes from someone who has direct experience of the law as it currently stands where information assurance and, where relevant, intellectual property are concerned.

This contract should ensure that there is no misunderstanding between the organization and the third party and should not be signed until the organization has satisfied itself as to the indemnity and insurance arrangements and/or the financial strength of the third party. It must also satisfy itself that the third party is capable of implementing the terms that have been agreed. Obviously, both parties to the contract will need to agree it and some terms may have to be negotiated in detail. As a rule, all contracts should include the following (and a request for detailed information of this nature should be included in a pre-tender questionnaire or in the request for proposal (RFP) guidance), and the organization should not be prepared to conclude a contract that does not at least deal with:

- The organization's policy on information security (which was discussed in Chapter 5).
- The organization's policies about asset protection (which are covered later in this book) including:
  - procedures that it has in place to protect organizational assets, including information, hardware and software;
  - procedures that will be used to identify whether or not any asset has been lost or compromised;
  - controls that are designed to ensure the return or destruction of information and assets at the end of, or at an agreed point within, the contractual relationship;
  - procedures to ensure integrity and availability of information;
  - restrictions on copying or disclosing information.
- A description of the service that the third party is to provide—which should be written in clear English and which both parties should agree

is a comprehensive description of the service. Where there may be an issue as to what is and is not included in the service, there should be a statement along the lines of: "For the avoidance of doubt, [activity] is not included in the service to be provided."

■ The target level of service and a definition of unacceptable service. These should be both meaningful and reasonable; some flexibility should be built in to allow for the unexpected or simply to accommodate the vicissitudes of the real world.

■ Verifiable performance criteria, and a clear statement on the process for monitoring and reporting. Again, these should be cost-effective and practical and should allow room for the service to operate. If the performance criteria are too tight or the monitoring regime excessive, the costs to both the organization and the third party of maintaining the agreement may exceed the benefits that they are getting from it.

■ The prospective liabilities of the parties to the agreement; the host organization will be particularly interested in identifying those of the third party and, if possible, avoiding their being capped.

■ Legal responsibilities (e.g. privacy of personal information legislation). These clauses must take into account differing federal and state legislation around these issues.

■ Intellectual property rights, copyright and protection of rights in any collaborative work.

■ The right to audit contractual responsibilities or to have a third party carry out such an audit.

■ The escalation process for dispute resolution. A dispute resolution process, possibly including binding arbitration, may be more cost-effective than to resort to the law courts.

Most contracts should also include, as appropriate to the circumstances of the contract and the service that is to be provided, one or more of the following:

■ Provision for the transfer of personnel, and associated costs, where appropriate.

■ Protection against the poaching of employees, particularly where they retain skills or knowledge that is critical to the organization.

■ Access control agreements (which will be discussed in Chapter 18), covering:

- — permitted access methods, control and use of passwords, user IDs, etc. and the process by which these are surrendered at the end of the contract;
- — the authorization process for user access and privileges;
- — a requirement that the third party maintains an up-to-date list of which personnel have been given what level of authorizations.

▪ The right of the host organization to monitor user activity and revoke user rights.

▪ Responsibilities regarding hardware and software installation and maintenance.

▪ The reporting structure and reporting formats, so that third party personnel know who within the organization is responsible for what and how they have to report on those issues for which they have been retained—for example, on attendance, or absence, or project progress, etc.

▪ The specified change management process; this is particularly relevant to software and hardware projects, where it is vitally important that the organization should be able to trace and audit changes to the original specification on the basis of which the third party contract was drawn up (and see Chapter 12).

▪ Any physical controls that are required (see Chapter 10).

▪ Training that is required in respect of methods, procedures and security. This section should specify who is responsible for providing the training, who pays for it, what steps must be taken to maintain the identified skill or competence and what evidence is necessary to demonstrate that it exists.

▪ Controls against malicious software and viruses (see Chapter 13).

▪ Procedures for reporting security incidents (see Chapter 25).

▪ Involvement with any other subcontractors.

Clause 6.2.3 of ISO/IEC 17799 sets out an even longer list of contractual requirements and this list should be referred to for an even more exhaustive schedule than we have provided; all business-critical issues have, however, been included above.

8

Asset management

Control A.7 of the standard deals with asset management, including classification and acceptable use. The objective of this control is "to achieve and
maintain appropriate protection of organizational assets." Clause 7 of ISO/
IEC 17799 expands on this.

Asset owners

Control A.7.1.2 says that all information assets should have a nominated
owner ("an individual or entity that has approved management responsibility for... the assets") and should be accounted for. Clearly, the "owner"
is the person, or department, that has responsibility for the asset—the
"owner" has no property rights to the asset. This control requires the organization to maintain, amongst the ISMS documentation, a schedule that
shows all the information assets of the organization. These should be the
same ones as were identified during the risk assessment, which was discussed in Chapter 6. Each of these assets should have a nominated owner,
an employee whose seniority is appropriate for the value of the asset which
he or she "owns." This person's responsibility for the asset should be set

out and described in a letter, or memorandum, to him or her. He or she should sign it to acknowledge agreement to it and this signed original should be placed on his or her personnel file. Either a copy should be retained along with the asset schedule, or the schedule should name the owner and refer to the personnel file for it.

This letter should describe the asset(s) for which the person is responsible and its (their) location(s). It should describe the security controls (including the security classification and access restrictions) that are required for the asset and set out the owner's responsibility for maintaining (and periodically reviewing) them. The owner may be allowed to delegate responsibility for implementing or maintaining controls to staff directly responsible to him or her, but should not be allowed to delegate accountability. This should rest squarely and clearly with the nominated owner.

Inventory

Control A.7.1.1 specifically requires the organization to identify all important information assets and to draw up and maintain an inventory of them. Of course, generally accepted accounting practice and legislation already require companies to maintain registers of all fixed assets within the organization. However, this requirement does not in practice automatically extend to public sector organizations. Furthermore, the assets that are covered by the fixed asset register do not necessarily include all the information assets of the company, particularly not the intangible information assets.

The information assets of the organization should be identified during the risk assessment process (see Chapter 6) and the resulting schedule should be checked against the fixed asset register to ensure that no assets have been missed. The inventory should have a nominated owner and the procedures for maintaining it and, in particular, for accessing it in a disaster recovery situation should be clearly documented. The fixed asset register can also provide historic information about the cost of the asset, and this information is necessary to help identify the relative importance and value of the assets. ISO/IEC TR 13335-3 provides more detailed guidance on how to value assets to represent their importance.

The asset inventory should identify each asset, including all the software, describe it or provide such other identification that the asset can be physically identified (wherever possible, it makes sense to reuse whatever fixed asset number has already been allocated) and full details (including maker, model, generic type, serial number, date of acquisition and any other numbers) included in the inventory. Its current location should be stated. Any other information necessary for disaster recovery (including format, back-up details and license information) should be listed. The nominated owner (and, if this is different, the name of the operator(s)) of the asset should be shown on the schedule, as should its security classification (see below). The inventory should be updated for disposals (when and to whom). Physical inventory checks should be carried out at least annually, by someone other than the nominated owner of the asset, to confirm the accuracy of the register. The types of assets that ISO/IEC 17799 identifies as needing to be inventoried include:

- **Information assets:** databases and data files, other files and copies of plans, system documentation, original user manuals, original training material, operational or other support procedures, continuity plans and other fall-back arrangements, archived information, financial and accounting information.
- **Software assets:** application software, system software, development tools and utilities, e-learning assets, network tools and utilities.
- **Physical assets:** computer equipment (including workstations, notebooks, PDAs, monitors, modems, scanning machines, printers), communications equipment (routers, cell phones, PABXs, fax machines, answering machines, voice conferencing units, etc.), magnetic media (tapes and disks), other technical equipment (power supplies, air-conditioning units), furniture, lighting, other equipment.
- **Services:** "groups of assets which act together to provide a particular function," such as computing and communications services, general utilities, e.g. heating, lighting, power, air-conditioning.
- **People:** their qualifications, skills and experience—the knowledge and skill capital of the organization. This is a particularly complex process for which external consultancy help might be sought.
- **Intangible assets** such as reputation and brand. There are established methods of valuing intangible assets and a range of issues to be taken into account, including whether or not the intangible assets should be listed on the balance sheet. Certainly, reputation is one of the most important intangible assets, and boards should make a constructive effort to establish its value.

Usually, whoever is responsible for the facilities management in the organization will be the nominated owner of the services (see "Services" in the list above) and a number of the physical assets. The IT manager will usually be responsible for the other physical assets and the software assets, although a number of individual users are likely to be responsible for the notebook or cell phone or any other, similar, item that they have been assigned.

It is much more difficult to determine the owners of the intangible information assets. It is important to get this right because the owner will have specific responsibilities. In terms of new documents, the organization could simply adopt the policy that the originator of an information asset will be defined as its owner. This is meaningful in terms of information assets that will have, generally, a specific and limited use, which is driven by the originator. This would cover, for instance, business plans, forecasts, client letters and project plans, etc.

There are other information assets, however, whose use through the organization will be widespread and whose origination is the result of a strategic or group decision. Examples might include customer relationship management (CRM) systems and their client data, workflow systems and the information they contain, accounting systems and financial information. The only practical approach to these assets is for the organization, at the time that it decides to create it, to decide who will be the owner and to write this into the person's job description. Usually, the owner should be the person who uses it most, or has most control over it: the financial controller might be the nominated owner of the accounting system and the sales administrator might be the nominated owner of the CRM system.

It may be practical for this defined ownership to be time-bound. Sensitive incoming mail from a client may first, for instance, belong to the corporate services function until the relevant sales/customer relationship manager is identified and the ownership is then passed to him or her. It would also not be unreasonable to state that, once archived, the ownership of data passes to the facilities function, and that the value of the archived information will start to diminish from this point.

The process of identifying owners for information assets needs to be sensible. The organization is likely to have many items of information that have little or no practical value; there is little point in nominating owners for this information and going through the steps covering classification and control, for it will be time-consuming and the exercise will fail any cost–benefit test. It would be better for the organization to implement a procedure that defines the threshold above which information will be considered an asset and above which, therefore, it will be subject to the controls specified in this section of the standard. Some organizations opt for a catch-all default level for such information.

The way to do this is through the information classification procedure, which is discussed below; information with a specific low-level classification, assigned by its owner, may be defined as not being an asset worth protecting, and information with any other classification may be defined as an asset and worth protecting. For instance, a file of press cuttings might be classified such that it is clear that it is not an asset worth protecting; statutory accounts, once filed with the SEC, become public domain information, which there is no point in protecting from a confidentiality angle (although the integrity and availability of these data could still be of concern).

Acceptable use of assets

Control A.7.1.3 of the standard, introduced freshly in 2005, requires organizations to document and implement rules for the acceptable use of information assets, systems and services. These rules should apply to employees just as much as to contractors and third parties, and the particularly important areas for which acceptable use policies should be drawn up include e-mail and internet usage, mobile devices (telephones, PDAs and laptops) and usage of information systems beyond the organization's fixed perimeter. Chapter 17 deals with this issue in detail and provides sufficient guidance to enable the organization to draw up and implement adequate acceptable use policies.

Information classification

Control A.7.2 of the standard specifies that an organization must have a procedure for classifying information that will ensure that its information assets receive an appropriate level of protection.

Control A.7.2.1 of the standard provides guidelines on classification and these are expanded further by clause 7.2.1 of ISO/IEC 17799. The standard simply requires that classifications should be suited to business needs (including legality, value, sensitivity and criticality), both to restrict and to share information, and to the business impacts associated with those needs. It is important to note that sharing is as important an objective of this section as is restricting; it is possible to draw up a set of guidelines that are too restrictive for the business and that are therefore regularly breached. This is not a useful outcome. Organizations (particularly in today's environment) depend on sharing information; it is essential that information is classified in such a way that this can be done consistently and appropriately. Whatever classification scheme is adopted by the organization should be extended to cover the level at which users can access data in the system (read only, write, and delete).

Information classification is a key concept in the structuring and development of an effective ISMS. The classification given to a particular information asset can determine how it is to be protected, who is to have access to it, what networks it can run on, etc. "Confidentiality" is, after all, one of the three key objectives of an information security management system.

The benefits of adopting a consistent procedure are clear. The organization will:

■ reduce the risk of damage to its reputation, profitability or interests due to loss of sensitive information;
■ reduce the risk of embarrassment or loss of business arising from loss of another organization's sensitive information;
■ increase confidence in trading and funding partnerships and in the outsourcing of sensitive activities;
■ simplify the exchange of sensitive information with third parties, while ensuring risks are appropriately managed.

Classified information is marked so that both originator and recipient know how to apply appropriate security to it. The classification is based on the likely impact on the organization if the information is leaked or disclosed to the wrong third party organizations or people. It does not matter what system the organization adopts, providing it is clear, clearly documented and clearly understood by all staff and everyone who uses it.

The simplest approach is usually one that has only three levels of classification. The first level might be to identify that information which is so confidential that it has to be restricted to the board and specific professional advisers. Information that falls into this category might be marked "Confidential," with the names of the people to whom it is restricted identified on the document. Some organizations also number documents that have this level of classification, so that each person who is sent a copy receives a numbered copy. Usually, all pages of such a document would show the classification in capital letters at least ¼ inch high and, if it exists, the individual number. This information should be included in the document header, which should be set to appear on all pages of the document. Examples of confidential information might include information about potential acquisitions or corporate strategy, or about key organizational personnel, such as the chief executive. The amount of information that falls into this category should be carefully limited; the cost and operational inconvenience of protecting it properly is such that it needs only to be information whose release can significantly damage the organization.

A second level of classification might cover documents that are to be available only to senior or other specified levels of management within the organization. These might be marked "Restricted"; the related procedure should specify a level of employee above which anyone can access the document. Examples might include draft statutory accounts, which might be available to everyone in senior management, or implementation plans for corporate restructuring, which senior managers need to work through prior to their being rolled out. These documents are usually not numbered, but the decision to release them (which is, by definition, a decision to release them to everyone in the organization who is entitled to receive information of this level) should not be taken lightly.

The final level of classification might be, simply, "Private" and this should cover everything that has value but that does not need to fall within either of the other categories. Everyone employed by the organization should be entitled to access information with this classification. At the same time as adopting such a system, the organization should make clear how it will treat any internally originated documents that carry classifications (e.g. "Private and confidential," or "Restricted—commercial in confidence," or any other variations on the theme) other than those described in the procedure. Such incorrectly classified documents could be either automatically destroyed, or automatically reclassified, or automatically treated as having no classification at all; the policy decision should reflect the risk and cultural environment within which the new classification system is being adopted. The organization also needs to consider how it will appropriately reclassify third party sensitive documents that it receives and that it will be responsible for protecting.

It will be important, in deciding which employees will have access to which levels of information, to resolve what is to be done in respect of those employees who have to support senior management but who, themselves, might fall into a lower classification in terms of information security. An implication of this might be the rather farcical one of people, such as personal

assistants and secretaries, working on or distributing documents or supporting meetings whose content they have to try not to be aware of. Far
better, frankly, to allow these people the same level of access to confidential
documents as their managers and to take all the necessary steps to ensure
that only appropriate persons are recruited into these roles.

ISO/IEC 17799 also suggests that the "effects of aggregation" should be
considered; it is possible for a series of non-confidential items to become
confidential when they are aggregated. For example, individual pages of a
set of accounts might not, in themselves, be confidential (because they carry
incomplete information) but together they might be valuable and confidential. The best way to deal with these types of issues is to apply from the outset
the aggregate-level classification to all the component parts of the information asset.

The US government classification system

The United States government classification system was established under
Executive Order 13292, which was issued by President George W. Bush in
2003. Executive Order 13292 lays out the system of classification, declassifi-
cation and handling of national security information generated by the United
States government and its employees and contractors, as well as for information received from other governments.

The United States government classifies information according to the
degree to which the unauthorized disclosure is considered likely to damage
national security:

- **Top secret.** This is the highest security level that is publicly disclosed,
  and is defined as information that would cause "exceptionally grave
  damage" to national security if publicly disclosed. It is said that little
  information is classified as top secret when compared to the other levels
  of classification. Only that which is exceptionally sensitive (weapon design, presidential security information, nuclear-related projects and various intelligence information) is classified at the top secret level. The
  nature of the gathering method used to obtain the information can also
  cause the information to be classified top secret, though the information
  itself may be mundane and unimportant. Examples include signal inter-
  ceptions (SIGINT) and human intelligence (HUMINT).

- **Secret:** the second-highest classification. Information is classified secret when its release would cause "serious damage" to national security. Most information that is classified is held at the secret classification level.
- **Confidential:** the lowest classification level. It is defined as information that would "damage" national security if disclosed.
- **Unclassified.** "Unclassified" is not technically a classification. It is the default, and refers to information that can be released to individuals without a clearance. Information that is unclassified is sometimes restricted in its dissemination as, for instance, FOUO (For Official Use Only).

Organizations can model their own information classification system on that of the US government, or can turn elsewhere for guidance on the detailed aspects of information classification. There is, for instance, a set of rules on information classification available on the UK DTI's Communications and Information Industries Directorate website (www.dti.gov.uk/cii/) that was developed by business organizations.

These are called the unified classification markings, and the principle behind them is similar to that outlined above. The impact, however, is different and would reflect a different organizational culture than the version set out above. The organization must choose a classification system that is suitable for itself, or develop one on the basis of the options set out in this book.

Unified classification markings

SEC1 is defined as information whose unauthorized disclosure, particularly outside the organization, would be inappropriate and inconvenient. This is routine information that an organization simply wishes to keep private. This classification may not need to be marked on information; it refers to the majority of the organization's information. This information is, usually, commercially valuable and, while SEC1 may be an appropriate classification in a low-risk business environment, there will be other business environments in which this may be too low a classification.

SEC2 is defined as information whose unauthorized disclosure (even within the organization) would cause significant harm to the interests of the organization. This would normally inflict harm by virtue of financial loss, loss of profitability or opportunity, embarrassment or loss of reputation. This information might include:

- negotiating positions;
- marketing information;
- competitor assessments;
- personnel information;
- customer information.

SEC3 information is defined as information whose unauthorized disclosure (even within the organization) would cause serious damage to the interests of the organization. It would normally inflict harm by causing serious financial loss, severe loss of profitability or of opportunity, grave embarrassment or loss of reputation. This information might include:

- details of major acquisitions, mergers or divestments;
- high-level business or competition strategy;
- very sensitive partner, competitor or vendor assessments;
- high-level business plans and scenarios;
- secret patent information.

Information that is required, under the policy adopted by the organization, to be classified must be appropriately marked. This marking must appear wherever the information appears, be it on paper, cassette, disk, flip chart, film, microfiche, etc. Where information carries no classification, it is regarded as having no value.

When organizations are going to exchange information, they should ensure that each understands the other's classification system. The ISO/IEC 27001-organization will want to ensure that it has in place a methodology for applying to information received from a third party a classification that is in accordance with both the originator's and its own system. No organization should under-protect another organization's information; in circumstances where the receiving organization would classify particular information at a lower equivalent level than that applied by the originator, the recipient should apply a higher classification than it would to an internal document. Those companies that apply a SEC1 level of classification should make it clear to third party organizations that this type of information is freely available within the organization; those organizations that do not even apply a SEC1 classification should make it clear to third parties that this sort of information is not handled securely.

Information does not always have to remain classified at the same level at all times. Financial accounts, for instance, are confidential until they have been signed and filed with the SEC. The classification applied to them should be appropriately reviewed and the organization's procedure should require originators to review the classification of key documents on a regular basis. Some information is only sensitive for a specified period. Where this is the case, the information should show the date beyond which it will no longer be sensitive. This is common practice with, for instance, press releases, which are usually sent out with a legend along the lines of "embargoed until 0000 hours on x day."

Organizations that handle a considerable amount of information that falls into the SEC2 or SEC3 categories should go to the CII website (contact details above) and draw down a copy of the guidance entitled "Protecting business information—keeping it confidential." This booklet is free and is in Adobe Acrobat format; it describes the unified classification markings and sets out, in more detail, actions that organizations should consider in respect of infrastructure, distribution of confidential information, siting of workstations and other issues. It is likely to be particularly useful to government organizations and to organizations dealing with government. For most other organizations, the summary set out in the section on information labeling and handling, below, will prove to be adequate.

Information labeling and handling

Control A.7.2.2 of the standard requires the organization to implement a set of procedures for information labeling and handling that reflects the information classification scheme (as above) that it has adopted. As ISO/IEC 17799 says, these procedures need to cover all formats of information asset, both physical and electronic. There should be procedures for the following types of information processing activity:

- acquisition of information;
- copying (electronically, by hand and through reading and memorizing);
- storage, both electronic and in hard copy;
- transmission by fax, post, e-mail and infrared synchronization;
- transmission by spoken word, including mobile phone, voicemail and answering machines;
- chain of custody and logging of security events, particularly important when dealing with computer-related crime;
- destruction when no longer required.

The types of procedure that should be adopted for each of the unified classified markings are set out below. They should be adapted as necessary and incorporated into a simple organizational classification procedure within the ISMS, and everyone responsible for handling the information should be trained in how to apply them. Specific consideration needs to be given to the labeling of electronic assets, and the input of the IT team will be required to define an effective means for applying the chosen classification to electronic assets and media in a way that is rigorous and reliable.

SEC1

■ Information that has no marking can also be treated as information that has a SEC1 classification. It can be released to anyone outside the organization at the discretion of the information owner. It should be handled and processed within a secure perimeter and, at the end of the day, should be cleared away. Removable material should be put away when it is not in use and electronic equipment that is not being used should be switched off.

■ External mail should be sealed.

■ Electronic mail should only be sent over networks that are considered to be secure to at least this (SEC1) level and should not contain attachments that are classified at a higher level.

■ Destruction of papers should be through an approved office waste disposal company that has a contract that meets the requirements in Chapter 7.

The final items that need to be considered in terms of information classification are faxes and e-mail. Faxes are widely used and e-mail is ubiquitous; both are so unreliable that secure documents could easily be delivered to the wrong person. A part of dealing with this risk is the use of standard disclaimers on both faxes and e-mails, although these do nothing to control the likelihood of such a threat and are of little practical use in addressing the impact of such an incident. Policies on the use of faxes, enforced in the appropriate fashion, need to complement the disclaimer as a control. The fax disclaimer should be clearly printed on the fax cover sheet and it should be a procedural requirement that all faxes use the standard cover sheet. For preference, the disclaimer should be included in the standard fax cover sheet template on the desktop system; where the organization uses pre-printed cover sheets, the disclaimer should obviously be pre-printed on to them.

On e-mails, the disclaimer should be built into the standard organizational signature that is attached to all e-mails; the network administrator can set this up so that the organization's chosen disclaimer is included as a standard default in all e-mails, irrespective of the wishes of the e-mail originator, but so that the individual's chosen signature can also appear on the e-mail. A possible e-mail disclaimer is set out below, and is likely to need the additional statement (that any opinions expressed are those of the author and do not reflect in any way those of the organization) that is discussed in Chapter 17. Any version of this disclaimer actually deployed by any organization must first be approved by its own legal counsel to ensure compliance with current legislation.

Legal disclaimer

This message contains confidential information and is intended only for the individual named. If you are not the named addressee you should not disseminate, distribute or copy this e-mail. Please notify the sender immediately by e-mail if you have received this e-mail by mistake and delete this e-mail from your system. E-mail transmission cannot be guaranteed to be secure or error-free as information could be intercepted, corrupted, lost, destroyed, arrive late or incomplete, or contain viruses. The sender therefore does not accept liability for any errors or omissions in the contents of this message that arise as a result of e-mail transmission. If verification is required please request a hard copy version. This message is provided for informational purposes only.

Additional statements should be added to this to protect the organization against libel actions, and these are discussed in Chapter 17.

SEC2

SEC2 material needs more stringent controls:

■ All pages of, and physical media containing, SEC2 material should be clearly so marked. Access to it should be limited to those with a need to know and should be stored in a way that makes it unlikely that it will be compromised by accident or through opportunism and that should deter deliberate compromise of it.

■ Destruction should be done in a way that makes its reconstitution difficult.

■ Personnel who will handle this classification of material need to have had appropriate security checks carried out.

■ It should be handled within a secure perimeter and steps should be taken to ensure that material cannot be observed by unauthorized people.

■ IT systems handling this level of information should themselves be located within a managed security perimeter; effective access controls should be in force and appropriate monitoring procedures that deter unauthorized access should also be in place.

■ This material should only be disclosed on a need-to-know basis and steps should be taken to ensure that the recipient is aware of the sensitivity level and the implications for its protection.

■ SEC2 information should not be verbally disclosed in a public place where it could be overheard by others.

■ Letters should be sealed and sent in such a way that the sensitivity level of the information cannot be deduced from the outside of the letter; it might be marked "To be opened by addressee only." If sent externally, it should probably be within a cover envelope that does not reveal the security level of its contents.

■ Faxes should only be sent once it has been confirmed that the receiving station is the correct one, and that it is ready to receive, secured to a SEC2 level and attended by a trusted person. The fax should only be sent by an appropriately trusted person.

■ Steps should be taken to ensure that conversations are not overheard, and telephones in public, or hotels, or obviously insecure locations (overseas, or competitors' offices) should not be used as they are easy to listen in on or overhear.

■ Any messages sent via the internet should only be sent once they have been appropriately secured by means of an approved encryption method. Internet connections should only be made via an approved and secure firewall. Internally, the information should only be shared on an electronic system that is secured to at least a SEC2 level.

■ SEC2 material should be destroyed by an approved person or organization that will shred or otherwise effectively destroy it. Removable media should be overwritten before reuse; media that cannot be overwritten should be destroyed by an approved company and not reused. All

back-up copies should also be destroyed at the point that the original is
destroyed.

■ SEC2 documents and notebook computers carrying information of this
level of sensitivity should be supervised at all times and, when not in use,
should be safely locked away, including in secure facilities in hotels when
traveling.

SEC3

SEC3 material needs much more stringent safeguards. It requires the SEC2
controls, plus additional ones, as described below:

■ SEC3 material should be so marked. Access should, clearly, be limited to
those authorized to see and use the information. It should not be disclosed unless there is a good business, contractual or legislative need to
do so. Assurance (by means of a signed form) should be sought from the
recipient that the sensitivity of the information is understood and appropriate protection is available.

■ Copying should only be carried out with the permission of the information owner and should only be carried out by staff who themselves are
authorized to see and handle information with this level of security. Care
must be taken to ensure that additional or spoilt copies are destroyed.
There should be clear distribution lists with numbered copies and they
could also be marked "Not to be copied further."

■ It should be stored under conditions that make accidental compromise
unlikely, offer a degree of resistance to deliberate compromise and make
actual or attempted compromise likely to be detected. It is practical to
display a warning that any compromise will be detected and violators
pursued. The way in which the material is handled, used or transmitted
should make accidental or deliberate compromise unlikely.

■ When not in use, the material should be locked in approved security
containers, within a managed security perimeter. A clear desk policy
should be rigidly enforced.

■ IT systems, within a managed security perimeter, should be strongly secured with approved access controls that are highly resistant to penetration by a capable hacker. Highly effective surveillance and monitoring
procedures should be in place to detect unauthorized access.

- Discussions of information with this level of security should only take place where there is no likelihood of being overheard or monitored by surveillance equipment.
- Mail should be sealed and sent in a way that ensures its sensitivity level is not apparent from the envelope. There should be safeguards to prevent and detect attempts to read the information. It should, therefore, be delivered by a trusted individual or an approved courier in a double-sealed envelope and there should be a receipt for it.
- Faxes should only go over secure connections and telephone conversations should only take place over secure links. Steps should be taken to ensure that neither party to such a conversation can be overheard.
- IT systems should be fully physically secure and any messages sent via the internet should be encrypted. Information should not be stored on a network that is connected to the internet, however strong the firewall connection.
- Destruction of SEC3 material should be done in a way that makes attempted or actual compromise, accidental or deliberate, unlikely, reconstitution difficult and any attempted compromise likely to be detected. Destruction should be recorded.
- Hard disks should be overwritten with a secure approved utility. Media that are to be destroyed should be destroyed by an approved company and their destruction recorded. All back-up copies and files also have to be destroyed.
- Home working facilities should be organizationally approved and appropriately secured.
- This sort of information should never be discussed in airplanes or other forms of public transport or where any untrusted person is present. It should not be discussed in public places, hotel rooms, competitors' premises or restaurants.
- Notebook computers carrying this information should be kept secured to SEC3 standards at secure offices and kept supervised at all times. They should not be left in taxis or airports or anywhere else.

Non-disclosure agreements and trusted partners

There will be circumstances where the organization needs to share confidential information, of either a SEC2 or SEC3 level, with a third party organization. This might be as part of a series of commercial negotiations or other important circumstances. An appropriate risk assessment should be carried out prior to sharing any information with the third party organization and the results of this risk assessment should be reflected in a non-disclosure agreement (NDA), which the third party is asked to sign. The NDA should be drafted by legal counsel and should include the appropriate controls identified in Chapter 7 and in this chapter. The controls should be selected to ensure that the third party organization is able to respect the information security classification that has been assigned to the material to be shared. The majority of the controls that should be listed in the NDA will be drawn from the list of information-handling requirements shown in this chapter, and some controls might be drawn from the list in Chapter 7 for third party contracts, where the risk assessment identifies them as necessary. No information should be released until the NDA has been returned, signed by the appropriate authority in the third party.

Those organizations that have to share confidential information regularly will have a well-developed procedure for carrying out these risk assessments (probably based on a standard questionnaire drawn up by the internal information security adviser) and a standardized but customizable NDA. This should enable the process to be completed expeditiously; the organization will certainly want to ensure that it can be dealt with quickly and effectively, as otherwise either the information will be shared without safeguards or the organization will struggle to achieve its own objectives.

9

Human resources security

Clause 5.2.1 of the standard requires the organization to provide appropriate and adequate resources to carry out all the PDCA phases of IS management. Clause 5.2.2 requires that whoever is assigned an ISMS-related task has the necessary competence. These two clauses can be satisfied at the same time as the required controls are constructed. It will be necessary to demonstrate, in the documentation, how the competences were determined, and why.

Section 8 of IS0/IEC 17799 is structured to deal with human resources security in a way that covers the three stages of employment: pre-, during and post-employment.

Control A.8.1 of the standard deals with pre-employment security issues. The objective of this clause is to reduce the risks of loss of information through human error, fraud or misuse of facilities. Control A.8.1.1 requires the organization to define and document, for employees, contractors and other third party users, their role and responsibilities in respect of the ISMS and information security within the organization. ISO/IEC 17799 makes it clear that this statement should include both *general* and *specific* responsibilities.

Job descriptions and competence requirements

Every job description should contain 1) a description of the competences required for the role, and 2) a statement to the effect that every employee is required to be aware of the organization's policy on information security (a copy of the policy might be attached to the job description) and to take whatever actions may from time to time be required of him or her under the terms of the organization's ISMS. In particular, the employee's attention should be drawn to the responsibility to protect assets from unauthorized access, disclosure, modification, destruction or interference, the information classification and handling rules, the access controls (both physical and logical), the incident reporting procedure, the requirements to carry out any other specific procedures and processes, the requirement personally to improve competence and skills in this area and the fact that the employee will be held accountable for his or her acts of commission and omission. The job description should set out clearly that breach of information security controls may be considered a misdemeanor under the organization's disciplinary policy and that breach of them might, under specific circumstances, result in dismissal.

Specific requirements should in addition be included in the job descriptions of particular individuals. If the organization prefers not to identify required competences for *all* roles, it will at least be necessary to do so for those involved in the ISMS. The people who should be considered for such specific requirements include:

- chief information officer;
- information security adviser;
- members of the information security management forum;
- IT management;
- network management;
- IT and helpdesk support staff;
- premises security staff;
- HR, recruitment and training staff;
- general managers;
- finance staff;
- company secretary/legal staff;
- business continuity/emergency response team.

People in each of these functions (and there are likely to be others—each organization is different and each organization needs to make arrangements that are appropriate to it) are likely to have a direct impact on the effectiveness of implementation of the information security policy and the ISMS. While Chapter 4 had an initial discussion of the generic responsibilities that apply to particular functions, the only effective way to ensure that all information security responsibilities are captured will be for the members of the information security management forum to work through all the clauses of the standard, identifying which members of staff will be responsible for implementing the clause or will be affected by it. These responsibilities should then be included in the job descriptions for these people.

This analysis should be underpinned by a review of all the roles, functions and employment levels of staff within the organization; this review should consider what responsibility, if any, people in given roles will have in assuring the confidentiality, integrity and availability of information in the organization. The conclusions of this review should be compared with those generated by the analysis carried out on the basis of the clauses of the standard. A statement of information security responsibility that combines both outputs should then be the final form of the amendment to the job description.

This statement of information security responsibility could either have a separate, headlined and complete paragraph in the job description, in which case the member of staff affected should sign and date a copy of the amended job description, or there should be a separate statement, attached to the job description and referred to in the job description, in which case both documents should be signed and dated by the employee. The signed document should then be retained on the individual's personnel file.

As part of any arrangements with third parties that involve their access to the organization's information assets, security roles and responsibilities that match those required by the organization should be implemented by the third party.

Screening

Control A.8.1.2 of the standard requires the organization to carry out verification checks on permanent staff, contractors and third parties at the time of job applications. The organization should identify who will be responsible for carrying this out, how it will be done, how the data will be managed and who will have what authority in respect of the data and the recruitment process. Any screening and data collection activity must be carried out in accordance with the relevant local legislation. There is, in some roles, a legal requirement to carry out criminal screening and there are clearly risks in taking unknown staff into the organization, not just in terms of fraud and confidentiality, but also in terms of integrity and availability. An inadequately experienced IT staff member could mismanage a vital server or application in such a way that information availability and integrity are compromised. ISO/IEC 17799 (clause 8.1.2) provides more information about the type of verification envisaged. It sets out four basic checks that should be completed:

1. Character reference checks, one personal and one business. These should, for preference, be written, but a substitute might be a signed and dated detailed note of a telephone reference given by a nominated third party to a competent (i.e. experienced in carrying out telephone reference checks) member of the organization's staff.
2. A completeness and accuracy check of the employee's résumé; this is usually carried out by means of written references supplied by previous employers or third party organizations, and most employers will already have standard documents that are sent out to guide these third parties in replying. It is critical that the employer is methodical in ensuring that all facts are corroborated and that all forms are returned, duly completed, by previous employers. Where they are not returned within a defined time period (which should be short—perhaps 10 days at the outside) the organization should arrange to complete the form by means of a telephone interview with the previous employer.
3. Confirmation of claimed academic and professional qualifications, either by means of obtaining from the candidate copies of the certificates or other statement of qualification or through an independent résumé checking service. These firms can, for a nominal sum, carry out detailed résumé checks (including checking academic and other qualifications) that would satisfy the requirements of both point 2 above and point 3.
4. There should be an independent identity check, against a passport or similar document that shows a photograph of the employee.

Where a job, either on initial appointment or on promotion, involves access to information processing facilities and particularly if it involves processing sensitive (financial or highly confidential) information, there should also be a credit check. Where individuals have considerable authority in their position, this check should be repeated regularly, either quarterly or annually as appropriate.

Normal practice would be that, while a draft employment contract (or employment agreement) is agreed between the prospective employee and the organization, it is not signed and the employee does not commence work until the checks have been completed. Depending on the outcome of a risk assessment, some organizations might choose to allow people to commence work, particularly in roles that deal with only a low level of information, subject to satisfactory references; in these circumstances, it is necessary to set a time limit within which the reference checking will be complete. The contract of employment would usually not be signed by the organization until the reference checks are completed and, if they are unsatisfactory or not completed within the allocated time, the employee is dismissed. A similar process should be carried out for temporary or agency staff and contractors.

Where the staff are supplied by another organization (and this is often the case with IT staff, who are directly employed by or contracted to the agency concerned) the contract with the third party should set out clearly its responsibility to carry out checks to a similar level. The contract also needs to set out what steps the agency has to take where answers to the screening process have been unsatisfactory or the process itself has not been completed. At the very least, these should include informing the employing organization, and in full, without delay, offering to replace any individual who has already started work immediately and at no additional cost. The contracting organization should have adequate professional indemnity insurance and this should be checked by obtaining and keeping on file a copy of the current insurance certificate.

While this may be relatively easy to implement for future hires, the organization has to decide what to do in respect of existing staff. It will not be sufficient simply to adopt the approach that, because the staff are already there, there will be no problems. Undoubtedly, the correct approach to this situation is to ensure that the organization has records of equivalent completeness for existing staff as for new hires. It will be important that existing staff are made aware that this process is to be carried out and that it will be done openly and quickly.

Statistically, the likelihood is that every organization will discover that one or more members of its staff have incorrect or false résumés. Each of these instances will have to be tackled, and the organization will have to judge the extent to which the individual threatens its information security; the organization's direct experience of the employee in the work environment may provide sufficient evidence to act on or to set aside the inaccuracy in the résumé. If it is to be set aside, the employee should certainly be made aware that the inaccuracy was uncovered and the reasons for its being set aside should be explained; this simple step can help the employee avoid such behaviors in the future.

New and/or inexperienced staff may, at certain times, have to be authorized to have access to sensitive systems. The company should identify what level of supervision will be required in such circumstances and ensure that it has in place a procedure for providing the appropriate level of supervision. The performance of all staff in respect of information security, particularly those who have access to sensitive information, should be reviewed on a regular basis (at least annually) and appropriate steps taken to ensure that the standards set by the organization are maintained. This review can be by means of one or more questions that are incorporated into an existing annual appraisal system.

At annual reviews, and on a day-to-day basis, line managers within the organization should be aware of unusual behavior from members of staff that may be signs of stress, personal problems or financial challenges. Apart from the human benefits of helping employees deal with these challenges, such issues have been known to affect people's performance negatively (which may, of course, have implications for information security) and may also lead some individuals to commit crimes or fraud. Managers should be appropriately trained to spot and handle these situations within the restrictions of the relevant legislation.

Terms and conditions of employment

Control A.8.1.3 of the standard requires the organization to ensure that employees, contractors and third parties all agree and sign an employment contract, which contains terms and conditions covering, *inter alia*, their and the organization's responsibilities for information security. These terms and conditions should include a confidentiality agreement, constructed in accordance with local legal guidance, that covers information acquired prior to and during the employment and whose effect should continue beyond the end of the employment.

This confidentiality agreement should be drafted by the corporate counsel, as described in Chapter 8. It should form an integral part of the contract of employment, so that acceptance of terms of employment automatically includes acceptance of the confidentiality agreement.

There are circumstances in which someone who is working for the organization will not have signed an employment contract; he or she might, for instance, be working on a temporary or interim management basis, or even for short-term work experience. Anyone who has not signed a contract of employment should sign a confidentiality agreement of some description. This might form part of a contract for the provision of services or it might be a stand-alone confidentiality agreement. It should reflect the terms that are set out in the contract of employment with any additional terms and sanctions that are recommended by the organization's lawyers in respect of these third party relationships.

This confidentiality agreement is designed to cover situations in which a person is exposed to confidential information in the ordinary course of the employment or project, and it sets out the organization's requirements in these circumstances. It should cover legal responsibilities and rights in protection of copyright, intellectual property, data protection legislation, confidential and sensitive (particularly financially sensitive) information and any other relevant information issue. A different and specific non-disclosure agreement (NDA) should be signed by any organization to which confidential information will be disclosed pursuant to a business transaction; this was discussed in Chapter 8.

The agreement should be signed and dated and the original returned to the organization before the individual is granted any access to confidential information. The terms of specific agreements should be reviewed when an employee's circumstances change, particularly when he or she is due to leave the organization; it is often sensible to remind a departing employee (particularly someone who has had access to substantial amounts of confidential information in the course of the employment) of his or her obligations under the contract of employment and, in particular, of which obligations will survive termination of the employment. It is normal practice for compromise agreements to restate key confidentiality clauses.

Standard confidentiality agreements and NDAs should be reviewed after specific instances where loopholes in an existing agreement appear to have been found, and steps should be taken both to amend the document for the future and, where the loophole is a significant one, to replace and re-sign existing confidentiality agreements and NDAs.

The contractual clauses should make clear that the employee has a responsibility for information security. This responsibility must be described.

The simplest way to handle this is to attach the job description (and the separate statement of information security responsibilities, if this is the route that the organization has gone) to the contract of employment and for the contract of employment to refer explicitly to the responsibilities set out therein. As long as the information security clauses of the job description have been drafted in accordance with the guidance at the beginning of this chapter, and cover confidentiality, classification, responsibilities in regard to information received from third parties, responsibilities in respect of handling personal information, how the responsibilities are applied outside normal working hours and in any non-work (e.g. home) environment and action to be taken in respect of anyone disregarding the organization's requirements, this requirement of the standard will have been met.

It also recommends that an employee's responsibilities in respect of compliance with relevant legislation should also be clearly stated. This is particularly important in terms of GLBA, HIPAA, EU Safe Harbor arrangements, and a variety of state legislation, such as SB 1386 and OPPA, as well as copyright law, and the CAN-SPAM Act. The contract should contain a clause (drafted by the organization's lawyers, and forming part of the contract of employment) that states that the individual will be personally responsible for ensuring that his or her activities in respect of information are not at any times or in any way in breach of these specific laws.

There is also the requirement to set clear rules for acceptable use of e-mail and the internet and, in the contract of employment, to set out very clearly the consequences for breaches of them. The rules do not need to be included in the contract, but the contract can refer explicitly to a section of the ISMS that contains them. E-mail usage rules are set out in detail in Chapter 17, as are acceptable internet use rules. Such policies must be consistently and firmly enforced; this sends a clear message to the organization that breaches will not be tolerated and helps build an environment of compliance.

During employment

Clause 5.2.2 of the standard and control A.8.2 of the standard require the organization to ensure that its employees, contractors and third party users are aware of information security threats as well as their responsibilities and liabilities and that it has appropriately trained its personnel. The objective of this clause is, simply, to ensure that all users of the organization's information assets, or who are assigned responsibilities in the ISMS, are aware of information security threats and are competent and adequately equipped to perform the requested tasks and to support the organization's information security policy in their work.

Control A.8.2.1 is a new clause, requiring management to ensure that everyone applies the organization's security policies and procedures; it is, in other words, an extension of the principle that management should be visibly committed to supporting the ISMS. There was a substantial discussion, in Chapter 3, around leadership, change management and communication, all of which is relevant to this control. ISO/IEC 17799's guidance on this control includes ensuring that staff (employees, contractors, third parties) are properly briefed on their roles and responsibilities before they are granted access to sensitive information or information systems (evidenced by their signature on their access rights document (see Chapter 18); are motivated to fulfill their roles and conform to the policies (evidenced through the internal audit process); and are aware of information security threats, risks and vulnerabilities.

Control A.8.2.2 deals with information security awareness, education and training and follows on from the previous control. All employees of the organization (including third parties) must receive appropriate awareness training and other training, as well as regular updates and communications.

Traditional training, which relies on someone delivering subject matter from the front of the classroom, is not a particularly effective method of ensuring that all of a large number of employees acquire the information, skills or competencies that are needed. It is certainly not a method that reliably demonstrates that this requirement of the standard has been met. The best way of delivering this sort of training is via e-learning that is run on a recognized learning management system (LMS).

E-learning can be delivered directly on to the desktop workstation of the targeted employee. It can be delivered in a way that improves uptake and retention over traditional classroom training. It can be rolled out quickly and to a consistent standard across an entire organization, and geography is no real barrier. The learning can be accessed by employees at a time to suit them and, because trainees are not required to go away on a training course, productivity is not affected by e-learning. In fact, e-learning can be less expensive as a method of rolling out training than traditional classroom training, both because of these productivity benefits and also because none of the usual costs of attending courses (whether internal or external) need to be incurred. There are a number of suppliers of e-learning products; one that can supply an appropriate suite of ISO/IEC 27001 or privacy-related products virtually off the shelf is likely to be less expensive as an option than an organization that makes a bespoke package specifically for its client. The website www.27001.com indentifies some suitable suppliers.

Any recognized LMS will both support the e-learning and provide a real audit trail that produces records of who has completed which e-learning modules and when they were done. The LMS can also run tests that can demonstrate the level of competence that the trainee has acquired in the subject matter. Administration of these systems can be done cost-effectively online.

E-learning is particularly cost-effective for training large numbers of staff. Small numbers of staff, particularly those who need detailed and extensive training, often involving feedback, questions and answers, coaching, etc., are better dealt with in the classroom. The areas of information security and the ISMS that are best dealt with through e-learning and that commence as part of the induction process are as follows:

■ all staff briefing—ISMS awareness, known threats and the importance of information security and the ISMS, including general controls;
■ asset classification and control;
■ reporting events and responding to security incidents and malfunctions;
■ e-mail and web access awareness and rules;
■ user access control and responsibilities;
■ mobile computing and teleworking;
■ legal compliance awareness and related issues;
■ business continuity awareness and procedures.

There are also a number of staff who will require user-specific training. These include the staff identified at the beginning of this chapter as needing specific statements in their job descriptions and contracts of employment about their information security responsibilities. These include:

■ chief information officer;
■ information security adviser;
■ members of the information security management forum;
■ IT management;
■ network management;
■ IT and helpdesk support staff;
■ webmasters;
■ premises security staff;

- HR, recruitment and training staff;
- general managers;
- finance staff;
- company secretary/legal staff;
- internal quality assurance/system auditors;
- business continuity/emergency response teams.

These staff should be exposed to the same all-staff training as was discussed above. In addition, user-specific training will be required. The necessary training is best identified through an individual training needs analysis (TNA). The organization is likely to have a TNA process in place and this should be applied to the security training issues. Those organizations that do not already have a TNA process in place have the choice between designing and implementing a process that will cover all of its training issues going forward and implementing one that simply works for the information security training needs. Information security training is better tackled, on an ongoing basis, as part of a structured approach to employee training. However, in situations where it is necessary to get specific training started, it will be simplest to apply a TNA process that will deal specifically with information security training.

Any handbook on corporate training, or a training professional, could provide appropriate support on a step that is fundamental to well-designed training delivery. The principle underlying a TNA is that, once the knowledge, skills and competence requirements of a particular role have been clearly established, and documented in the job description, the role holder's own knowledge, skills and competence can be compared to the requirement and a gap analysis, or TNA, completed. The next step is to map out an individual learning path that will meet the requirements of the TNA and close the knowledge, skills and competence gap. This individual learning path will contain a mix of self-learning, instructor-led training and experience. It should identify clearly where the training is to come from and should set out the dates by which specific steps are to be taken, identified skills or competencies acquired and proof of acquisition generated. There is far more to a TNA than this, so do make use of a training professional to do the job properly.

While most organizations will have a TNA process in place for groups of staff, which identifies the gap between the individual's skills and those of the generic role, there are individuals who, for information security purposes, must have very specific knowledge, skills and competencies that are in addition to those needed by a group of employees of which they may be a part. Clause 5.2.2 expects that there will be an individual TNA, based on an individual or additional assessment of the knowledge, skills and competence required for each of these roles, for each of the people in one of the individual or specialist roles identified above. Where this is being put together for a new employee, the offer letter might make permanent employment conditional on achieving certain stages within certain time-frames.

Clause 5.2.2 also requires the organization to maintain records of education, training, skills, experience and qualifications, and this is satisfied by following the recommendations of this chapter and attaching these records to the individual's personnel file. More importantly, the effectiveness of the training must be evaluated, and this requires the specific objectives for each piece of training, and the criteria for measuring its effectiveness, to be identified and agreed in advance. This is in line with best practice for effective staff training.

Training should clearly be delivered by competent trainers and this is a requirement of clause 5.2.2.b. In Chapter 4 there was an initial discussion on appropriate training for specialist information security advisers and the specialist training qualifications available for advisers.

Those IT staff charged with systems administration should be appropriately trained, by either the software supplier or by an approved training vendor, as system administrators for the software for which they are the nominated administrators. Evidence of this training should be retained on the individual's personnel file. Those responsible for firewall, antivirus, encryption and any other security software should have appropriate training certificates and should be required to keep their skills and knowledge current by attending regular refresher and update courses. These should be booked into the individual's training calendar in advance and there should be evidence that they were attended. Certainly, in any Microsoft environment, there should always be a systems administrator who has a Microsoft certificate, such as the MCSE.

Webmasters, in particular, need to be thoroughly trained and have their skills regularly updated. Their training needs to cover the security aspects of all the hardware and software for which they are responsible; in particular, they need to be capable of ensuring that the web servers are fully secured. Whether the server software is Microsoft's Server 2003 or whether an Open Source product is used, it is essential that organizations run the most recent versions of the server software, that all service packs and (where relevant) the latest hot fixes are installed as soon as they become available, and that the servers are all locked down in line with the recommendations available from NIST.

Information security staff, company officials/legal staff and HR/personnel staff will also need specific legal training. There are a number of specific legal issues to do with information security (all discussed in Chapter 27) and the organization needs to know how to handle them, using standard template documents wherever possible. It does not need to employ an in-house lawyer, as this can be unnecessarily expensive; external expertise can be brought in where and when necessary to deal with specific legal issues.

Staff dealing with telephone systems and network hardware and software will all need specific, supplier-certified administration and security training that covers these products. The organization will need access to regular updates on information security issues relating to these products.

There is a discussion about training for auditors in Chapter 27.

The most effective way (particularly for a multi-site organization) to make information about information security available to everyone in the organization is either to put it on an intranet or to deploy a specialist software product that is designed to deploy and manage policies across a corporate network. Either the organization already has an intranet, in which case it simply needs to create an information security sector on it (or within the quality assurance sector), or it could consider either setting up an intranet or acquiring and deploying an appropriate policy management tool. This does not need to be an expensive step, but it is undoubtedly the best way of dealing with information sharing.

There are a number of new media companies that can set up an intranet; the organization's existing webmaster or IT manager might also have the skills necessary to do this. Of course, it will be necessary to ensure that appropriate guidance on procedures is available to any affected staff in case of a system or intranet crash. This could mean that paper versions of the procedures should be available or, alternatively, a notebook computer with an up-to-date set of procedures that is part of the emergency response equipment.

The benefits of using either an intranet or a policy management tool are that they can be the single repository of controlled documents; the information security manual and procedures can all be stored there and staff can be trained to access it for anything to do with information security. It is easy to keep the controlled documentation up to date and to ensure that document control is effective. It is then easy to alert all relevant members of staff about changes to procedure simply by sending out an internal e-mail, with an appropriate link, that tells them which sections of the ISMS have been changed.

The intranet can also have a section that carries information about information security developments and issues of which staff need to be aware. Someone within the organization needs to have the responsibility for keeping the site up to date, and this person, obviously, will need to be appropriately trained. The people who might have this role include the information security adviser, the quality manager, the marketing manager (if the marketing department has responsibility for internal communications) or the webmaster.

One of the key benefits of deploying an off-the-shelf policy management tool ought to be its capabilities to provide version control and an audit trail for the deployment of policies and procedures as well as an e-learning function that provides evidence that individual users throughout the organization have been appropriately trained. This sort of evidence can be an essential part of demonstrating compliance with legislation such as GLBA and HIPAA. The KnowledgeBank has information about current policy management tools.

Disciplinary process

Control A.8.2.3 of the standard requires the organization to deal with employee (and contractor and third party) violations of its information security policy and procedures through a formal disciplinary process. Obviously, the organization should use its existing disciplinary process and, in employee contracts (as discussed earlier in this chapter) and in the ISMS itself, should be clear about this.

Clearly, no disciplinary process can start until the existence of breach has been verified (and control A.13.2.3 deals with evidence collection), and formal commencement criteria may need to be documented that are legal in the local jurisdiction. The organization should ensure that those who are carrying out a disciplinary hearing in respect of a reported violation of an information security procedure are given the professional and technical support that they might need in order to deal fairly with the person and the issue. This might require the organization's information security adviser to be involved in the process. On no account should inexperienced, uninformed managers attempt to deal with information security matters that are beyond their knowledge or experience as this will be unfair on the employee concerned and potentially dangerous for the organization if the full impli-cations of an incident are not understood quickly enough. It could also, depending on the outcome of a disciplinary hearing conducted by an inex-perienced manager, potentially expose the organization to time-consuming and expensive industrial tribunal actions or trade union challenges for unfair treatment of an employee.

Termination or change of employment

ISO/IEC 17799:2005 introduces this new control area (A.8.3) and its three controls. Previous experience using the standard suggested that adminis-tration of employee termination was, in information security terms, often sloppy; as a result, organizations were creating new vulnerabilities that needed to be assessed. The control objective of this chapter is to ensure that termination of employment (or a change in job role) is carried out in an ordered, controlled and systematic manner, with the return of all equipment and removal of all access rights.

Control A.8.3.1 deals with termination responsibilities and simply requires the organization to document clearly who is responsible for per-forming terminations and what these responsibilities are. These responsi-bilities should clearly include dealing with the ongoing clauses in the contract of employment. Usually, the HR department will be responsible for ensuring that all the termination aspects of an employment contract have been dealt with (usually in conjunction with the ex-employee's line manager) and these may be standard aspects of a termination interview, which is car-ried out in a standard way, using a standard checklist.

The termination of contractors and third parties needs also to be dealt with; the organization simply needs to determine how it will achieve, with these personnel, the same clarity it seeks with ex-employees and who (agency, third party organization) will be responsible for performing the task.

Control A.8.3.2 wants to see all employees, third parties and contractors return all organizational assets upon termination. As well as financial (e.g. credit cards and purchase orders) and HR/fixed assets (e.g. motor cars), these assets fall into four categories: software, hardware, information and knowledge. Subject to local employment law, the contract of employment should have a clause that allows the employer to withhold any outstanding payments of any description until all organizational assets are proven to have been returned and, after a suitable interval, to deduct from any such outstanding amounts the cost of replacing assets that haven't been returned. Of course, this will tend to push the majority of resignations to the day immediately after monthly or other substantial payments have cleared the employee's bank account, but such is life.

The first two asset types are best dealt with procedurally through a centralized recording and authorization process; there should be a record for each employee (maintained by HR and IT), which lists all laptops, PDAs, cell phones and other hardware issued to employees. This list should be integrated with the asset inventory discussed in Chapter 8, and the nominated owner should clearly be the person to whom the asset is issued. There should be an acceptable use document for each asset, describing what has been provided (and laptops should have a standard, documented "kit"—while laptops are often returned, the accessories are often missed), setting out clearly the organization's expectations for the proper use of the asset, including (for example for cell phones) any expectations about how costs are to be split between employee and organization.

Information—classified documents, whether electronic or paper—should also all be returned. In fact, it is difficult to identify what documentation any individual has removed during the course of employment (unless they were limited-circulation numbered documents), and this control is, in practical terms, best met through the termination interview. One standing item on the schedule for this interview should be a question as to whether or not the employee has any classified information and, if none, a reminder that any such documents must be returned.

Knowledge—the skills and competence that a terminated employee may have—should be retained in the organization. This is, in real terms, not easy to achieve. In the case of people who have critical knowledge, there should be a risk assessment prior to commencement of any termination action, to identify any knowledge that must be retained and to plan methods of retaining it. Unless this step is taken, one can assume that the knowledge— particularly if it is held by someone who is being unwillingly terminated— will leave the company with the employee. It is not unknown for organizations to delay commencing termination procedures with employees until they have successfully transferred their knowledge.

Control A.8.3.3, removal of access rights, is critical, as access rights may enable a disgruntled ex-employee to compromise a system; this section should be read in conjunction with Chapter 18. The organization needs a clear documented procedure to ensure that, upon (and sometimes—subject to risk assessment and local legislation—before) termination, an employee's (or contractor's or third party's) access rights are also terminated. Similarly, any change in employment should also lead to a review and adjustment of existing access rights.

These access rights include passwords, tokens and other authentication rights, e-mail and internet user accounts and user names, electronic files, etc. and should be extended to include any identification cards, including calling cards and headed notepaper. It may be necessary for ex-employee e-mail accounts to continue in use for a period after termination, and this should be covered by a standard policy that sets out how the e-mail auto-responder should be set up, who should have ownership of the account and how any incoming e-mails should be treated.

10

Physical and environmental security

Control A.9 of ISO/IEC 27001 deals with physical and environmental security. It deals with what might be called geographic or area security, with equipment security and with general controls to protect physical assets. Large or multi-site organizations might, as discussed in Chapters 5 and 6, need to break themselves down into a number of physical domains (giving due consideration to any communication links between them) and then consider each domain on its merits.

Secure areas

Control A.9.1 of the standard deals with secure areas. Its objective is to prevent unauthorized physical access, damage or interference to business premises and information. It has four sub-clauses. Critical or sensitive information and information processing facilities should be housed in secure areas, protected by a defined secure perimeter, with appropriate security barriers (e.g. walls, fixed floors and ceilings, card-controlled entry gates) and controls (e.g. staffed reception desks) that provide protection against unauthorized access or damage to papers, media or information processing facilities. The protection implemented should be commensurate with the assessed risks and the classification of the information and should take into account out-of-hours working and similar issues.

Physical security perimeter

Control A.9.1.1 of the standard requires the organization to use a security perimeter to protect areas that contain information processing facilities. It may be appropriate, depending on the risk assessment and the classification of the information being protected, for an organization to use more than one physical barrier, as each additional barrier increases the total protection provided.

The first step is to use a site or floor plan to identify the area that needs to be secured. A copy of this document should be found with the property title deeds. The plan that is with the deeds is there to show clearly the premises that the organization owns or leases, and it is the most appropriate base document to use for defining the secure perimeter as it identifies clearly the property over which the organization has control.

A continuous line needs to be drawn around the premises on the site plan, including all the information and information processing facilities that need to be protected. This line should follow the existing physical perimeter (and a perimeter in this context is something that provides a physical barrier to entrance) between the organization and the outside world—walls, doors, windows, gates, floors, fixed ceilings (false ceilings hide a multitude of threats), skylights, etc. Special attention should also be given to lifts and lift shafts, risers, maintenance and access shafts, etc. This site plan, showing the defined physical perimeter, should form part of the ISMS records. The ISO/IEC 27001 auditor will almost certainly want to see it and then to test the effectiveness of the perimeter.

A comprehensive risk assessment should be carried out to identify the weaknesses, vulnerabilities or gaps in this perimeter and, from this assessment, the appropriate physical controls—the additional physical barriers, such as doors, card-controlled gates, staffed reception desk, etc.—can begin to be identified. While not all organizations will have information as valuable as that obtained by Tom Cruise's character, Ethan Hunt, in the film *Mission Impossible*, the way in which he gained access to the room within which it was kept indicated that the guarding organization's risk assessment had not been sufficiently thorough. There was a vulnerability in the physical perimeter that Ethan Hunt identified and then exploited in a way that demonstrates that "difficult to imagine someone coming in through there" was an inadequate approach to securing the physical perimeter. The ISO/IEC 27001 auditor will want to see the documented risk assessment and will analyze its thoroughness and effectiveness, initially by challenging the person responsible for defining it and then, after inspecting likely vulnerable areas, by probing to see how secure it actually is.

The following controls should form part of the implemented security perimeter:

■ The perimeter itself is defined (and should have been the subject of a risk assessment) in a document and, if possible, by means of appropriate signage, and staff are aware of what and where it is.

■ The perimeter (particularly of a building containing information processing facilities) should be physically sound. There should be no gaps in the perimeter (risers, lift shafts, air-conditioning vents, etc. should all be assessed) or areas where a break-in could easily occur. The external walls should be of solid construction and all external doors should be protected against unauthorized access using appropriate control mechanisms, one-way bars, alarms, locks, etc.

■ There should be a staffed reception area or other means to control physical access to the site or building. Access to secured premises should be restricted to authorized personnel only.

■ Physical barriers should be extended from real floor to real ceiling (i.e. below and above any false floor or false ceiling, particularly those installed to provide effective ducting for cabling) to prevent unauthorized entry or environmental contamination such as that caused by fire or flood.

■ All fire doors on a security perimeter should open outwards only, should slam shut (because they have working door-closing mechanisms fitted to them) and should be alarmed (and this fact should be advertised on the doors to try to prevent inadvertent false alarms). Some organizations site CCTV cameras to cover these doors to watch for deliberate false alarms that might be designed to distract security staff attention from a planned point of real break-in elsewhere or to enable a perimeter breach before security staff can attend.

■ Appropriate intruder detection systems should be professionally installed and maintained. All external doors and accessible windows should be covered and unoccupied areas should always be alarmed. The alarm cover should also be specifically extended to include computer and communications rooms. Copies of test certificates, schedules of key holders and alarm response procedures (who is to do what when an alarm goes, including out of hours) should be retained as part of the ISMS records. Key holders should receive training in how to respond to alarms, what to do to secure the site after a break-in or other incident, and what the escalation procedure is. The alarm response procedure should be reviewed after every alarm incident and, where a police response service is part of the security set-up, every effort has to be made to avoid false alarms as these can lead the police to withdraw their cover. This is particularly important where the organization includes a manual alarm trigger at, for instance, the reception desk to help deal with unwanted intruders during opening hours; these alarms can easily be triggered accidentally. However, making them awkward to trigger detracts from their effectiveness in addressing the reason for having them in the first place.

There are particular problems where two or more organizations share physical premises. In these circumstances, more than one secure perimeter may be necessary. For instance, there may be a staffed reception desk that lets employees of both organizations on to the property according to jointly agreed procedures. Each organization might then restrict access to its own floors, either through key cards or through its own reception desk. Where this type of additional perimeter is not possible, there may need to be individual security perimeters around individual information assets or information processing facilities in order to ensure that the organization's information processing facilities are physically separated from those managed by any third parties.

Physical entry controls

Control A.9.1.2 of the standard requires secure areas (see A.9.1.3, which is discussed below) to be protected by appropriate entry controls to ensure that only authorized personnel are allowed access to the premises. ISO/IEC 17799 recommends specific controls, some of which are more difficult for smaller companies, but which are nevertheless worth considering and, wherever possible, implementing:

■ Visitors to secure areas—whether the site itself or specific areas within the site—should be supervised, or cleared in advance, and their date and time of arrival and departure recorded. Access should only be granted for specific, authorized purposes and all such visitors should be issued with instructions on the security requirements of the area and on emergency evacuation procedures. These instructions are usually recorded on a standard visitor's pass, which, itself, records the date and time of arrival into a ledger on which the departure details can be recorded when the visitor leaves. Good practice would usually require the security staff issuing the visitor's pass to confirm by telephone that the visitor is expected and the purpose of the visit. A more secure set-up would be for visitor details to be notified to the reception desk in advance and for a telephone check to take place when the visitor arrives. In high-security areas, these visitor lists might have to be approved by a senior line manager before they are forwarded to the security desk. Visitors should be accompanied everywhere by a member of staff and, where necessary, their identity should be reconfirmed prior to access to other sections of the secure area being granted. Visitor passes should use some visible system of demonstrating whether or not they are still valid; for instance, all passes issued on Monday might have a black dot, a red square on Tuesdays, etc.

■ The selection of security services is, itself, a security risk. Not all such companies take appropriate steps to vet and train their operatives and it is therefore essential that the controls identified in Chapter 7, in respect of external parties, are fully implemented. No matter what their prior training or experience, security guards should also receive training in the internal security procedures of the organization for which they are providing security services.

■ Where access for unauthorized people to the site or building is controlled remotely from the reception desk, there should be an effective communication tool that enables the receptionist to identify (both verbally and visually) the visitor before allowing access.

■ Access to sensitive information, and information processing facilities, should be controlled and restricted to specifically authorized persons only. This is particularly important for the computer server room(s), access to which needs to be severely limited. Authentication controls, such as a swipe card and/or individual PIN codes, should be used to authorize and validate access to secure areas, and to secure areas within the security perimeter. If possible (and if required by the risk assessment), the swipe card entry system should also provide an auditable trail of access. The record of visitor passes issued should be maintained in a secure location, as it might, at some point in the future, be required to identify an intruder.

■ All personnel should be required to wear some form of visible identification (which could be incorporated with an access card—which might work through either swiping or physical proximity) and should be encouraged to challenge unescorted strangers or anyone not wearing visible identification. A visible identification badge is a control far more important in a large organization than in a small one but, in any size organization, unidentified and unaccompanied visitors should always be challenged. There are many organizations for which this, on its own, will require a significant culture change and this could significantly contribute to improved security. Of course, even in a small organization, visitors having to wear badges acts as a deterrent to opportunist trespassers/intruders, as they will realize that they are obviously out of place without the appropriate visual "stamp" of approval.

■ Access rights to secure areas should regularly be reviewed, updated and, where necessary, revoked. This is particularly important for access rights to computer server rooms. The record should be reviewed on a regular basis by the information security management forum and a record of their review should form part of the ISMS documentation.

■ Third party support personnel should have access rights that are, to the greatest extent possible, restricted to those secure areas or information processing facilities they need to access for specific times, and these access rights should be monitored, reviewed and, where necessary, revoked.

Securing offices, rooms and facilities

Control A.9.1.3 of the standard requires the organization to create secure areas within the security perimeter to protect offices, rooms and facilities that have additional, special security requirements. A secure room may contain lockable cabinets or safes. Secure rooms could be any rooms within the premises but will certainly include server rooms, telecoms rooms and plant (power and air-conditioning) rooms. Some areas (such as accounts or HR, or VP offices) might also need to be secured. Many chief executives' offices should also be treated as secure rooms.

There could be a clash, within organizations that are strongly committed to open-plan working, between the desire for openness and the need for security. This will have to be addressed and solutions found that can be consistently and coherently applied across the whole organization. Part of the solution will lie in what sort of meeting rooms or available secured areas can be used by employees, and part will depend on how information is classified and what facilities are made available for its storage.

ISO/IEC 17799 provides very common-sense advice on the selection and design of a secure area, and this section should be read in conjunction with "Protecting against external and environmental threats" below. Secure area design should take account of the possibility of damage from fire, flood, explosion, civil unrest and other forms of natural or human-created disaster. This should include considering the risks posed by neighboring premises, such as potential leakage of water from outside the secure area. Secure storage facilities, such as safes and high-security document stores, need also to be sited in such a way that they can be located on a site map within the business continuity documentation and quickly and easily recovered (as described in Chapter 26) after a disaster. This will require consideration to be given to issues such as the fire resistance period of surrounding doors and floors; the organization wants to avoid scenarios where, for example, after an explosion in the building, a safe containing all the organization's insurance documents falls from its location on the first floor right through into the basement of the building and has to be recovered (when it can be found) from amongst the debris of fire and flood.

The controls that ISO/IEC 17799 recommends should be considered and, if appropriate, implemented include:

- Key storage areas and keyed entrance areas should be sited to avoid access by unauthorized persons and by the public.
- Buildings that contain information processing facilities should be unobtrusive and give as little indication as possible of their presence or purpose.
- Office machinery, such as faxes and photocopiers, should be sited within the secure perimeter in such a way that access to more secure rooms is not required—in other words, do not put the photocopier or fax machine in the same room as the computer servers.
- Doors and windows should be locked when the building or room is unattended. External protection, such as burglar bars, should be considered in the context of the risk assessment for first-floor and any other accessible windows. This is particularly important for the computer server and communications rooms, which should be accessible only to a

small number of authorized personnel, each of whom has an individual access code so that a record of access and egress can be maintained at an individual level. No one should be allowed into one of these rooms unless accompanied at all times by an authorized person. Externally, any special precautions taken for specific rooms (e.g. whitewashed windows or bars) should not stand out in comparison to other rooms as this would clearly indicate to a potential intruder where the most valuable assets might be stored. There should be no obvious signs outside the building to indicate how valuable or important it is.

■ As discussed earlier, information processing facilities managed by the organization should be physically separate from those managed by third parties, even if this means erecting a cage or some other form of physical security within a shared secure area.

■ Internal directories or telephone books or other guides that identify the location or telephone numbers of secure, sensitive areas should not be accessible by the public or unauthorized persons.

■ Hazardous or combustible material, particularly office stationery, should not be bulk-stored within a secure area. There should be a separate area, some distance away, where these are stored. Regular inspections of secure rooms, by someone other than those responsible for their day-to-day management, are usually necessary to ensure that this requirement is observed.

■ Back-up equipment and media should not be stored with the equipment that they will back up, in order to ensure that the organization can actually restore operations if it loses or otherwise has compromised its frontline facilities (through, for example, fire in the server room or terrorist activity affecting the whole of the premises).

Protecting against external and environmental threats

Control A.9.1.4 encourages organizations to protect themselves from damage due to fire, flood, earthquake, explosion, civil unrest and other forms of natural or human-created disaster. The discussion, above, about external threats to secure areas should be applied to the organization's general physical locations. In a sense, this control is asking the organization to ensure that it has complied with health and safety and fire regulations and that it has carried out all the relevant risk assessments required by these regulations, while the comments, above, about controls against threats to secure areas apply more generally. In particular, there should be an appropriate site-level risk assessment covering the possibility of all these natural or human-created disasters; premises in a known earthquake area, for instance, face a greater threat than ones elsewhere, and the organization's business continuity plan will need to take appropriate account of the threat. Similarly, likely local activity (including that of neighbors) should be considered, as should the risks of particularly high-profile locations—for instance, there might be protest marches, terrorist atrocities or police activity near federal or state buildings. In particular, choice of fall-back locations should be driven by consideration of likely repercussions of particular events: the diameter of a bomb explosion, the likely effect of a police cordon, etc.

The auditor will want to see, and the board will want to know, that an appropriate risk assessment has taken place and that appropriate controls against such disasters have been implemented. Of course, these controls must be consistent with the corporate risk treatment plan.

Working in secure areas

Control A.9.1.5 of the standard requires the organization to implement "controls and guidelines for working in secure areas" to enhance the security provided by being within a secure perimeter and/or a secure area. These additional controls are largely common-sense extensions of the controls discussed earlier. ISO/IEC 17799 wants the organization to consider the following additional controls:

■ Only allow employees (or contractors or third parties) to know about the existence of, or activities within, a secure area on a "need-to-know" basis.

■ Avoid unsupervised working within secure areas so as to avoid the opportunity for malicious activities. The extent to which this control is worth implementing does depend on the risk assessment and the size of the organization. At the very least, staff who are being disciplined, or who are on notice, should not be allowed into secure areas unsupervised. This also reduces the health and safety risk for a lone worker, who might have an accident or become ill in an area to which trained first-aiders may not have access without one of a restricted number of authorized staff being available to open secure doors.

■ Vacant areas should be kept locked and periodically checked. This activity should form part of the schedule of activities of a security guarding company or individual guard.

■ Personnel of contracted third party service providers should be given restricted access to secure rooms and this should always be under supervision.

■ Recording equipment (i.e. cameras, videos, photocopiers, etc.) of any sort should not be allowed within secure areas; the records could (accidentally or deliberately) come into the hands of someone who wants to gain unauthorized access to the organization's sensitive information.

■ Additional security restrictions may become necessary when the organization is working, in a specific area of its site, to develop something that needs to be kept confidential for a period of time.

■ Finally, specific controls might be necessary to ensure that executive toys (e.g. MP3 players) or other recording devices (digital cameras, handheld video cameras, cell phones with or without still photography or video capabilities, USB flash sticks) do not collect information from secure areas.

Public access, delivery and loading areas

Control A.9.1.6 of the standard requires the organization to control delivery and loading areas as well as any other areas to which unauthorized persons (such as members of the public) might have access and, if possible, to keep them isolated from information processing facilities in order to limit the danger of unauthorized access to those facilities. This control will have a different importance for different types of organization. A manufacturing or retailing organization is, for instance, likely to have more significant public access, loading and delivery issues than a straightforward office-based organization. The risks range from unauthorized personnel (customers, delivery drivers, etc.) to dangerous deliveries (e.g. bombs, anthrax), any of which might compromise the organization's information security. A risk assessment should, as with every other area to be controlled, be used to determine the security requirements.

The controls, which are primarily for larger organizations that have substantial delivery activity to deal with, that ISO/IEC 17799 wants considered are:

■ Access to a holding area from outside the secure perimeter should be restricted to identified and authorized delivery staff or other personnel.

■ The delivery and holding area(s) should be designed so that delivery staff cannot gain access from it to other parts of the building.

- The external doors of a delivery or holding area should be closed when the internal one is open.
- Incoming material should be inspected for potential hazards or threats before it is moved elsewhere or to the point of use.
- Incoming material should, if appropriate, be registered on arrival.
- Incoming and outgoing shipments should, where possible, be physically segregated.

Implementation of these controls can require significant reorganization of existing delivery facilities and procedures with potentially a significant capital expenditure on the physical set-up. The risk assessment should reflect the fact that, as security controls are improved in other parts of the organization, so remaining vulnerabilities become more significant because they provide the few remaining ways in which unauthorized access to information can be gained. In other words, once an organization has started down the road to ISO/IEC 27001 certification, it should be thorough and complete the journey.

11

Equipment security

Control A.9.2 of the standard deals with equipment security. It wants the organization to take steps to prevent the loss, damage, theft or compromise of its assets and the consequential interruption to its activities. It is broken down into six sub-clauses, each of which deals with aspects of equipment security and disposal.

Equipment siting and protection

Control A.9.2.1 of the standard requires equipment to be sited, or protected, in such a way that risks from environmental threats and hazards, or unauthorized access, are reduced. ISO/IEC 17799 identifies a number of controls to be considered, including:

■ Siting equipment so as to minimize unnecessary, unauthorized access into work areas—for example, refreshment units or office machinery designed for use by visitors to premises should be sited within a designated and supervised public area; unauthorized personnel should not have to access secure offices in order to use these facilities. Consideration needs to be given to how access to washrooms will be managed in respect of visitors to the premises. Clearly, if the only washrooms are within a secure area, visitors will either have to be denied the use of them or will have to be escorted at all times! Doors to computer facilities should have, depending on the risk assessment, mechanisms for ensuring they are kept shut and locked at all times, with any deviations notified on an alarm system.

■ Information processing and storage facilities handling sensitive data should be positioned so as to reduce the risk of being overlooked while in use. This applies, for instance, to workstation monitors in a first-floor office, where passers-by could look through a window and see what is on the screen. This may not be relevant if the information that is likely to appear on the computer screen is not sensitive but, if it is, a simple solution might be the installation of window blinds. It would apply to a wall or floor safe, in retail premises, whose location could be seen by a member of the public on the premises unless it is hidden in another room. Entrances to computer server rooms, and the security locks that protect them, should not be visible from the street, or through a window that would enable someone with a telescope potentially to see a code being input into a door lock. It all depends on the risk assessment; one should be carried out for each circumstance in which this control might need to be implemented and action then taken in the light of that assessment and in proportion to the risk identified. Decisions should, as usual, be documented.

■ Items requiring special protection should be isolated so as to reduce the general level of protection required. Only a risk assessment will establish what type of equipment falls into this category; it is clearly sensible that, for instance, the fuse board that controls the power into the computer server room should be sited away from public places and away from places that even authorized staff access on a regular basis. An opportunist thief passing an office containing a notebook that is docked at a workstation but not otherwise secured might find it difficult to resist the temptation to add the notebook to his or her own briefcase.

■ ISO/IEC 17799 suggests that controls should also be adopted to minimize the risk of potential threats including fire, theft, explosives, smoke, water (or supply) failure, dust, vibration, chemical effects, electrical supply interference or failure, and electromagnetic radiation! The only way this can be complied with is to consider, in respect of each of the major systems and components of systems (see Chapter 6), what the risk of compromise will be for each of the risks identified in this section and, in the light of that assessment, to implement appropriate controls. Many of the controls that will be adopted will be simple common sense; there will be a further discussion of issues arising from this item in Chapter 26, which deals with business continuity. Certainly, in any office environment, consideration should be given to how workstations and, in particular, notebooks can be locked down so that they are not easily removed. Notebooks should, at the very least, be attached to the desk by notebook security cables, which have individual pass codes. There is a range of security products available, from a number of different suppliers (their advertisements can be found in most information security magazines), that are designed to secure equipment. These range from night safes for notebooks through security ties for workstations to safes of one sort or another. There are sufficient security products available for any piece of important equipment to be adequately secured such that there is little real risk of it being stolen, other than by properly equipped criminals who are ready, able and determined to overcome the controls that are in place.

■   ISO/IEC 17799 recommends that an organization should consider its policy toward eating, drinking and smoking in proximity to information processing facilities. Most IT specialists will probably say that eating and drinking should not be allowed anywhere near IT equipment. Somehow, sometimes, this does not also apply to them! Direct experience suggests that very little of any real significance ever happens in the general office as a result of people eating or drinking at their desks. Sometimes, paper-based information is damaged, but computers rarely are. The debris left by people eating in the office can attract rodents and often leaves unattractive odors, but these tend to be the limits of their impacts. The one place where all three of these should certainly be banned (apart, obviously, from clean facilities or anywhere that is specifically designated as a clean area) is the server room. Eating and drinking inevitably leaves debris, which, because the server room is not (or should not be) accessible to the cleaners, accumulates and can negatively impact stored data or the machinery. Smoking might trigger the smoke alarms and cigarette ash is not good for any server or other magnetic media. Smoking is, nowadays, largely confined to the street outside the offices, which does reduce the risks within them. Fire is also something that the organization might want to keep out of the server room, if not out of the office completely. Again, a risk assessment should be carried out and its conclusions should determine the controls implemented. Eating, drinking and smoking are obviously never allowed in clean rooms or similar facilities.

■ Environmental conditions should be monitored for conditions that adversely affect the performance of information processing equipment. The organization should be particularly concerned here with heat and cold, with smoke, with dust and with rain. IT equipment should not be exposed to any of these; server rooms should be equipped with heat, condensation/moisture, fire and smoke detectors that have alarms that contact duty personnel (wherever they are—i.e. the alarms must be able to trigger pagers or similar long-distance communications tools) who know what action to take to deal with the threat. Fire suppression equipment could also be installed.

■ Lightning protection should be installed in all buildings that operate information systems and there should be lightning protection filters on incoming power and communications lines.

■ Special protection methods, such as protective keyboard membranes, might be necessary for equipment in industrial environments.

■ The impact of a disaster in nearby premises or sites (such as the street) should be considered, as was mentioned in Chapter 10 and will be touched on again in Chapter 26.

Supporting utilities

Control A.9.2.2 of the standard requires the organization to protect its equipment from power failures, failures in supporting utilities and other electrical anomalies. This is obvious common sense, as all information processing equipment is electrically powered and is dependent on one or more of water supply, sewage, heating/ventilation and air-conditioning, but most organizations make inadequate contingency plans to deal with this. All support utilities should have a rota of regular inspection by an appropriately qualified engineer to ensure that they are still operating as required and are likely to continue doing so. For a start, every item of equipment should have a power supply that conforms to its maker's recommendations.

An uninterruptible power supply (UPS) is essential to support equipment running critical business applications. The UPS should enable continuous running or, under specific circumstances, orderly close-down. The UPS will need to be of adequate power to support the equipment that relies on it for as long as necessary to allow orderly shutdown or the provision (if possible and appropriate) of alternative power and, if necessary, the manufacturers of both should be consulted. There should be contingency plans for a failure of the UPS; these might include provision of a back-up UPS. UPS equipment should be regularly tested in line with the manufacturer's recommendations and it should certainly be stress-tested in a simulation of the worst possible combination of power and service-interruption circumstances that can be dreamed up, to ensure that the continuous running or system close-down plans work effectively.

UPSs must also be considered for workers in home offices. Appropriate equipment needs to be provided to home office users to ensure that data are not lost; this might include read/write CD ROM drives or floppy disk drives, supported by a standard procedure requiring home office users to take at least daily back-ups of data. Users (both in the home office and mobile, with notebooks) should be trained to save the document on which they are working manually at pre-defined intervals or, alternatively, to have an autosave (which is standard on some later Microsoft packages) facility that does this; this will reduce the amount of work lost in the event of a sudden power outage or battery failure. Home office UPSs also need to be tested on a regular basis and a procedure for doing this will need to be designed and implemented.

A back-up generator should be considered if processing has to continue through a prolonged power failure. Just like the UPS, back-up generators should be regularly tested and stress-tested. Adequate petrol or diesel supplies should be immediately available and stored in accordance both with applicable health and safety legislation and with the outcome of a specific risk assessment.

While Chapter 26 will deal at length with business continuity planning, this is an appropriate point at which to suggest that consideration might also be given to the impact a power outage could have on the working environment. In winter a building will rapidly become too cold for staff to continue working unless alternative sources of heat are easily accessible and ready for use when needed; a visit to the local camping shop should offer some ideas for solutions.

In addition, emergency power switches should be located near emergency exits in equipment rooms to facilitate rapid power-down in the event of an emergency. Emergency (non-electric) lighting should be available in the case of mains power failure at night or in winter. This may be no more than will be sufficient to enable the computer room to be secured and other secure areas or rooms also to be secured. Torches, issued to identified personnel and maintained in a state of constant readiness, may be sufficient—it will all depend on the risk assessment. Gas-operated lamps may also be required.

Lightning protection should be supplied for all buildings, and lightning protection filters should be fitted to all external communication lines. This can be particularly challenging for external communication lines that are without the control of the organization, and due consideration will have to be given to appropriate contingency plans for circumstances where there is a power interruption as a result of a lightning strike to a utility company's unprotected lines.

Finally, consideration needs to be given to all the other supporting services: critically, air-conditioning, humidification and fire suppression equipment needs to be regularly tested and have appropriate alarms fitted to alert staff when they have become inoperative. Telecommunications services should have two different methods of connection to the service provider, to ensure that there is no single point of failure for a critical service, and there should usually be an analog telephone service available as well to deal with emergencies where the digital service is unavailable.

Cabling security

Control A.9.2.3 of the standard wants to protect any cables that carry data or that support information services from interception or damage. With a bit of luck, some of the controls recommended by ISO/IEC 17799 will have been implemented at the time your building was put up because, if they weren't, it's going to be difficult to implement them now. The controls ISO/IEC 17799 wants considered are:

■ Power and telecommunications lines into information processing facilities should, wherever possible, be underground or subject to alternative adequate protection. If they are not already underground, it is probably too late. However, it may still be possible to ensure that cables are adequately protected; specialist information from the utility company concerned will be necessary to help identify a way to protect them. Seriously, where highly sensitive data are being handled, the way in which the utility company handles its telecommunications cables may be critical. Where the risk assessment highlights this issue, there should be a discussion with the utility company about what extra protection they could provide. This protection is important; facilities that are otherwise protected could be penetrated simply because it is possible to tap into the telecoms cable or cut the power cable. The sheer difficulty in implementing appropriate controls means that this becomes a particularly vulnerable area as everywhere else becomes more secure.

■ Cabling in work areas should be appropriately organized and protected. The tangle of cable that often hangs out the back of workstations and lies around on the floor is vulnerable to breakage and can, of course, be a health and safety risk. Cables should be tied away with cable tidies, power splitter boxes should be sensibly sited and, where possible, desks with cable handling systems should be used.

■ Network cable should be protected by using conduit or avoiding routes through public areas. This is a lot simpler to bring about; the network cabling contractor can be instructed to install new cabling— or to strip out and reinstall old cabling—in such a way that it will be protected from unauthorized interception or from damage.

■ Power cables should be separated from communications cables to prevent interference—while the risk of electric interference is self-evident, keeping the two services clearly separate ensures that the risk of losing both power and telecommunications simultaneously is reduced.

■ There are additional controls that should be implemented for particularly sensitive data: armoured conduit, locked rooms/boxes at cable inspection and termination points, fiber optic cabling, electromagnetic shielding, sweeps for unauthorized devices attached to cables, and controlled access to patch panels and cable rooms. Risk assessments should be carried out, expert advice taken and controls that are identified as necessary through this process should be implemented.

Equipment maintenance

Control A.9.2.4 of the standard requires the organization to maintain all its information processing equipment in accordance with the manufacturer's instructions and/or documented organizational procedures to ensure that it remains available and in working order. This clearly means that the organization should retain copies of all the manufacturer's instructions and should identify the recommended service intervals and specifications, and to enable a quick call-out for corrective action in the event of a breakdown they should be displayed together with the supplier's contact details on the equipment. Only authorized and trained personnel should carry out repairs/services; records of all work done should be retained (in a book attached to the machine) and there should be appropriate procedures (dealing with saving, deleting or erasing data, particularly sensitive or confidential data) for controlling equipment sent off-site for repair. Any insurance requirements should be identified and complied with.

There is a more important issue around older equipment. Equipment that works faultlessly for long periods can suddenly fail; it is important, at that point, that there are detailed records of qualified maintenance and repair organizations. More sensibly, a documented record of the service history of equipment should be maintained so that, as it becomes older, properly informed decisions can be taken about the right time for it to be replaced.

Security of equipment off-premises

Not surprisingly, control A.9.2.5 of the standard requires the organization to use security procedures and controls to secure equipment used outside an organization's premises. In particular, use off-site of any equipment should be formally approved (particularly notebooks, personal digital assistants (PDAs) and cell phones, together with any other information processing equipment that will be used away from the office) by line management. The process for this approval should be standardized and can be determined in the light of a risk assessment that considers the possible risks to the organization of its equipment when used off-site. Some of the controls that ISO/IEC 17799 says should be considered are:

■ Equipment (and media) taken off premises should never be left unattended—notebooks should always be carried as hand luggage and, wherever possible, disguised. Notebook computers should not be left in cabs, on planes or anywhere else—but they often are, and the organization needs to think through the consequent risks. Possible controls include placing a limit on the data that can be carried on the C: drive of a notebook, requiring back-ups to be carried out at regular intervals (through Microsoft's "My briefcase" function, for instance) and limiting the period of time that confidential information can be stored on the notebook. Preferably, password protection (including screen savers) should be standard, and confidential information should be encrypted. PDAs should be backed up regularly, and access to both PDAs and cell phones should be restricted by means of access codes.

■ Staff should be trained in how to protect equipment from risks identified by the manufacturer, such as electromagnetic fields, and these requirements should be built into the user authorization requirements.

■ A risk assessment in respect of home working should lead to designation of standard—and, where necessary, special—controls, such as lockable filing cabinets.

■ Certainly, adequate insurance should be taken out to protect equipment off-site and this should be from an insurer that properly understands the market and whose cover is adequate for the risks identified in the risk assessment.

Secure disposal or reuse of equipment

Control A.9.2.6 of the standard wants information and licensed software to be erased from equipment prior to its disposal or reuse. The standard delete function in software packages is inadequate; when equipment is to be disposed off, it should be completely wiped of all data. Even so, the data image may still be on the disk; as disk drives are so inexpensive now, it may be better to destroy disk drives completely before selling PCs. Storage devices (tapes, floppy disks or CD ROMs) should, for preference, be destroyed rather than reused. Workstations, servers and laptops should have their hard disks overwritten prior to their disposal and all software should be removed. Software may be copied and sold; the original license holder for the software could thus be open to a charge of illegal software copying. Destroy any software before disposing of the hard media.

Removal of property

Control A.9.2.7 requires the organization to ensure that equipment, information or software is not removed from its premises without authorization. This is clearly a basic control that is useful in deterring theft of assets. The procedure for obtaining authorization should be clearly laid out in the ISMS, and the steps that are required should be proportionate to the sensitivity or value of the asset. Valuable assets should be logged out of the premises and logged back in again; staff who are regularly carrying valuable assets in and out (such as notebook computers) should have a written authority to do so, which they should carry with them at all times and be able to provide on challenge. Spot checks should take place to detect unauthorized removals, and all staff and contractors should be made aware of this policy and that breach of it may be considered as a disciplinary matter, perhaps involving the police. Remote workers, who have company assets at home, should be required annually to endorse an inventory of items in their possession, commenting on their current state of repair. There also need to be specific procedures for ensuring that portable equipment is recovered from staff who leave. The best way to do this is to withhold final salary payment until all company property is returned; the only way to set this up properly is to have this specific right written into employment contracts initially. Indeed, subject to the value an organization puts on the data accessed by an employee during day-to-day activities, it may be sensible to alter a person's duties at the point of resignation. Removing the right, as well as the need, for a departing salesperson to access sensitive client data has obvious benefits. The early retrieval of company assets from such staff will also assist both the organization and individual concerned—and will prevent any untoward suspicion if an asset is stolen, damaged or corrupted during the notice period.

12

Communications and operations management

Control A.10 of the standard has a number of major sub-clauses. The first of them is control A.10.1, which deals with operational procedures and responsibilities. Its objective is to ensure the correct and secure use of information processing facilities.

Documented operating procedures

Control A.10.1.1 of the standard requires the organization to document the operating procedures that were identified as necessary in the security policy and which are being discussed at length through the pages of this manual. As discussed in Chapter 3 (system integration), the document control principles of ISO 9000 are applicable to ISO/IEC 27001, and all the operating procedures that are part of the organization's ISMS should be treated in accordance with these requirements, including appropriate management approval.

Again, as discussed elsewhere, the best way to make the entire ISMS available to staff is through an intranet and to third party contractors through an extranet. The key benefits of such an approach are that documentation can easily be kept completely up to date and users can be sure that they are seeing the most recent version of ISMS requirements.

While the organization will adopt those procedures that it finds most useful in implementing its information security policy, ISO/IEC 17799 recommends that there should be detailed procedures (and the level of detail should be appropriate to the size of the organization, with more detail required for larger and more complex ones), which should be worked out between the information security adviser and the responsible operational staff, for:

■ Processing and handling information—which covers, in particular, confidentiality requirements and information classification (see Chapter 8).
■ Back-up, which is dealt with in more detail in control A.10.5.
■ Work scheduling requirements, explaining where necessary interdependencies with other systems (so that no one has to find these out the hard way) and earliest job start/latest job completion times (for instance, for back-up procedures).
■ Instructions for handling errors or other exceptional conditions, including restricting use of system utilities, although the organization should have due regard for the comments in Chapter 4 and elsewhere about the need to recruit and retain an information security specialist who has sufficient skill and experience to respond flexibly to new and unusual circumstances. These instructions might, therefore, set out reporting requirements and general guidance, with more specific instructions for junior operatives and inexperienced staff to follow.
■ Contacting appropriate support in the event of unexpected operational or technical difficulties, and what records should be kept of the contacts.
■ Instructions for handling special outputs, such as special stationery, or what to do with failed output for special jobs. Uncontrolled versions of these instructions should be posted near the machines to whose use they relate.
■ Detailed system restart and recovery procedures to follow in the event of system failure. These procedures should be in the ISMS, and controlled copies should be visibly posted near the equipment to which they relate, to enable them to be easily used when required.

■ There should also be detailed procedures for all the basic housekeeping functions, including computer start-up and power-down, back-ups, equipment maintenance, mail handling, computer room usage, etc. These procedures should, wherever possible, be reflected in visible reminders as to requirements posted in the vicinity of where they are relevant. Staff should be trained in their use. Consideration should be given to the possibility that unauthorized staff could see these procedures, and therefore what their classification level is (see Chapter 8) would be relevant to how they are posted.

Remember that overly detailed or infrequently used procedures are as likely to lead to problems as no systems at all. Organizations that outsource their IT services should specify the requirement for proper and appropriate system documentation, to ISO 9000 and ISO/IEC 27001 standards, in the outsourcing contract.

Change management

Control A.10.1.2 of the standard requires an organization to control changes to its information processing facilities, operational systems and application software. These changes usually cause major disruption to the business even when they go well. Inadequate control of these sorts of changes is a common cause of system failures or vulnerabilities. It is also a common cause of unnecessary expenditure. Formal, documented change control procedures need to be in place, which could be adopted from or be the same as existing project management or change control procedures within the organization. What is important is that, for all changes to information processing equipment, software or security procedures, there should be a formal method of control, preferably within an appropriate project governance structure. There is further information about project governance on the website.

Procedure change is easy to control, particularly if the ISMS was set up with the information security management forum as the body that steers implementation of the ISMS. It will have to approve all procedural changes, which should be issued under formal document control and supported, where appropriate, by additional staff training.

Changes to operational programs and applications can impact on one another, and the change control process should ensure that this risk is considered. The specialist input of the IT manager, or vendor-certificated experts, should if necessary be considered as part of the change management process. There needs to be a clearly formulated policy dealing with updates, patches and fixes to major operational and application software; there is not always a valid business or information security reason for making the upgrade and, therefore, the organization's policy needs to set out the criteria for upgrade decisions and their timings.

In general, the change control procedure for operating programs and applications could be on a standard single-page document that includes:

1. an identification of significant changes, and the business reasons (including, if necessary, a cost–benefit assessment);
2. the planning process for testing changes and gaining user acceptance of the changed system;
3. an assessment of their potential (security and other) impacts, including their impacts on other operational or application software and any hardware changes that might be required;
4. formal approval for the changes to be made;
5. communication to all relevant people of the changes, perhaps by means of copying, or e-mailing to them uncontrolled versions of the change control form;
6. procedures for aborting and recovering from planned changes that go wrong.

On a more substantial level, any significant change to the network would necessitate a review of the main information security risk assessment and the statement of applicability that was derived from it. Provision should be made in the change control procedure to ensure that this possibility is considered. Any dependent records would need to be amended.

Segregation of duties

Control A.10.1.3 of the standard requires the organization to impose a control that should already be basic to its financial management system, which is the segregation of duties. ISO/IEC 27001 wants to separate the management and execution of duties or areas of responsibility in order to reduce the opportunities for unauthorized modification or misuse of information or services.

This control is difficult to achieve in smaller organizations but, just as with the financial version, it should be implemented to the greatest extent possible. Wherever it is difficult to implement, the imposition of management supervision, activity monitoring and collection of audit trails is essential. Audit (both financial and security) should at all times be independent.

A key objective of duty segregation is to separate event initiation from its authorization. This is designed to prevent fraud being perpetrated without being detected in areas of single responsibility. The key is to segregate activities that require collusion if fraud is to be committed (e.g. raising an order and signing that the goods have been received) and, where the risk assessment indicates that information assets may be at risk through fraudulent collusion, then two or more people need to be involved in order to limit this vulnerability by lowering the likelihood of conspiracy between one person inside the company and one person outside it. The purchase of IT supplies, or IT services, is one of the more obvious examples of areas where fraud might affect information security.

Separation of development, test and operational facilities

Control A.10.1.4 of the standard requires an organization to separate development and testing facilities from its operational ones in order to reduce the risk of accidental change or unauthorized access to operational software and business data. This clause will be relevant primarily to software development companies and secondarily to any organization that is having bespoke software developed in-house for use, rather than buying a commercial off-the-shelf (COTS) package, in its own operations. One might expect any reputable software development company to be certified to TickIT, the worldwide software industry version of ISO 9000.

This is a key segregation of activities; the rules for the transfer of software from development to operational status should be defined and documented. ISO/IEC 17799 sets out very clearly the ways in which software development should be separated from operations; any organization that is involved in developing software should refer explicitly to clause 10.1.4 of ISO/IEC 17799 for guidance on best practice in how to do this. Software developers may also want to consider the TickIT assurance scheme in this context.

Many companies that are not software companies are likely to be doing some limited development work even if it is limited only to intranet and websites. The controls of this clause of ISO/IEC 27001 are relevant in these circumstances. In essence, the requirement is that developing and testing activities should be separated to the greatest extent possible, preferably running on different computers, or on different domains, and certainly running in different directories. Access methods and passwords should be different between development, test and operational environments. The test environment should be a known, stable one, that emulates as closely as possible the live, operational one and in which meaningful testing can take place and any attempt by a developer or webmaster to introduce malicious code or Trojans or build in vulnerabilities can be detected. Developers should never have access to the live site.

Third party service delivery management

Control 10.2 is a new control in ISO/IEC 17799:2005, addressing the management of services and information security in line with external party contracts (which were discussed in Chapter 7). Control A.10.2.1 requires the organization to ensure that all the security controls, service definitions and delivery levels identified in the third party service contract are carried out. This usually requires the dedication of adequate, appropriately skilled resources on either a full-time or part-time basis. Substantial third party contracts might require the creation of a management team and mechanisms for monitoring contract performance.

When an outsourcing contract is concluded, substantial information will need to transfer to the outsourcing supplier from the organization, and this transfer should be planned in detail and adequately resourced. A complete inventory of those information assets (hardware, software and information) that are to be transferred should be agreed between the parties prior to finalization of the agreement and this inventory list (which might conform to the layout and content detail identified in Chapter 8) should be used to ensure that all the assets are actually transferred.

Prior to transfer, there should be a risk assessment to identify the risks that there might be in the transfer process. These could range from access by unauthorized personnel through to accidental damage or loss. They should be listed in a project-level risk register (which is linked and subsidiary to the corporate-level risk register), and an appropriate control (within the organization's risk treatment framework) should be adopted for each of these risks.

Properly, the organization should carry out a risk assessment prior to entering into a contract within an external facilities management company and incorporate, after agreeing them with the contractor, those controls identified through the risk assessment into the contract. In addition, the contract should contain a clause that enables security enhancements to be required should there be a breach of any of the agreed controls during the contract period. The risk assessment has to take into account the fact that data will be stored at the contractor's premises and consider the possibility of it being compromised there. Chapter 7 dealt with the issue of third party contracts, and the controls identified by the risk assessment as necessary should be built into the contract.

Issues that should receive particular consideration include:

■ sensitive or critical applications that might be better dealt with in-house;
■ the approval of application owners and software vendors for the outsourcing process;
■ implications for business continuity plans;
■ the security standards to be required of the third party and how compliance is to be measured;
■ how activities and individual responsibilities are to be monitored;
■ how security incidents are to be handled and how the contractual procedure to be adopted is to meld into the organizational policy that was adopted earlier in this chapter.

Again, there will be a judgment that the organization will have to make between the benefits it expects to gain through the outsourcing contract and the risks that the contract will bring. The controls that are adopted are, of course, designed to reduce this risk. It will also be important to ensure that the controls are not so tight that the contract is stifled from the outset because that, in its own way, can be as big a risk as allowing too lax a regime to be implemented. This is an extremely difficult balance to strike and the assistance of someone really experienced in negotiating long-lasting outsourcing contracts might be sought early in the process.

In the outsourcing of IT, particular care will be necessary. A carefully thought-through control framework will be required. This should be specified in the outsourcing contract and should concentrate on staffing, access control and ensuring that, on an ongoing basis, an adequate level of assurance is obtained that systems, and system security, are being managed according to the contractually agreed standards. Thought should also be given to what other steps should be taken to ensure compliance with the contract. Comprehensive documentation of the relationship (including agendas and minutes of meetings, agreements on specific issues, etc.) should be maintained in case of future dispute.

Monitoring and review of third party services

Control A.10.2.2 requires an outsourcing organization to monitor and review, on a regular basis, the performance of its third party contractor. As mentioned above, the key requirement is to create a third party contract management resource and process (including standard reports, meetings, etc.) with a designated individual or (depending on the size and complexity of the contract) a department that is responsible for ensuring the contract requirements are met. Key responsibilities should include:

- monitoring performance to ensure that the contracted service levels are actually achieved, identifying shortfalls and agreeing how they should be rectified;
- reviewing all records of security incidents (including audit trails), operational problems, failures, fault tracing and anything else likely to create a risk for the organization and ensuring that appropriate corrective action is taken. This may sometimes lead to escalation through the contractual escalation clauses, and the contract management team should have the skills and experience to manage such an escalation.

It is important that the third party designates an individual or, depending on importance, a team with whom the organization's contract management personnel can deal. The third party unit needs to have sufficient authority to ensure the third party's adherence to the terms of the contract and sufficient skill and experience to deal effectively with issues arising. The agreed contract management process should, for preference, be agreed and documented in the outsourcing contract; this ensures that there is no room for vagueness about what is required and, in any case, the organization may need to specify its right to monitor the third party's change management processes, incident reporting and handling, and vulnerability identification and correction processes.

Legally, the outsourcing organization must remember that ultimate accountability for data processing rests with it and cannot be transferred under an outsourcing contract. It is therefore essential, if the organization is to conform with applicable privacy regulations, that it ensures the processes and systems inside the third party contractor are adequate.

Managing changes to third party services

At the point that it transfers services to a third party, an organization loses the power to make direct changes to those services, whether to respond to changing business needs or to new information security risks. Equally, once they are under the control of a third party, it is possible that changes that suited the third party might be inappropriate. It is important, therefore, that the outsourcing contract ensures that any changes are properly managed, and this is what control A.10.2.3 requires.

This control, which recognizes the central importance of risk assessments to effective management of information security, also recognizes that changes should be assessed in the light of how critical the affected business systems and processes actually are. The change management process should be an extension of that discussed earlier, with the exception that it will be an inter-organizational change process. It must therefore allow for approvals on both sides of the organizational barrier, and any barriers to the process must be identified and designed out as early as possible. Professional, experienced advice on change management within an outsourced function should be deployed early in the negotiation process.

The changes (all of which have information security implications and therefore are likely to need a risk assessment followed by the identification and deployment of appropriate controls) that the organization might require of its third party contractor include: enhancements or changes to systems to handle changes to the current service offering; development of new applications or systems to meet new business needs; and changes that reflect changes in the organization's own internal policies and procedures, including those around information security and information security incidents. The third party may want to make changes to the services it provides to take account of network enhancements; new technologies (particularly those that reduce cost or improve efficiency); new products or new releases of existing products; new development tools; changes in its product or service suppliers (e.g. a telecoms supplier); and changes to (or in) physical locations. Again, all these should be identified in the outsourcing contract, and provision should be made for how possible changes that haven't been identified should be addressed, to ensure that the organization doesn't come to a standstill.

System planning and acceptance

The objective of control A.10.3 is, like so many others, to minimize the risk of systems failure. It has two sub-clauses, capacity planning and system acceptance.

Capacity planning

Control A.10.3.1 of the standard requires the organization to monitor its capacity demands and then to make projections of future capacity requirements so that it can ensure that it has adequate power and data storage facilities available. The utilization of key system resources (file servers, domain servers, e-mail servers, printers and other output devices) should be monitored so that additional capacity can be brought on-stream when it is needed. The projections should obviously take account of predictions of levels of business activity, and there should therefore be an overt link between this activity and the annual business planning cycle. The trends that should be considered are the increase in business activity and, therefore, in transaction processing, and the increase in the number of staff and, therefore, in the number of workstations and other facilities. E-commerce businesses should also consider the expected increase in website activity and plan sufficient capacity to ensure that the site remains operational, particularly at times of peak activity.

All of this should enable network managers and webmasters to identify and avoid potential bottlenecks that could threaten system security or the availability of network or system resources or data.

System acceptance

Control A.10.3.2 of the standard requires the organization to establish acceptance criteria for new information systems, for upgrades and for new versions, and to carry out appropriate tests prior to acceptance.

This is a clause that is more important for an organization that uses bespoke software or relies on a third party (or internal supplier) to deliver a large IT project than for an organization that uses commercial off-the-shelf software. Nevertheless, it is important, even for such an organization, to establish the basis on which it will accept upgrades and new versions. The key requirement must be that the acceptance criteria for new systems should be clearly identified, agreed and documented. There should be a significant element of user testing against these criteria, which should be clearly related to the requirements specification that was used in initiating the project. The acceptance criteria must be capable of objective and, if necessary, independent testing to prove whether or not they have been met. There should be a formal acceptance process for new software, once it is said to have met its acceptance criteria; this process should involve management authorization.

All off-the-shelf packages have regular upgrades, and Microsoft tends to issue new versions of its software every couple of years, service packs on a regular basis and patches monthly. A number of other major suppliers have adopted similar upgrade delivery profiles. One issue that needs to be resolved is that of when upgrades or new versions will be deployed. Many IT managers take the view that it is safer to upgrade to a new version (particularly of a Microsoft package) only after it has had a period in the marketplace during which its initial set of bugs can be diagnosed and fixed. Others take the view that, the faster the upgrade is implemented, the faster the organization will be able to have in place software without the known security weaknesses of earlier versions. Of course, it will soon have its own vulnerabilities exposed!

Our view is that users of commercial off-the-shelf software packages should subscribe to the websites of all their software suppliers, should be aware of upgrades, patches and fixes as they become available and of any new weaknesses or flaws that implementation of the upgrades might cause and, unless they can identify compelling data security reasons not to, should upgrade at the earliest opportunity. Microsoft service packs should be installed virtually as soon as they are available (unless there are compelling reasons—such as the need to test their impact on a range of other software that is run on the corporate network—not to) through the organization's current change control procedure, and regular upgrades (now at least weekly and usually daily) from security software providers should also be accepted, on the same basis, as soon as they are available.

Networks running non-Microsoft applications (e.g. ERP software) should confirm with their vendor that the upgrade will not negatively impact the software and, if there is any doubt, a test upgrade in an isolated environment should be performed before the live system itself is upgraded.

Fixes and patches tend to have little or no impact on users, other than to continue securing their information. Across the web, they are usually free. Version upgrades, other than to antivirus software, may have significant user impacts, and there are usually cost implications. There are a number of controls that should, therefore, be considered. The first is budgetary. The organization should ensure that it has a sufficient budgetary provision to deal with upgrades planned by software vendors. Strategically, it is sensible for organizations to move relatively soon after the issue of an upgrade to its implementation, as the weight of developer resource and support tends to shift away from older packages toward new ones over time and, eventually, support for older versions tends to be withdrawn. There are also likely to be compatibility issues between organizations that are using significantly different releases of the same software. There should also be competitive advantage for organizations in upgrading, in that it enables staff to increase their productivity. Users should also be involved early in any upgrade process, to ensure that their needs and wants are identified and, if possible, accommodated.

All of these factors should be taken into account in deciding whether or not to upgrade. There may well be hardware or capacity issues (and, therefore, further budgetary issues) that arise from a decision to upgrade a software package, and these need to be considered and taken into account as part of the decision-making process.

Once budgetary issues, user requirements and hardware implications have been accounted for, and if the decision (which should be made through the information security management forum) to upgrade has been made, then there are a number of controls that should be implemented. These controls, recommended in clause 10.3.2 of ISO/IEC 17799, should also be implemented when a new software package is to be rolled out, to meet a specific business requirement:

- Computer performance and capacity requirements should be assessed and taken into account in planning a roll-out.
- Revisions to, or establishment of new, error recovery and restart programs may be required.
- Routine operating procedures will have to be (re)drafted and tested to ensure that they are adequate.
- Appropriate new security controls will have to be put in place, consequent upon a risk assessment, for the new software system, of all aspects of the security arrangements upon which it impacts.
- New user manuals may be required.
- New business continuity requirements may have to be dealt with.
- The impact on other software systems and processes should be considered and evidence sought that it will not adversely affect the running of existing systems, particularly at peak or critical periods such as month-end.

■ Consideration should be given, in the risk assessment, to the possible effect that the new system may have on the overall security of the organization.

■ Users should be trained in the use of the new system and the impact that it will have on their current working practices.

It is often argued that it is safe for new, off-the-shelf systems to go live without any period of "parallel running." The risks of doing this should be very carefully assessed, back-up and contingency plans carefully thought out and tested, and appropriate insurance arrangements made. Where the organization has any uncertainty over the likelihood of the new system running "out of the box," it should insist on stress-testing it by running it in parallel with the existing system in a safe test environment (that duplicates the operational one), until each of any key pre-identified stress points has been successfully overcome. Organizations should form their own views on these issues, not simply take the advice of external suppliers. This is particularly important for accounting and ERP systems, failure in the implementation of which can have devastating effects on the company concerned.

It is also important to have clear acceptance criteria (which clearly account for information risks) for any new communications systems and for anything that is connected to the internet. These systems should be demonstrably secure, and the system security risks analyzed and appropriate steps taken, prior to connection.

Major system developments should be subject to a comprehensive project governance framework (for more information, see the IT Governance website) and, in terms of testing and acceptance, this framework should at least include operational, stress and user acceptance testing. Depending on the risk assessment, the organization may even require an independent testing, verification and certification process, particularly to establish that the information security requirements have been met.

13

Controls against malicious software (malware) and back-ups

Control A.10.4 of the standard requires the organization to protect the integrity of software and information, by implementing detection and prevention controls against malicious software and mobile code and to ensure that appropriate user awareness procedures have been implemented. The importance of this control is highlighted by the finding, in the FBI/CSI 2002 survey, that 85 percent of organizations detected computer virus threats. Many organizations think that, because they have some form of antivirus software in place, they have a data security system. This book, and ISO/IEC 27001 itself, makes it clear that antivirus controls are just one part of an effective data security system; they are also an extremely important part.

Viruses, worms and Trojans

An overall understanding of the world of computer viruses, their different types and their characteristics, would be useful ahead of a discussion of how to resist them. Technically, the most useful generic term to use is "malware." "Malware" is a term that denotes software designed for some malicious purpose. It may be written in almost any programming language and carried within almost any type of file. Common forms of malware include viruses, worms and Trojans. "Antivirus" and "anti-malware" are terms that are used interchangeably in this manual.

A virus has at least two properties: it is a program capable of replicating, i.e. producing functional copies of itself, and it depends on a host file (a document or executable file) to carry each copy. It may or may not have a "payload," the ability to do something funny or destructive or clever when it arrives.

A worm, however, is autonomous. It does not rely upon a host file to carry it. It can replicate itself, which it does by means of a transmission medium such as e-mail, instant messaging, Internet Relay Chat, network connections, etc. Polymorphic worms are capable of evolving in the wild, so that they can more effectively overcome evolving virus defenses.

A Trojan is hostile code concealed within and purporting to be bona fide code. It is designed to reach a target stealthily and be executed inadvertently. It may have been installed at the time the software was developed. The objective is often to achieve control over the target system (see also Chapter 24).

These definitions can overlap. Some malware can exhibit properties of both viruses and worms. Some worms deliver Trojans. Whatever the malware, it is usually a well-defined entity, within a single file or part of a file. However, it is predicted that new generation malware will involve cooperation between several entities split over several files. This is scary.

Virus writers, mostly, do it for fun and because they enjoy the challenge of writing clever code. Sometimes they do it out of loneliness, or because they want to have some impact on the world. They often work together and have online groups, websites and communities through which they share work and ideas. They also compete with one another, and certainly their relationship with antivirus companies is often extremely hostile. Virus toolkits are now available online, so that anyone with limited code-writing skills can also create a virus.

Increasingly, virus writers are cooperating with hackers and spammers; spammers want to get their messages past corporate anti-spam filters; virus writers and hackers are good at breaking defenses; and the spam industry is a very lucrative—albeit increasingly illegal—one. Of course, many electronic messages are actually simply virus delivery vehicles and therefore very similar to spam anyway.

The result is that, in today's computer environment, the only way to avoid completely the danger of viruses getting on to the organization's network is to refuse to allow access to the network. An internet connection, a USB flash stick, a CD ROM reader, a floppy disk, an individual user—these are all possible sources of virus infection. Most infection is accidental; in other words, the virus wasn't directed specifically at the now infected organization. It just happened. Refusing access to everyone is obviously not the business-orientated solution that might be expected from most risk assessments.

Anti-malware software

The common solution is to install appropriate anti-malware software. Choosing anti-malware software needs to be done carefully, because poor software will not provide adequate coverage. Malware protection is a complex issue and is not easy for amateur users to navigate. It has been argued that it is probably impossible for ordinary users to perform a meaningful anti-malware product test, to evaluate their comparative efficiencies or to carry out a quality evaluation of the many competing malware detection products. There is also not much correlation between price and quality where anti-malware software is concerned.

Anti-malware products need to be tested over long periods of time, to ensure that they can handle the rapidly changing nature of the malware threat on an ongoing basis. However, most organizations need to make decisions about what to buy and install in much shorter time-frames. The vendor's own marketing material is, not surprisingly, an inadequate basis for choosing software. While there are some commercial approval schemes for anti-malware products, these usually only test detection rates without carrying out a proper scientific evaluation. They are not therefore the best sites to start with when choosing anti-malware software.

An anti-malware product should be chosen from amongst those companies that clearly have the resources to compete and survive in an increasingly competitive marketplace. Size of organization is not, however, a guarantor of anti-malware quality, and there are some substantial organizations whose malware detection rates are consistently demonstrated as being very poor. Under no circumstances should a software product from a small or new producer be chosen either. The organization needs to have the resources to develop its technology, to research malware, to stay on top of developments in a dynamic environment and to develop and produce countermeasures.

A site worth visiting is www.virusbtn.com, which publishes the *Virus Bulletin*. It contains single reviews of many anti-malware products and, occasionally, comparative reviews. It contains up-to-date information about viruses, about spam, about new viruses and about methods of countering them. It contains a list of viruses live in the wild and has tables showing the prevalence of virus reports each month. It also has a list of hoax viruses; there are many hoaxes, and the sensible information security adviser will want to deal effectively with them.

Anti-malware software needs to be integrated with the network or system firewall and needs to deal with spam and instant messaging as well as being capable of dealing effectively with endpoint security issues. The "endpoint" is the point at which the organization's security potentially breaks down: the home worker's own computer, the laptop, the smart phone, BlackBerry or other PDA, the USB stick or even the digital camera or MP3 player.

Hoax messages

Virus hoax messages are reducing in frequency, and are familiar to most e-mail users. One of the main reasons for this is that they play on people's ignorance. Users are understandably concerned about viruses, and so consider it "helpful" if, as suggested by the majority of hoaxes, they forward the message on to their entire address book.

Such an action, although well meaning, is not helpful. Aside from the imposed network load, the consequence is that the hoax becomes "well known" and listed on web pages that list hoax viruses. This fame (of sorts) no doubt leads to some degree of satisfaction for the hoax perpetrator.

The organization should train all its users to respond appropriately if they receive a "new virus" warning message. New virus hoaxes are, more often than not, merely recycled old hoaxes, with the addition of a few minor changes. As such it is possible to spot the tell-tale signs of a hoax. Typical phrases in the body of a virus hoax might be:

■ "Do not open! Doing so will result in the deletion of all of the files on your hard drive!"
■ "Forward this message to all your friends!"

Warning messages encouraging the recipient to forward the information to all his or her e-mail contacts will typically be hoaxes.

Following a standard procedure will enable organizations to ascertain quickly if the warning is genuine, and decide what action it should take. Users should be required to report the (hoax) virus to their information security adviser immediately, by telephone or in person, and on no account should it be forwarded, or copied on, to anyone, whether inside or outside the network.

The organization's information security adviser can ascertain whether or not this is a hoax virus by looking at the www.virusbtn.com list of virus hoaxes. Additionally, the two sites below carry useful up-to-date virus hoax information, and are worth consulting:

■ www.vmyths.com;
■ www.sophos.com/virusinfo/scares.

Anti-malware controls

ISO/IEC 17799 recommends, in clause 10.4.1, a number of common-sense controls to limit the risk of malware infection:

■ The ISMS should contain a formal policy and a procedure that requires compliance with software licenses and that forbids the use of unauthorized software. There is an extended discussion of how this control should work in Chapter 27.
■ There should be a policy that protects the organization against the risks of importing malware on disks, files or software that come from outside the organizational network. Such a policy has to be drafted in the light of a risk assessment and current technical advice about anti-malware capabilities and is likely to be a combination of required activity and technical controls. This policy should, for any network deploying Microsoft products, take into account the security components of XP2, as it is important

that the default firewall, antivirus capability and software automatic updates are configured correctly and in line with corporate policy. The policy could include disabling the disk and CD ROM drives and USB ports on network PCs and notebook computers, requiring any data that arrive on such media to be loaded by an IT team that is able to check the media first for viruses. Alternatively, antivirus software that is capable of checking files that are being uploaded from such sources could be deployed. The policy could ban downloads of software (such as screen savers and utilities) from the internet and/or set up controls on its firewall that make it impossible for such software to be imported, which automatically ensures that such downloads are not carrying malware. It could extend to making the unauthorized use (where the organization requires it, there should be a method for authorizing and verifying it) of external software a disciplinary matter. There is a discussion of related issues in Chapter 21.

■ Anti-malware software should be installed on the network, and updates should take place in line with the vendor's update policy—which should be closely tied to the availability of the updates. The ISMS should retain records of the planned updates and of their actual occurrence. The discussion, earlier in this chapter, about how to select anti-malware software is relevant here, as the evolution of malware happens quickly and leads the evolution of anti-malware products. Failure to update can expose the organization to severe threats, as new malware may be substantially more lethal than older variants. It is important that appropriate consideration is also given to endpoint security: protecting notebook computers, PDAs and cell phones (particularly where they can be synchronized with data on the network such as diaries, contacts, etc.). Wireless networks pose particular challenges, as there are airborne viruses that can infect these wireless networks. In other words, anything that transfers a file, or a part of a file, is also capable of transferring malware, and appropriate technical support plus a risk assessment and the subsequent implementation of appropriate controls are necessary steps to ensuring that they are secured.

■ All patches, fixes and service packs that are published by Microsoft on its website, and those published by other vendors for their products, should be applied as they become available. They are usually published to deal with either a bug or a known vulnerability that could be exploited either by a hacker or by malware and, if the malware doesn't already exist at the point the patch becomes available or the vulnerability is publicized, it soon will—sometimes within a matter of hours. There should be a record of what has been downloaded and applied, by whom and when.

■ There should be a regular review of the software and data on all systems that support critical business processes. There is software that is designed to identify all software running on the system, and this should be used to support the review process. The presence of any unauthorized files or software should be formally investigated and, if appropriate authorization is not forthcoming, they should be deleted.

■ All files from external sources, particularly from untrusted, uncertain or unauthorized sources or over untrusted networks, should be checked for malware before use, and the organization should have a centralized, automated process for carrying out and documenting this check. The process needs to be intelligent if it is to be business focused; simply blocking all unknown senders is not helpful.

■ All e-mail attachments and software downloads (where permitted) should be checked for malware at the point of entry to the network. The firewall is the place to do this, and there will be a detailed discussion of firewall and related issues in Chapters 18 and 19. Further checks against malware could and should be carried out on the desktop and on the servers as well. In other words, the anti-malware software should be installed on the print and file servers, the e-mail server and the workstations (integrating effectively with the endpoints), and all these should be kept up to date. A software package that enables updating to be driven centrally across the network is the most useful method of dealing with this.

■ Users should be trained to recognize, and respond appropriately to, possible virus-infected e-mails that have bypassed anti-malware defenses. E-mails from unknown people, or from known individuals, that are either unexpected or that have unusual content lines, should be suspect. Virus writers play to the curiosity, egotism and fear of potential recipients, and subject matter lines like "Hi," "I love you," "This is approved," "Happy Christmas" or "Here's your new password" are likely to mask potentially destructive viruses. The same e-mail message appearing multiple times from the same sender or from different senders is extremely likely to be a virus and should be recognized as such. User training should include *not* opening the e-mail at all, and using the organization's alternative, non-e-mail, incident reporting procedure to report its arrival as fast as possible.

- There should be clearly documented management procedures that set out responsibilities for running the anti-malware software, for dealing with a malware incident and for recovering from one. Training in all these aspects should be carried out and records of the training, which should be kept up to date, should form part of the ISMS records. A virus incident is a security incident and is covered as part of control 13: information security incident management.
- There should be appropriate business continuity plans (see Chapter 26) that enable the organization to recover from malware attacks. Back-up procedures are discussed in detail below.
- Information security managers should have appropriate sources of accurate and up-to-date information on malware, which they should use both to analyze incidents and to plan ahead to ensure that the organization avoids such incidents. The website www.virusbtn.com was mentioned earlier. The organization might also subscribe to *Security Wire Digest*, available by e-mail from www.infosecuritymag.com. There are other journals, magazines and sites that provide regular, up-to-date information, and the information security professional should ensure that he or she remains fully up to date.

Airborne viruses

Personal digital assistants (PDAs, BlackBerries), smart phones and 3G or web-enabled cellular phones (together often referred to as "handhelds") are increasingly targets for hackers and virus writers. By the end of 2001, there were only about a dozen forms of handheld malware (Trojans and viruses) in the wild, but this has gone on increasing. Viruses can get into PDAs from host computers, when PDA and PC files are synchronized. They can also transfer from PDA to PDA via infrared ports and Bluetooth technology. They can be picked up over the air, using wireless modems. They can spread by telephone connection, and web phones are particular targets. However, the risk of damage to data stored on handhelds is much less than the risk of damage to networks as a result of viruses (written to be innocuous to handhelds but infectious to desktops and networks) that are transmitted to networks by handhelds when users synchronize PDAs and PCs. Handhelds that have wireless connections to the internet can be used to mount denial-of-service attacks, and could be used for defrauding phone networks or other malicious activity.

Most users of handhelds are relatively unsophisticated in their understanding of malware issues and will take little or no action to protect their handhelds. Multiple platforms mean that it is difficult to produce generic anti-malware (AM) software. Handhelds are small, with limited memory and processing power, which limits the options for anti-malware development. The only secure approach for the organization to adopt is a layered one, which installs AM software on the handheld (the endpoint), to concentrate on the handheld viruses, and installs an AM solution on the desktop that scans handhelds during each synchronization. These needs will have to be taken into account when selecting an antivirus software package, and the network will need to be appropriately configured. Organizations should also consider, as part of the user access statement, including a warning about airborne viruses and the need for users to be as alert about possible infections on handhelds as they are about the desktop.

Controls against mobile code

Mobile code is defined, in the *Internet Security Dictionary*, as a "program that can execute on remote locations with any modification in the code. [It] can travel and execute from one machine to another on a network during its lifetime." Mobile code includes ActiveX, Java, JavaScript, VBScript, MS Word macros and PostScript. These codes can be used to collect information from a target system, to introduce malicious code or a Trojan, or to modify or destroy information. Macros are usually found in documents; JavaScript runs on websites and drives most pop-ups and a host of other more important features; ActiveX enables a PC to download critical plug-ins plus their secret payloads. Control A.10.4.2 of the standard requires that mobile code execution should be restricted to an intended environment so that it won't violate information security policies.

The simplest way of dealing with mobile code is to have a policy banning it and installing blocking software on the firewall that stops all mobile code dead. The drawback of this is that this also makes it difficult for users to use properly many legitimate websites that rely on mobile code to operate efficiently.

The organization does, therefore, need to draft a policy (within the context of a risk assessment and current technical advice) that enables users to access websites and reduces the risks of dangerous mobile code executing. This may involve blocking all mobile code, or blocking it simply for some sites—in which case there should probably be a link between the way in which the organization controls surfing and the mobile code policy. Once the policy has been decided, and appropriate software installed on user machines and on the network, and correctly configured, the user authorization and internet acceptable use policies should be adjusted to set out the requirements in respect of mobile code. User awareness training will be necessary, and there will need to be planned monitoring of system resources to detect and eliminate any rogue mobile code that has bypassed these controls.

Back-up

Control A.10.5 of the standard requires the organization to take regular copies of essential business information and software. This is one of the most basic and most important of all controls. It is important not just because it enables an organization to recover from a disaster or media failure, but because it can also enable individual users to recover from unforced errors. Where back-ups have not been taken, it can be impossible to recover from disaster.

An essential first step in making a back-up policy work in most offices is to ensure that most information is filed on the organization's servers, not on individuals' C: drives. Unless specific software is installed, C: drives cannot be backed up, while servers can be, automatically and centrally. This is particularly difficult to do with notebook users, who often work on the move and who need immediate access to their files. Unless a web-based file back-up application is installed on the laptop, the requirement should be for regular back-ups from portable devices to network file servers and for the use of the file server rather than the fixed C: drive to be part of the initial staff training on data security. One step that might be considered in order to illustrate the importance of this particular control would be to make storage of digital data on a desktop a disciplinary offense.

A second essential step is ensuring that the back-up policy is comprehensive. Mobile users have information stored in cell phones and on PDAs. Office-based users use a range of software products, sometimes on single machines only, which might be outside the normal range of Microsoft products. Organizations have websites, intranets and extranets. They use accounting systems, ERP systems and project management systems. They have voicemail systems, which also carry data, particularly in all those voice mailboxes that substitute more and more for real people. Increasingly, organizations use the services of application service providers (ASPs), and this leads to data being stored outside the organization's secure perimeter in situations where the organization has no direct control over the security of its information. It is critical, in these relationships, that the controls discussed under A.6.2.3 are carefully considered. All digital data storage needs to be considered.

So do paper files. The fact that data are stored in paper files or in other books does not make them any less important to the organization than data in digital form. A fire, a flood, an explosion or even simple straightforward theft can deprive an organization of its paper files. They need to be taken into account, and those that are assessed as important to the organization need to be backed up in some manner.

Once the organization has identified all the data assets that need to be backed up, it can decide on a method, and frequency, for carrying out the back-up. This exercise should be comprehensive and should link back to the list of assets that was put together as part of the initial asset inventory discussed in Chapter 8. Each of these methods of backing up and storing data should be risk-assessed in the light of the highest security classification that is likely to be given to data stored in this medium or a particular file or device. There is an early decision to make, for electronic data, between dual-writing (making the copy at the same time as the original) and once-per-day copying. Once a decision has been made as to what data are to be protected, and the necessary level of back-up information has been defined, the controls that ISO/IEC 17799 would like to see considered are:

■ The minimum level of back-up information, together with accurate and complete records of what has been backed up and a copy of the documented recovery procedure, should be stored at a remote location. Accurate records of what has been backed up are necessary in order to facilitate finding what is required for a restore operation. The minimum information would be details of precisely which servers have been backed up and the date and time of back-up. It does need to be sufficiently remote, so that if, for instance, the base city ceased to exist the remote site could take up the burden. The remote location should be sufficiently remote to avoid any disaster that takes place at the main site (or which affects the environs of the main site) but not so remote that it cannot be easily accessed. Back-up tapes might also be stored with a storage company, which collects one tape (or set of tapes) every day and leaves behind the next tape (or tapes) in the cycle. Such an organization would, of course, be subject to the controls discussed in Chapter 7, for third party contracts. At least three cycles of back-up information should be retained for important applications. A typical back-up cycle, of digital media to a digital audiotape (DAT), is called *grandfather, father, son*. These three generations refer to monthly, weekly and daily back-ups, with the "son" an incremental back-up running every day (one tape for each day of the week) and being overwritten on the same day the following week. The "father" back-ups are full back-ups, done every week (one tape for each week of the month) and then overwritten in the same week of the next month. The "grandfather" back-ups are done every month (one tape for each month of the year) and overwritten in the same month of the next year. Autochangers and additional software might be necessary to ensure that back-ups are done fully and effectively.

■ Back-up information should be given the same level of physical and environmental security as the original data; it is just as important and, therefore, the controls that were discussed in Chapters 9, 10 and 11 must also apply to the back-up data. Where necessary, back-ups should be protected by encryption.

■ Back-up media (e.g. the tape unit) should be regularly tested to ensure that they are working. The back-up should be set to happen at a regular time each 24 hours, or whatever shorter or longer cycle the organization chooses in the light of its assessment of its risks of data loss. It should take place at a time of limited or zero network usage, as the network will run slowly while the back-up takes place and those sections being backed up are unlikely to be available to users while the back-up is taking place. It should be demonstrated that the equipment and media used have the actual capacity to complete the required back-up within the allotted time. If they don't, the back-up may be flawed and critical data may be lost. Details of these tests should be retained with the ISMS documents and are critical evidence that the back-up system will be able to help when it needs to.

■ Restoration procedures, which should be documented in the ISMS, should be regularly tested. This should involve those staff who will be responsible for carrying out the restoration, as it is critical that restoration can actually be completed within the time allotted. Tests should be carried out to restore data from every single one of the servers and for every single one of the applications that are supported; it is only through such exhaustive testing that the organization can be sure that it will have what it needs when it needs it. Deficiencies should be put right either through training or through reassessing the software, hardware or back-up procedure itself. The wrong time to discover the deficiencies in this procedure is in the middle of an attempt to restore either an important document or an entire system. The records of these tests, and their outcomes, should form part of the ISMS business continuity documentation. Like all critical tests, they should be reviewed by the information security management forum on a regular basis. Restoration of files from historic records will become increasingly difficult as organizations update or change their software; they will need to remember to retain the ability to access old electronic records for as long as their data retention policy requires and that this might necessitate retention in a working state in a secure environment of software that has otherwise been superseded.

■ Critical paper files should also be backed up, with complete photocopies stored at a remote location. The comments about physical security for back-up documents, and the controls over copying paper documents that were discussed in Chapter 8, should be applied.

■ RAID (Redundant Array of Independent Disks) should be considered for all servers running critical applications. This will provide a level of protection if one of the server drives fails. There are six basic RAID levels, providing different levels of data protection and performance improvement. A risk assessment should be the basis on which selection and implementation of a RAID solution takes place. RAID 5 is the usual level of RAID array implemented, and this combines a good level of protection and performance. Expert advice should be taken on the implementation of a RAID array.

■ The retention period for business information should be defined and applied to the backed-up data. It is particularly important to recognize that legal requirements (see Chapter 27) now increasingly require that e-mails are retained as business records. Data vaults may be an appropriate solution to this requirement.

14

Network security management and media handling

Any organization that is pursuing ISO/IEC 27001 is likely to be a reasonably complex one, with one or more networks of computers, usually across a number of geographic locations. Effective network management is essential to the stability of its operations and, therefore, this is a key area for control.

Network management

Control A.10.6.1 of the standard requires the organization to implement a range of controls to achieve and maintain security in its networks, particularly in those that span organizational boundaries. This is also designed to protect the supporting infrastructure and to protect connected services from unauthorized access. Four controls are recommended for consideration by ISO/IEC 17799:

1. Following the principle of segregation of duties (discussed in Chapter 12), operational responsibility for networks should, wherever possible, be separated from computer operations. The organization should describe within its ISMS (perhaps through a minute of the forum, or the job descriptions of the individuals) how this is achieved.

2. There should be clear responsibilities and procedures for the management of remote equipment, including in remote user areas. These are discussed in Chapter 21 and elsewhere.

3. There should, if necessary (i.e. if a risk assessment identifies it as so), be special controls to protect data passing over wireless and public networks. These could include cryptographic techniques (see Chapter 23), controls to protect the network from access (see Chapter 19) and controls to maintain the availability of computers connected to the network.

4. Close coordination of management activity (a key role of the forum discussed in Chapter 4) should ensure consistent application, across the entire network, of the ISMS controls.

Neither the standard nor ISO/IEC 17799 helps much in this section in terms of network management. This is partly because of the speed with which networking has evolved since the standard was drafted. Many of the requirements of this clause are met by controls introduced in response to other requirements of the standard, as indicated above. Network management is, however, one of the most critical roles within the organization and, of course, how it is to be carried out does depend very much on the type of network that is installed. There is a discussion at the beginning of Chapter 19 about networks. The architecture of the network should reflect the organization's needs and resources, and expert assistance may be required to design and implement it. One of the most useful books for anyone tackling networking issues is still *Networking: The Complete Reference* by Craig Zacker (2001), published by Osborne/McGraw-Hill.

The recruitment of an experienced and effective network manager is a key step for the organization. External assistance may be required in the recruitment process. This person's job description should include a clear description of the network(s) for which he or she will be responsible, and the standard to which it/they will have to be maintained should be set out explicitly, with objectives and measurable standards of performance. Those aspects of the ISMS for which the job holder will be responsible should also be specifically identified. The job description should contain a clear reference to the job holder's responsibility for maintaining the integrity, availability and confidentiality of data on the assigned network(s).

The network architecture should be specifically documented, including the planned detailed settings of all its hardware and software components. This plan should reflect a risk assessment (as described above) and should be carried out with the assistance of a specialist network engineer. The implementation of the plan should also be in the hands of specialists and, both once it is finished and at periodic intervals thereafter, should be subject to technical audit (see Chapter 27). Developments in networking technology should, where appropriate, be integrated into the existing network, subject to the change management controls discussed in Chapter 12.

Security of network services

Control A.10.6.2 of the standard requires the organization to provide a clear description, in its ISMS and in the network services agreement (even where the services are provided internally), of the security attributes (as well as the expected service levels and management requirements) of all the network services that it uses. This is referring to the wide range of public or private network services available, which may have simple or complex security characteristics. A clear description of these characteristics should be provided so that appropriate risk assessments can be carried out and so that, when security incidents involving these services take place, adequate information is available to deal with them. Increasingly, the most common source of network service is the internet, and its security characteristics are non-existent.

In addition, as organizations outsource technology and buy other critical services on application service provider (ASP) models, these control requirements become more important. Internet service providers (ISPs), server farms, hosting services, managed service providers, dedicated information services and so on can all be critical to the security of the organization. It is therefore necessary to identify and document their security characteristics.

The characteristics in which the organization should be interested include:

▪ security technology, such as encryption, authentication and network connection controls;
▪ the technical parameters for connecting with the service provider securely;

- procedures for restricting access to the services, where necessary;
- controls relating to any data (particularly personal data) stored on the system.

It is particularly important to check the resilience of the supplier's systems and to understand and check its fall-back procedures. The organization should establish the extent to which the supplier will maintain security controls when it is in fall-back mode. There should, therefore, be a risk assessment for every outsourced provider that identifies these sorts of risks and proposes additional controls to offset any observed security weaknesses.

Media handling

Control A.10.7 of the standard wants to prevent damage to or disclosure of the assets of the organization and any consequent interruption to its business activities. It has four sub-clauses, dealing with removable computer media, disposal of them, information handling procedures and system documentation security.

Management of removable computer media

Control A.10.7.1 of the standard requires the organization to control removable computer media, such as tapes, disks, cassettes and printed reports, so as to prevent damage, theft or unauthorized access. ISO/IEC 17799 recommends that documented procedures should be included in the ISMS as follows:

- It should be required that the previous contents of any reusable media that are to be removed from the organization should be erased. The erasure must operate across the totality of the media, not simply across what appears to be the existing content, as otherwise there is a danger that information may leak to the outside world.
- Authorization should be required for all media that are to be removed from the building and an audit trail should be retained. Some media, such as back-up tapes, are removed on a daily basis, and the authorization for such standard removals should be documented in the ISMS. Other media, such as USB sticks, are more easily portable, and the organization's overall policy on these will need to be determined.

- All media should be securely and safely stored in line with the manufacturer's recommendations. Media safes that have an appropriate fire resistance should be installed, in line with the guidance set out in Chapter 10. Library procedures should be considered to ensure that media are properly tracked and controlled.
- Information that is likely to be required at some point beyond the media lifetime (check the manufacturer's statement about media longevity) will need to have appropriate arrangements made to ensure its future availability—including alternative storage, so as to avoid the impact of media degradation.

Disposal of media

Control A.10.7.2 of the standard requires the organization to dispose safely and securely of media when they are no longer required. Careless disposal of media (which includes throwing floppy disks into waste bins or losing USB sticks) could enable confidential information to leak to outside persons. There should be documented procedures in the ISMS that ensure disposal is done securely.

The items that should be considered for secure disposal under such a procedure are: paper documents, voice or other recordings, carbon paper, output reports, one-time printer ribbons, magnetic tapes, removable disks, USB sticks or CD ROMs, optical storage media, program listings, test data and system documentation.

Media such as these, containing sensitive information, should be disposed of securely. Some organizations may wish to separate media carrying sensitive information from those that don't and will need to carry out a risk and practicality assessment to decide how to deal with them. Other organizations will simply treat all disposable media in the same way, so as to avoid any risk of sensitive data bypassing secure disposal arrangements. This means shredding or incineration or, for magnetic media, overwriting. It is usually sensible for all media to be gathered together and disposed of simultaneously rather than attempting to separate out sensitive media. The best way to do this is through a series of disposal bins and baskets, located throughout the organization's premises, into which identified types of media go when they are no longer required. A specialist contractor would normally supply these bins and an associated removal and destruction service. Contracting with such an organization should obviously be subject to the disciplines set out in Chapter 7. A log of disposals should be maintained.

Information handling procedures

Control A.10.7.3 of the standard requires the organization to establish information handling and storage procedures that will protect its information from unauthorized disclosure or misuse. These procedures should apply to all information: documents, computing systems, networks, mobile computers and PDAs, snail mail, e-mail and voicemail, all other forms of communication, multimedia, faxes, checks, etc. The control requires the organization to do a number of things that it has already tackled under other headings, and one or two new ones. As a starting point, information should be labeled and handled consistently with its classification (see Chapter 8), irrespective of the media that contain it. In addition, ISO/IEC 17799 recommends that the procedure should cover:

- handling media (discussed further below);
- access restrictions to identify unauthorized personnel (Chapter 10);
- a formal record identifying authorized recipients of data, which lines up with the classification of the data;
- in data processing operations, ensuring that input data are complete, processing properly completed, output validation applied and spooled data protected to a level consistent with its sensitivity;
- ensuring media are stored in line with manufacturers' recommendations, which are usually common sense;
- keeping data distribution to a minimum, in line with their classification, and clearly marking all copies of media for the attention of the authorized recipient;
- regular review of distribution lists and authorization lists to ensure that they still contain appropriate people. This is particularly important with automated circulation lists and e-mail directories, which can easily survive the departure of one or more of their members. Outlook e-mail directories should be regularly audited (monthly, for organizations of any size) to ensure that all staff who have left the company have been removed and that the only names appearing in the directory are still authorized to be there.

Security of system documentation

Control A.10.7.4 of the standard requires system documentation to be protected from unauthorized access. This does not refer to off-the-shelf manuals and similar documentation that would be available as standard with each and every instance of the software. It does refer to bespoke documentation, which would contain descriptions of applications processes, procedures, data structures and authorization processes. Such documentation should be securely stored, with a restricted access list authorized by the application owner; and where it is held on or supplied by a public network, other protection (such as access control or encryption) may be required.

15

Exchanges of information

Control A.10.8 of the standard exists to prevent loss, modification or misuse of information exchanged either within or between organizations. Such exchanges of information should also comply with any relevant legislation. There are five sub-clauses, one of which (10.8.4: electronic messaging) is addressed in Chapter 17.

Information exchange policies and procedures

Control A.10.8.1 of the standard requires the organization to put in place procedures and controls that protect the exchange of information through the use of any communications facilities including letter, e-mail, voice, facsimile and video communications facilities. The risks associated with these methods of communication have been discussed earlier in this book and are summarized here. E-mails can go astray and are a widely used medium for harassment, information leakage and so on. One could be overheard while talking on a cell phone in a public place, such as on a train. Answering machines can be overheard by someone physically present in the room as the caller leaves a message. Unauthorized access to dial-in voicemail systems is a clear danger, as is unauthorized dial-in to teleconferences. Facsimiles can accidentally be sent to the wrong person.

So, information security could be compromised by any of these events. It could also be compromised by the theft or disappearance of critical cell phones or by the failure of communications facilities (whether through overload, interruption or mechanical failure or even through failure to identify and pay appropriate service provider invoices in due time). Information can also be compromised if unauthorized users can access it. A cell phone that carries a list of pre-programmed contact telephone numbers can, in the wrong hands, reveal sensitive information.

There should, therefore, be a clear, formal policy, procedures and controls within the ISMS to protect information exchanges through all possible routes and that set out to employees what is expected of them when using any of these communications methods. These requirements should be part of the training for all staff that was discussed in Chapter 9. Users of cell phones should receive a mini-restatement of the current version of the procedure when they are issued with corporate cell phones.

The controls should cover the following:

- There should be procedures designed to protect exchanged information from interception, copying, modification, mis-routing and destruction. Subject to the risk assessment, these are likely to include technological controls, such as digital watermarking, encryption and other cryptographic techniques to protect confidentiality, integrity and authenticity, etc. The organization's policy should link the method of protection to the level of classification (as discussed in Chapter 8) and should have regard to any applicable legal requirements.
- We have already discussed (in Chapter 13) the need for procedures to protect against malware, and the organizational policy on information exchange should reference the anti-malware policy and controls, just as it should reference the acceptable use policies (Chapter 17) and the formal guidelines for the retention and disposal of information. Sensitive documents should not be printed to, or left on, widely accessible printers or fax machines; the usual way to deal with this is for there to be a small number of personal (or otherwise supervised), dedicated fax machines and printers to which sensitive information can be printed.
- The dangers of wireless communications should be clearly identified and the policy and controls implemented in this regard clearly referenced in the SoA.

■ The acceptable use policies and any external party agreements for use of the organization's facilities should set out clearly the responsibilities not to compromise the organization through harassment, obscene messages, defamation, impersonation, forwarding chain e-mails, unauthorized purchases, etc.

■ Remind staff that they should not reveal confidential information (for classification issues, see Chapter 8) when using cell or fixed phones other than from secure locations. Public places, open offices, offices with thin walls, competitors' premises and crowded trains are all places from—or to—which confidential information should not be communicated. The best way to do this is to avoid having these sorts of conversations other than from a secure location. In fact, the same rules apply to confidential discussions: they really should only take place in secure rooms that do have soundproofed walls. Subject to the risk assessment, there are many conversations that should not take place until the designated discussion venue has been swept for bugging and other espionage devices.

■ Avoid using communications equipment that may be compromised; telephone systems in competitors' premises may be wire-tapped or have conversations otherwise recorded. Many telephone calls to and from investment banks and other institutions are automatically recorded ("for training purposes"). Analog cell phones can be scanned and messages intercepted.

■ Messages containing sensitive information should not be left on answering machines or voicemail systems that might be overheard or replayed by unauthorized persons, or which might be re-routed to an inappropriate person or stored in some communal database. It is even possible that a caller might misdial and leave a compromising message on an unknown voicemail system.

■ Faxes can easily arrive at the wrong recipient and, every day, many do. Confidential faxes should be dealt with in line with their security classification as set out in Chapter 8. Any faxes that are sent out should not contain information that the sender would not want to arrive unsolicited at a wrong number or that might be stored in a fax message store to which unauthorized access can be gained. Fax senders should check to ensure that they are using the correct stored number and/or have correctly dialed the intended destination number. If the fax has started sending when the error is discovered, dispatch should immediately be halted. Fax machines should be checked to ensure that they have not been programmed to copy faxes automatically to alternative, unauthorized numbers. Fax machines also often have page caches from which pages can be printed after repair of a fault or restoration of power: beware!

Exchange agreements

Control A.10.8.2 of the standard requires the organization to have (primarily) formal agreements for the electronic or manual exchange of information and software between organizations. These might include escrow agreements, which are particularly important where one organization relies on the software developed by another and there is even the slightest chance that the developer might go out of business at some point.

The sensitivity classification of the data to be exchanged should govern the security conditions to be included in the agreement. Where necessary (i.e. where there is uncertainty about the appropriate level of protection) a risk assessment should be conducted. The issues that should be addressed in inter-organizational agreements for information exchange do depend on the sensitivity of the information. Information exchange agreements should reference any of the relevant policies and procedures that the organization applies to information exchange and could, according to clause 10.8.2 of ISO/IEC 17799, include:

- identification of who is responsible for controlling and notifying transmission, dispatch and receipt on either side of the agreement;
- notification procedures to ensure the other side knows that sensitive information has been dispatched or received and associated (primarily technical) controls to ensure traceability and non-repudiation;
- minimum technical standards for packaging and transmission;
- courier identification procedures;
- responsibilities and liabilities if data are lost or there are information security incidents;
- the agreed labeling system, to ensure that the appropriate protection required is immediately obvious and provided—the preferred system should (practically) be the same as that used by the receiving organization internally, as this will ensure that there is consistency of understanding;
- where relevant, responsibilities for information and software ownership, and for data protection, software copyright and ownership and similar issues;
- where relevant, technical standards for recording and reading information and software;

▪ any special controls (such as cryptographic) that may be necessary for particularly sensitive information.

The person(s) responsible within the organization for the maintenance, dispatch and receipt of such information and software should be asked to draft the procedures; it may be necessary after that to ensure that the procedures are made as practicable as possible. There may be other controls (discussed in Chapter 7) that may also need to be included in such agreements.

Physical media in transit

Control A.10.8.3 of the standard requires the organization to protect any media being transported beyond the organization's physical boundaries from unauthorized access, misuse or corruption. As back-up tapes are amongst those media most regularly transported and as the organization's survival could depend on their protection, it is particularly worth getting this right for the back-up tapes. The mail and casual courier services are not necessarily secure transport services. There are a number of controls, whose benefits are self-evident, which ISO/IEC 17799 recommends should be considered in relation to the security requirements for the media in transit:

▪ A list of authorized, reliable and trusted couriers should be established, and contracts following the pattern described in Chapter 7 should be negotiated. The contract should include some method by which the organization can satisfy itself as to the background checking processes applied by the courier company to all its staff, particularly its temporary and part-time staff. There should be an agreed method of identifying the courier on arrival at the dispatching organization.
▪ Packaging of hardware should be in line with manufacturers' specifications and, in any case, sufficient to protect the contents from any likely physical damage, including environmental factors such as heat, moisture or electromagnetism.
▪ Where necessary, appropriate physical controls should be adopted to protect particularly sensitive information. These could include delivery by hand, the use of special locked containers (with keys sent by alternative routes), tamper-evident packaging, split deliveries (so that neither single delivery will give the whole story) and use of cryptographic controls.

Business information systems

Control A.10.8.5 of the standard requires the organization to prepare and implement policies and guidelines (and therefore documented procedures within the ISMS) to control the business and security risks associated with the interconnection of business information systems. The modern distributed network dramatically improves communication between employees of an organization and provides frequent opportunities for information to be shared electronically that previously required face-to-face communication.

Face-to-face communication is inherently more secure than using electronic business information systems. The range of appropriate controls for electronic information sharing that should be considered covers the number of ways in which information can be lost, misappropriated or improperly used. The range of communication methods that should be considered includes paper documents, desktop computers, mobile computing, mobile communications (phones and pagers), PDAs, mail, voicemail, multimedia, postal services/facilities, fax machines, printers and photocopiers. Many of these risks are increased by operating in an open-plan office.

Risk assessments will identify vulnerabilities in the organization's office systems, particularly where information is being shared between two (or more) parts of the organization. These include the recording of phone calls, conference calls, call confidentiality, fax receipt and storage, mail opening and mail distribution, photocopying, printing, etc. All of these systems provide easy opportunities for information to go astray, whether accidentally or deliberately. An inadvertently hit print command could lead to a confidential document being printed to an insecure printer without its owner being aware of it. A copy of a confidential document could be left in a photocopier in error; a confidential fax could be received at an insecure fax machine; a confidential voicemail could be listened to by someone not authorized to receive the information; common diary systems could expose the confidential movements of senior staff engaged on acquisitions or disposals, etc. Such risks should all be considered. One way of dealing with the potential risks is, of course, to improve dramatically the extent to which employees of the organization are taken into the confidence of the management. This approach, which was indicated in Chapter 8 in the context of data classification, relies on management establishing a culture of trust inside the organization as a result of which every member of staff is highly committed to maintaining the confidentiality, integrity and availability of its information. New employees and potential third party contractors are subjected to rigorous security vetting and the organization concentrates significant resources on maintaining its secure perimeter and network security. Such an approach can work well in a smaller company where management has a very personal and direct relationship with the majority of employees, but is more difficult to implement in a larger or multi-site business.

The key message, in today's business environment, is that employees who believe that they know what is going on, and who are involved in maintaining the security of the organization's data, are less likely to be internal security threats than are staff who are disconnected, disaffected and uncommitted, and this can be taken into account in the risk assessments.

The additional controls that ISO/IEC 17799 recommends should be considered are:

- There should be a clearly stated and implemented policy on information sharing that reflects the policy on information classification (see Chapter 8) and that deals in particular with what information is to be posted on corporate noticeboards, electronic information bulletins and corporate intranets or in e-mail released to one or more general circulation lists.
- Where the system provides inadequate protection against outside interference in, or access to, information whose classification level requires such protection, then it should not be made available on internal noticeboards even if its classification would allow it to be.
- Diary information that, in Microsoft Outlook, can be made available to any other user of the system should be restricted for those working on sensitive projects. This is because someone who wants to access the documents or records of such a project prefers to plan an attempt to do this when the owner is not on-site or is otherwise occupied.
- Business information systems include workflow applications such as purchase systems, goods inwards systems, sales contracting and invoicing systems, resource planning and scheduling systems, payroll systems (including salary increases and other payroll alterations), etc. Any one of these systems is potentially a target for someone who wishes to commit fraud or otherwise interfere in the operation of the organization. It is therefore important that the suitability and security of the existing system is considered before such applications are rolled out. If these systems are already in place, an assessment of vulnerabilities needs to be carried out and appropriate controls implemented. These might have to include

hardware upgrades and should certainly review the workflow steps, access to the system and authorization levels and user authentication.

■ The ISMS needs to identify the categories of staff, contractors and partners allowed to access the system and the locations from which it can be accessed. External party access was discussed in Chapter 7 and access control will be discussed in Chapter 18.

■ It is likely to be necessary to restrict particular facilities to particular members or categories of staff. For instance, payroll should be accessible only by payroll staff and specified accounts staff and management. Accounting records should be accessible only by staff reporting to the chief financial officer (CFO), and certain functions should probably be restricted to the CFO alone. Administration of salesforce automation and customer relationship management software should be restricted to the sales administrator; salespeople may just want to make changes to the system that won't entirely suit the organization.

■ E-mail and user access directories should distinguish between employee and third party user names and user groups that contain external members; they should also distinguish between internal and external e-mail addresses. Such distinctions enable users to take appropriate steps to restrict circulation of information.

■ Information back-up and retention was discussed in Chapter 13.

■ Fall-back requirements will be discussed in Chapter 26.

16

Electronic commerce services

The growth in electronic commerce led, in ISO/IEC 17799:2005, to the elevation of what had been a single control into a comprehensive control area. Control A.10.9 of the standard requires any organization involved in e-commerce to ensure the security of its e-commerce activities and to protect its services against fraudulent activity, contract dispute and disclosure or modification of information.

E-commerce issues

E-commerce can involve electronic data interchange (EDI) as well as e-mail and, increasingly, web-based trading and online transactions. There are a number of issues that need to be tackled and controls introduced; web transactions take place within a rapidly changing environment in which some fundamental security principles are beginning to emerge. There are also specific issues that need to be considered in the use of extranets by businesses in trading with supply chain partners.

The e-commerce world is changing rapidly. This has immediate and constantly changing implications for information security. Organizations are changing and becoming more open; they are also becoming more complex. As companies acquire others, or develop business partnerships, so they want to share information across spaces that are no longer strictly limited to an organizational domain. The drive toward more open business models is driving forward greater interconnection and greater sharing of information. Technology is contributing to these changes, as more and more powerful applications are developed to push information around the world and to overcome any barriers in its way. Content is no longer limited to text; it now includes documents and active content (mobile code, such as Java or ActiveX) that download and run on users' desktops; it includes voice, sound, animation, streaming video, instant messaging, file transfers and a whole range of multimedia applications. All these changes help the development of e-commerce, so organizations, and users within them, want to respond to and use all the new capabilities; they also create a whole new and fast-changing series of risks and vulnerabilities and a very porous organizational security perimeter.

Technology changes are at the heart of these changing threats. Applications are increasingly written to assume that information will be shared across networks, regardless of the organizational boundaries or firewalls between them. Many vendors are now actually building their applications to overcome or circumvent the firewall controls, which are often viewed as barriers to e-commerce and which must be overcome in the pursuit of open, networked working. One ongoing change is that most internet application developers now make new applications run via the firewall port that is mostly open (port 80, traditionally enabled on 99.9 percent of firewalls to run HTTP). This means that a diversity of media types try to navigate port 80, making it difficult for firewalls to filter out malware or to control access to specific data channels. Of course, as new applications are developed and firewalls lag behind in their ability to handle the new application effectively, so organizations will take increasing risks by opening their firewalls anyway —particularly where the application is considered critical to the business.

The risk from hackers is growing all the time. There is a detailed discussion of the world of the hackers in Chapter 18, in the context of access control, and this is also highly relevant to the consideration of e-commerce. Organized crime, as was described in Chapter 1, is turning to the internet and e-commerce as a lucrative business area, and the growth of "phishing" attacks and spam mail are two of the most visible and high-profile indicators of the extent to which e-commerce is also a danger area for consumers and businesses. Equally important are the risks arising from industrial espionage and the value that transactional information can have to a competitor, even if it has only been inadvertently disclosed.

Non-repudiation is a major issue for online commerce. As commercial transactions take place over the internet, the same types of dispute that arise in the analog world arise in the digital one. Disputes can involve the specifics of agreements and performance, and there are digital equivalents of the postmarks, recorded delivery receipts and notarized documents that exist in the analog world. There are three key components to the non-repudiation issue:

- **Non-repudiation of origin.** There must be evidence for a receiving party that the sender is genuine, not an impostor. A vendor would, for instance, want to be sure that an order was from a genuine customer.
- **Non-repudiation of submission.** There must be evidence that the thing was actually sent at a particular time (such as a postmark).
- **Non-repudiation of receipt.** It must be possible to prove that the receiving party has actually received what was sent. Lesser issues include verifying the time and place of transmission.

There is a discussion of how these specific issues of non-repudiation should be dealt with in Chapter 23.

It is against this background that the issues identified in clause 10.9.1 of ISO/IEC 17799 should be considered. The standard's control objective, in A.10.9.1, is that electronic information passing over public networks should be protected from fraudulent activity, contract dispute and unauthorized disclosure and modification. In implementing this control, there are a number of interlinked issues, many of which should be addressed in formal agreements between parties:

- Authentication, to ensure that there is some confidence that customers or traders are who they say they are.
- Authorization, to ensure that trading partners know that prices set, or contracts agreed, have been agreed by someone authorized to do so, and that trading partners know what each other's authorization procedures are.

- Dealing, in online contract and tendering processes, with non-repudiation, with the confidentiality, integrity, proof of dispatch and receipt of documents.
- How confidential are discount arrangements and how reliable are advertised prices?
- How is the confidentiality of transaction details (including payment and delivery details) to be protected?
- What vetting of payment information is necessary?
- What is the most secure method of payment, and how is credit card fraud to be dealt with?
- How are duplicate transactions, or loss of transactions, to be avoided?
- Who carries the risk in any fraudulent transactions, and how is insurance to be dealt with?

As can be seen, these questions and the controls they should instigate are specifically designed for business-to-business (b2b) commerce; trading partners should incorporate their answers to these questions into an agreement between them. Trading partners operating through an internet exchange or via an extranet also need to resolve these issues. Many, but not all, of the issues listed above can be solved by implementing effective cryptographic controls. Cryptographic controls, encryption, digital signatures, non-repudiation services and key management are the subjects of control A.12.3 of the standard and are discussed at length in Chapter 23.

These controls need to be extended to cover business-to-consumer (b2c) commerce for all those organizations selling across the web, particularly in respect of the implications of the various personal privacy regulations, "phishing" attacks and credit card fraud. As will be discussed in Chapter 27, which deals with compliance, the organization also needs to determine which laws and whose jurisdiction apply to the transaction.

Security technologies

The speed of change, the range of threats and the variety of technology available mean that it is virtually impossible for an organization's information security specialist, let alone the business manager responsible for information security, to be adequately informed on the subject. It is essential that any organization implementing web-based services takes professional advice from a security organization that is technology-agnostic and that can provide completely up-to-the-minute advice on appropriate technology steps. In assessing an adviser, consideration should be given to its financial and business viability in the same way as the creditworthiness of a potential client might be assessed. This is trebly important for any potential supplier of security technology; not only does one need to have some certainty that the company will survive to service and develop its technology, but there also needs to be some certainty that the technology itself is, or will really be, part of the mainstream.

The Internet Engineering Task Force (IETF) is an open, international community of practitioners concerned with the evolution of internet architecture and its smooth operation. It has a number of working groups, which consider and propose official standards and protocols for use on the internet. Its website can be accessed at http://www.ietf.org. The fact that a protocol has been adopted by the IETF and by a number of supporting organizations does not, however, mean that every single organization in that space has to—or indeed will—use it. The internet is still wild. The four key security technologies (SSL, IPSec, S/MIME and PKIX) are briefly described below. There are a number of other technologies, with various derivations, but these four are still the technological basis of most internet security systems.

Secure sockets layer (SSL)

This is a handshake protocol that was developed by Netscape Communications to provide security and privacy to internet transactions. It is application-independent; after an SSL session starts, other protocols (like HTTP and FTP) can be layered transparently on top of it. It has become one of the most popular security protocols on the internet. Installation of a server ID, or digital certificate, will automatically activate SSL on the server, and this enables that website to communicate securely with any visitor using Microsoft Internet Explorer or Netscape Navigator. Client and vendor servers are able to authenticate one another automatically. Once this is complete, SSL will encrypt all communication (data such as credit card numbers and other personal information) between the web server and the visiting browser with a unique session key. The session key is not used again. SSL was designed to ensure that, even if information is intercepted, it cannot be viewed by someone who is not authorized to do so.

However, Achilles is a more recent tool, available to all on the internet, which can intercept http and https data (by acting as a proxy sitting between a browser and a server) and potentially allow an attacker to alter it before sending it on. SSL cannot be relied on in isolation; these sorts of "web application session tracking attacks" are constantly evolving and the organization's defenses have to evolve equally quickly. Cookies, which are the most widely used session tracking mechanisms, and which are stored in the browser, can be edited in such a way that the attacker can usurp another user's session on, for instance, an e-bank site. The organization's information security adviser and specialist technology advisers should (assuming that the risk assessment identifies this as an issue) take steps to ensure that the security of the session tracking mechanisms of web applications is assessed and any weaknesses repaired before an attacker takes advantage of them.

The default settings on Microsoft and other browsers should show the user a warning that the site to which information is about to be submitted is insecure, that the communication could be observed by a third party and that passwords, credit card numbers or other confidential information should not be submitted. The warning does not appear where there is a valid SSL connection. There are other signs that there is an SSL connection: the URL will change from http to https and a closed padlock will appear in the bar at the bottom of the browser window.

Internet Protocol Security (IPSec)

Where SSL allows two systems to communicate securely over an insecure connection, IPSec creates a secured connection between the two systems. IPSec defines how interoperable, secure host-to-host and client-to-host connections (known as virtual private networks, or VPNs) are to work, creating an encrypted tunnel over a public network that provides privacy as good as that available on a private network. There is more detailed information available for the technically inclined at http://www.ietf.org/html.charters/ipsec-charter.html.

S/MIME

Multipurpose Internet Mail Extensions (MIME) is a specification that provides a standard method for attaching to basic e-mail messages additional files such as pictures, audio and application files. Secure MIME adds security features such as digital signatures and encryption services to the basic MIME specification, thus protecting the privacy of e-mail and its attachments.

PKIX

The PKIX working group of IETF has been taking forward work on the definition of a standard, interoperable public key infrastructure and on fostering usage of public key security services. It has specified the mechanisms for encryption and described the structures of public and private keys, certificates and digital signatures. It has also addressed how certificates should be managed, hosts addressed, certificate authorities (CAs) run, and so on. Much more information is available from this section of the IETF website (http://www.ietf.org/html.charters/pkix-charter.html).

In addition, and of particular relevance for b2c trading, there is the SET (Secure Electronic Transaction) protocol, developed jointly by Visa and MasterCard as a method for enabling secure, cost-effective bank and credit card transactions over open networks. SET includes protocols for purchasing goods and services electronically, for authorizing payments and for requesting and obtaining digital certificates.

Server security

Control A.10.9 of the standard also requires the organization to protect itself against modification of information. This points to the need for organizations to take specific steps to protect their web servers from attack. There are a number of baseline security measures that the ISMS should require to be carried out regularly, and which should be documented. These are particularly important for server software, which should be specifically locked down in line with the baseline requirements published on its website by NIST. Microsoft's Internet Explorer (IE) browser also has significant vulnerabilities, and users should ensure that they are always using the most recent version of it, with the most recent service pack, or an alternative, possibly less vulnerable browser. It would make sense for there to be a specific risk assessment of browsers and for the organization to document a policy as a result of it.

In the context of a Microsoft (or any other server) system, baseline controls should include:

■ Someone should be appointed to be specifically responsible for the security of the web servers. This person should have adequate specialist training and should be patched into a completely up-to-date source of information about vulnerabilities, threats, attacks and defenses.

- The organization should run as recent a version as possible of both server and browser software. The more recent the version, the fewer the security-related bugs.
- The organization should install the latest service pack (SP) on each Windows NT/2000/XP host that houses any server software. Service packs are available, free, over the web from www.microsoft.com/downloads.
- The organization should install the latest hot fixes, as soon as they become available. These are usually also available directly from the Microsoft website.
- The organization should avoid installing an application or web server on the same physical platform as a domain controller.
- The organization should obtain and apply specialist technical advice on the secure set-up and operation of internet servers.
- The organization should ensure that the server host itself is correctly configured and patched so that any operating system vulnerabilities cannot be exploited to access the web servers.

Online transactions

While the credit card industry has introduced its own specific information security requirements for its merchants (the PCI standard, which is cross-referenced to ISO/IEC 17799 in the KnowledgeBank), control A.10.9.2 of the standard specifically addresses online transactions. The standard wants the same outcomes that any online customer, credit card company or supplier wants: online information to be protected so that it remains authentic, is complete, is not mis-routed, altered, disclosed or duplicated and, in particular, is not stolen so that it can be used in a fraudulent transaction elsewhere. The steps that ISO/IEC 17799 suggests should be considered, subject to the risk and cost–benefit assessments, include:

- Electronic signatures—which are not always practical for consumer transactions, as so many consumers have not set up digital signatures, and which are more appropriate for commercial transactions.
- Technical controls to verify user credentials, including requests for random components of (strong) passwords, to keep the transaction confidential (using SSL technology) and to protect privacy (in line with the privacy policy, which should be displayed on the website).

- Communications should be encrypted, even if only using the encryption technologies available inside the Microsoft Windows package (in the e-mail Tools/Security menu).
- Personal information storage should not be accessible from the internet, i.e. it should be stored on a secure server within the organizational perimeter.
- Security should be embedded end to end in a trusted authority relationship.
- Legal issues must be carefully considered: in which jurisdiction does the transaction occur and what legal arrangements must therefore be made to protect it legally? As discussed in Chapter 27, this issue needs professional legal advice.

The standard does not deal with online fraud or "phishing" attacks but, clearly, any organization (particularly a financial one) that operates a high-volume website must be prone to such an attack. Such organizations need, as a matter of course, to warn their customers about non-disclosure of passwords and to have a fast response mechanism for identifying fraudulent sites and arranging, through the computer security team of the FBI and their ISP, to have them taken down.

Publicly available information

Control A.10.9.3 of the standard requires the organization to have in its ISMS a formal authorization procedure for information that is to be made public and to protect the integrity of this information so as to prevent unauthorized modification. The key aspects of this issue are:

- the reliability and security of the system on which information is going to be made available;
- the control of information released in interviews and, directly or indirectly, into the public arena; and
- the control of electronically published information.

The first issue should have been dealt with in terms of how the organization has configured and secured its web servers, and as discussed elsewhere in this book. Access to the publishing system or website should not allow access to the network to which it is connected. Segregation should be demonstrably effective. This was referred to in the section on server security above; it is a principle of secure network design that every machine in a demilitarized zone (DMZ) should be accessible without depending on access to any other machine on the network. The systems should have been tested against failures, in line with their risk assessment and their known vulnerabilities.

The second is relatively straightforward to design and implement. The organization pre-authorizes particular individuals to release particular classifications of material, ensures that they have appropriate press training and experience and combines this with a specific process for documenting authorization to release specific highly confidential information such as information that might affect a share price, for instance.

The third is more complicated. Electronically published information (for example, on a web server accessible via the internet) will need to comply with legislation and probably with legislation in both the country in whose jurisdiction the web server is hosted and the country in whose jurisdiction the transaction takes place. This is still a gray area, particularly for organizations that supply their products and services internationally across the web, and specialist legal advice should be taken on what rules, regulations and laws should be observed, and where and how.

This advice should be incorporated into the risk assessment. It is possible, for instance, that an organization might decide that the risk of prosecution in a number of jurisdictions is such that it will not take particular steps to comply with local laws. What is important is that, through the risk assessment, the organization does decide what controls it needs to put into place to protect the information that it publishes.

Electronic publishing systems (i.e. websites) that permit users to provide feedback or otherwise to enter data, particularly while carrying out a transaction, should have a number of controls. These should include:

■ Any information that is to be published on the website should be approved in advance by someone appropriately experienced, against a pre-set checklist that ensures that whatever is published falls within the organization's commercial, marketing and legal criteria. It is particularly important to remember that publishing information electronically may have the same consequences as publishing it any other way. People may rely on it, and the laws covering libel will also apply! As it is published to the world, it is possible that the potential liability may depend on the jurisdiction where the information is read and relied on. It is certainly wise, particularly for websites that publish information from more than one supplier (or that have links to other sites, or act as portals, aggregating information from a number of organizations), for there to be a disclaimer making clear what material emanates from the publisher and what from other sources. This disclaimer should make it clear that the publisher accepts no responsibility for third party material.

■ Any information that is obtained from people using the website should be collected in accordance with data protection legislation, whether GLBA, SB 1386, OPPA or any other applicable state or federal law.

■ Information input into the site should be processed quickly, accurately and properly so that a third party does not have time to access it and so that the records stored are correct. This applies particularly to individual personal and financial information, and to corporate commercial information entered on to an extranet.

■ Web applications must filter user-supplied data. Raw user input could contain all sorts of things that the organization does not want on its system. Hackers can access corporate networks through websites. The application must therefore enforce the content type of data entered so that, for instance, a numerical input can only be a number and all non-numeric characters must be filtered to exclude string and query terminators, wildcard selectors and all sorts of other unusual input. Specialist advice should be sought to ensure that the most current technological defenses have been incorporated into the application.

■ Sensitive information (particularly individual personal and financial information) should be protected while it is being collected and while it is stored. Effective methods of doing this were discussed earlier in this chapter and, essentially, require the organization to process this sort of information on a secure server, using SSL, which should be advertised as such to the third party user.

17

E-mail and internet use

While e-mail is dealt with in ISO/IEC 27001 as a sub-clause of control A.10.8, it is a substantial and fundamentally important subject in the information age. The e-mail policy aspect of control A.10.8.1 and control A.10.8.4 of the standard have, therefore, been addressed together in this book, and this chapter will cover all the issues surrounding e-mail and its usage. In this clause, the standard requires the organization to develop and implement a policy, and put in place controls, to reduce the security risks created by e-mail. Obviously, the degree to which these controls will be required will be dictated by the findings of a risk assessment.

E-mail has almost completely replaced telexes and is well on the way to replacing faxes and traditional, or "snail," mail. Key differences between e-mail and snail mail are the speed of the former, its volume message structure, informality, ease of misdirection, ease of duplication and ease of interception. This means that there are a number of issues to be considered around the headings of security risk and user policies.

Internet access sits alongside e-mail as an issue that is directly related to the activities of individual employees, and there are similarities between some of the control principles in each area. This chapter therefore also deals with internet acceptable use policies (AUP).

Security risks in e-mail

ISO/IEC 17799 identifies a number of security risks in e-mail. These include:

- vulnerability of messages to unauthorized access or modification or denial-of-service attacks;
- vulnerability of messages to error such as incorrect addressing, misdirection or just the unreliability of the internet;
- issues around instant messaging and file sharing;
- legal issues, such as potential need for proof of origin, dispatch and receipt; and
- uncontrolled remote user and internet access to e-mail accounts.

More important than any of these is the risk to the company that e-mail sent between organizations by individual members of staff may lead to unauthorized exposure of confidential or sensitive information and a breach of confidentiality, leading to bad publicity and possibly legal action. There is already case history to show that organizations can be exposed to libel writs as a result of what a staff member has written in an e-mail message, probably informally and for internal distribution only. There is also the requirement for organizations to ensure that confidential information that may affect share prices is not leaked and that Stock Exchange regulations are all observed.

Organizations should draw up clear policies on the use of e-mail. These should be included in the ISMS, and all members of staff should be required, as part of the formal user access statement (Chapter 18, control A.11.2.1), to agree to abide by them. The first decision that the organization has to make relates to the private use of e-mail facilities by employees. The fact is that e-mail use is now so ubiquitous that it is virtually impossible to prevent employees from using a work e-mail facility for private communications; attempts to stop this can be very difficult to enforce and so it is more practical to concentrate on controlling the risks.

An e-mail policy should set out:

- Employee responsibility not to compromise the company, forbidding the use of company e-mail for sending defamatory e-mails, or for harassment, unauthorized purchases or publishing views and opinions about suppliers, partners or customers of the organization. All e-mails should have an automatic footer that contains the legal disclaimer set out in Chapter 8 (control A.7.2.2), with the addition of a statement to the effect that the views expressed in the e-mail are those of the sender alone and do not reflect the views of the organization.

- That e-mail is not to be used to communicate sensitive information with specific classifications. These were discussed in Chapter 8.
- That e-mail attachments should be appropriately protected, using (where necessary) cryptographic controls of some sort. These controls are discussed in Chapter 23.
- How to respond to viruses and hoax virus messages. This was discussed in Chapter 13. The incident reporting procedure and the requirement not to pass on hoax virus messages should be included in the e-mail policy.
- Employees should be required to delete non-essential e-mail messages as soon as possible and, on a regular basis, to clear e-mail boxes of correspondence that is no longer required. Clear guidelines, taking into account legal requirements around data retention and business records, must be drawn up to cover this. The archive facility should be used so that messages that need to be retained but that are no longer current can be removed from the inbox. These controls are necessary so as to avoid e-mail boxes becoming so full that more and more server space is required to support the system. E-mail archiving solutions should be considered instead of the more common-place automated restrictions on e-mail storage volumes. The procedures around e-mail archive management should be clearly documented and user training should include inbox management.
- That e-mail may not be used to purchase anything on behalf of the organization without specific prior authorization, and then only in accordance with the organization's current policy on purchasing.
- That the corporate e-mail address may not be used for personal purchases or any other personal transactions.

Organizational purchasing policy does need to take into account the ease with which purchases can be done by e-mail and lay down very specific guidelines for staff on this issue. Where e-mail is to be used between organizations as part of the purchasing process, the two organizations should document the basis on which trading will occur and precisely what weight is to be attached to e-mails. For instance, it might need to be agreed in a heads of agreement document that e-mails will not constitute an implied contract between the organizations and require that all contracts continue to be made in writing, signed and sent by post or fax. These issues were covered in more detail in Chapters 15 and 16.

Misuse of the internet

There are a number of issues associated with employees surfing the net during work hours and from organizational facilities. Seventy-eight percent of respondents to the FBI/CSI 2002 survey detected employee abuse of internet privileges. Each of these issues has implications for the confidentiality, integrity or availability of information.

Employee productivity can be significantly reduced (some research suggests that 30 to 40 percent of employee internet activity is not work-related) by the time demanded by the wide range of interesting activity, from stock markets to games to chat rooms, that is available on the internet.

Network traffic can be significantly affected, with resulting reduced business performance, by the combination of recreational surfing by employees and bandwidth-intensive activities such as accessing streaming video and audio, MP3 downloads, image downloads, sharing digital photographs (such as holiday snaps), etc. The bandwidth put in and paid for by the organization is designed for organizational use, not for individual benefit.

As already stated, the internet is wild; allowing employee access to the internet allows all sorts of malware to access the organizational system in return. There is a discussion of how an organization's defenses can be breached in Chapter 16's section on electronic commerce security.

Recreational surfing can lead employees to access inappropriate sites, such as pornographic sites (apparently something in the order of 70 percent of internet porn traffic occurs between 9 a.m. and 5 p.m.) and sites promoting violence, discrimination and all sorts of other inappropriate matters. They can also access sites that will download illegal or pirated software, pirated games, pirated videos or pirated music or hacking tools. The organization through whose network such downloads are made could find itself inadvertently liable for the criminal behavior of its employees. Free access to the internet can lead to lawsuits, harassment charges (sexual harassment charges can arise from objectionable or sexually explicit material being brought into the workplace by one employee and being seen by another, even where the other person was not meant to see it) and even criminal prosecution (an employee downloading illegal material, or forwarding it from the organization's computers, might create just such a risk).

Clearly, organizations that find themselves forced to dismiss employees for accessing illegal or offensive material can be severely damaged by the resulting negative publicity.

Organizations should counter these risks by a combination of surf control technology and a well-designed and enforced acceptable use policy (AUP). Surf control, or filtering, technology is widely available and can be installed both on organizational networks and on individual workstations. The software package should be chosen in the light of the AUP; the AUP should not be built around the limitations of the chosen package. An appropriate package should allow the organization to impose different restrictions at different times of day (e.g. possibly slightly more lenient outside normal work hours) and for different user groups (e.g. possibly slightly more lenient for senior management or research staff). It should allow blocking of specific sites, as well as broader categories or groups of sites, so that restrictions can be focused in the light of business needs, rather than over-blocking in a way that goes against the business needs. The package's reporting tools should enable the organization to know when there are unauthorized site access attempts, how many there are and by whom, so that the individual concerned can be helped to comply. The package must be able to work with the organization's chosen firewall; it must be scalable, so that it can support a growing organization from a central location; and it must be able to update for barring access to new websites regularly, even daily.

While there will be further discussion of the legal issues surrounding data security in Chapter 27 (and readers should refer to it, as well as to their professional advisers, for additional information), it is appropriate at this point to state that an AUP must:

- be in writing;
- be clearly communicated to all employees;
- set out permissible use of both internet and e-mail—e.g. for business purposes only;
- specify what uses are prohibited—e.g. downloading offensive, pornographic or illegal material;
- state what monitoring (if any) will take place;
- set out acceptable online behaviors;
- specify which online areas are prohibited—e.g. pornographic or hate sites;
- set out privacy rules in relation to other users, and in respect of the employer's right to monitor the employees' activity;

■ set out the likely disciplinary consequences of breaching the AUP.

One site worth visiting for more information is www.info-law.com/guide.html, for a comprehensive guide to internet and e-mail use in the workplace.

Internet acceptable use policy (AUP)

An AUP should combine statements on use of the internet and use of e-mail. E-mail issues were addressed earlier in this chapter. Variations to what is set out below will depend on the conclusion that the organization reaches regarding private usage of its internet facilities; this statement reflects a far-reaching restriction, and not all employers will consider all its components necessary. It is important that, as for all other components of the ISMS, the organization adopts and develops an AUP that reflects in detail the culture of the organization but that also provides the level of security required by a risk assessment:

■ General statement: this should start off with a reminder about the dangers of the internet and say that the company will not be liable for any material viewed or downloaded. It should continue by saying that use of the internet must be consistent with the organization's standards of business conduct and must occur as part of the normal execution of the employee's job responsibilities. Any breach of the AUP may lead to disciplinary action and possibly termination of employment. Illegal activities may also be reported to the appropriate authorities.

■ Organizational user IDs or websites (or e-mail accounts) should only be used for organizationally sanctioned communication.

■ Use of internet/intranet/e-mail/instant messaging may be subject to monitoring for reasons of security and/or network management and users may have their usage of these resources subjected to limitations.

■ The distribution of any information through the internet (including by e-mail, instant messaging systems and any other computer-based systems) may be scrutinized by the organization, and the organization reserves the right to determine the suitability of the information.

■ The use of organizational computer resources is subject to applicable law, and any abuse will be dealt with appropriately.

- Users shall not visit internet sites that contain obscene, hateful or other objectionable material, shall not attempt to bypass organizational surf control technology and shall not make or post indecent remarks, proposals or materials on the internet.
- Users shall not solicit e-mails that are unrelated to business activity or that are for personal gain, shall not send or receive any material that is obscene or defamatory or that is intended to annoy, harass or intimidate another person, and shall not present personal opinions as those of the company.
- Users may not upload, download or otherwise transmit commercial software or any copyrighted materials belonging to the company or any third parties, may not reveal or publicize confidential information (refer explicitly to the information classification levels selected by the organization and discussed in Chapter 8), and shall not send confidential e-mails without the level of encryption required in terms of the specified policy in the ISMS.
- Users shall not seek to avoid and shall uphold all malware prevention policies of the organization, shall not intentionally interfere in the normal operation of the network or take any steps that substantially hinder others in their use of the network, and shall not examine, change or use another person's files or any other information asset for which they do not have explicit permission.
- Users shall not carry out any other inappropriate activity as identified from time to time by the organization and shall not waste time or resources on non-company business. This includes downloading bandwidth-intensive content such as streaming video and MP3 music files, sharing digital photographs, etc.

The AUP should, if possible, be developed in a way that involves staff from within the organization; certainly, all staff will need to be trained to ensure that it is understood. The training activity should be detailed and ongoing and should include notifying employees of changes to the policy and its implementation. All employees should accept the AUP at the time that they sign the user access statement (control A.11.2.1). Copies of the AUP should also be prominently posted in any employee resource center or staff internet café from where activity to which the AUP applies will take place. Of course, the right filtering software, properly installed and dynamically managed, should help the organization avoid needing to take disciplinary action in respect of employee behavior on the web.

18

Access control

Control A.11 of the standard is extremely important; its objective is to control access to information, and a properly thought-through and thoroughly implemented access control policy, within the ISMS, is fundamental to effective information security. This clause deals with user access management and responsibilities, network access control, operating system access control and application access control. It provides for appropriate monitoring and also deals with mobile computing. It is a major clause in the standard and a major component of the ISMS.

The reader needs to understand that access control has become even more critical over recent years, not least because of the requirements of privacy legislation. Chapter 1 of this book set out the key reasons why cybercrime is on the increase. In particular, it pointed to the growth in hacking. It is worth understanding the world of hackers, as a background to the need for effective access control.

Hackers

It has been argued that hackers have four prime motivations: *challenge*, to solve a security puzzle and outwit an identified security set-up; *mischief*, wanting to inflict stress or damage on an individual or organization; *working around*, getting around bugs or other blocks in a software system; and *theft*, stealing money or information. Hackers like to talk about "white hat" and "black hat" hackers; the argument is that the "black hat" hackers are malicious and destructive while the "white hat" hackers simply enjoy the challenge and are really on the side of good, offering their skills to help organizations test and defend their networks. This differentiation is convenient for hackers, who seem able to change hats as easily as they evade most network defenses. The only sensible approach for any security-conscious organization is to assume that all hackers are potentially in the wrong-color hats, however they might initially present themselves. "Gray hats" is a term that is evolving to recognize the uncertain danger of so-called "ethical" hackers.

The term "cracker" evolved to identify black hat hackers who break into computer systems specifically to cause damage or to steal data. Hackers like to say that crackers break into computers but that hackers get permission first, and will publish their discoveries. Of course, hackers become crackers, crackers become hackers, and either could become a security consultant. "Script kiddies" are none of the above; most IT departments contain one or more individuals whose interest in testing the systems that they are employed to protect leads them from time to time beyond the law. They are not as sophisticated as hackers and so they haven't yet qualified for a hat but, using their own very simple code or, more usually, programs found on the internet, they can be just as lethal to unprotected systems as the "Cult of the Dead Cow." The Cult of the Dead Cow (CDC) is considered the most influential hacker group in the world; it has been operating since 1984, publishes an e-zine and believes that it provides an incredible service to the computer community by exposing weaknesses in computer systems and forcing organizations and developers to strengthen their systems.

Hacker techniques

The most common techniques that hackers use to gain access to networks are set out, alphabetically, below. The list, which includes common hacker terms, keeps growing and is therefore never up to date:

- **Abusing software.** Hackers, once they have gained access to a system, use the installed software for their own ends. This can include using administrative tools for uncovering network weak points for exploitation, abusing CGI (Common Gateway Interface) programs on web servers, exploiting vulnerabilities in internet server software and so on. The advice of a network security specialist should be sought to ensure that the organization fully understands the current level and type of risks arising from these types of activities.

- **Back door.** Programmers or administrators deliberately leave ways into software systems that can be used later to allow access to the system while bypassing the authorized user file. Sometimes, developers forget to take out something that was put there simply to ease development work or to assist with the debugging routine. Sometimes they are deliberately left in to help field engineers maintain the system. However they get there, they can provide any unauthorized user with access to the system.

- **Back orifice.** This program was developed and released by CDC. It is a remote administration tool that has great potential for malicious use. It is very easy to use, so that script kiddies have no problem using it. It is also "extensible," which means that it develops and improves with age. Most anti-malware systems should detect and remove back orifice, but new versions will become available on a regular basis.

- **Buffer overflow.** A buffer is an area of memory that holds data to be processed. It has a fixed, predetermined size. If too many data are placed into the buffer, they can be lost or can overwrite other, legitimate data. Buffer overflow vulnerabilities have for a number of years been a major source of intrusion. They provide hackers with an opportunity to load and execute malicious code on a target workstation.

- **Denial of service.** This sort of attack is designed to put an organization out of business for a time by freezing its systems. This is usually done by flooding a web server with e-mail messages or other data so that it is unable to provide a normal service to authorized users. A distributed denial-of-service attack uses the computers of other, third party organizations (which have themselves been commandeered by the cracker) to mount the attack.

- **Exploit.** This is either the methodology for making an attack against an identified vulnerability (the noun) or the act (the verb) of attacking or exploiting the vulnerability. Exploits are often published on the internet, either by black hats or by gray hats who claim that this is a good way of forcing software suppliers to develop more secure software or to provide fixes for existing software.

- **"Man in the middle."** A hacker gets undetected between two parties to an internet transaction, whether on a LAN or on an unsecured internet link. The hacker intercepts and reads messages between the two parties and can alter them without the intended recipient knowing what has happened. This is often recognized as a form of masquerading.
- **Masquerading.** A hacker will pretend to be a legitimate user, trying to access legitimate information, using a password or PIN that was easily obtained or copied, and will then try to access more confidential information or execute commands that are not usually publicly accessible.
- **Network monitoring.** This is also known as "sniffing" and involves deploying some code on the internet to monitor all traffic, looking for passwords. These, and other ostensibly confidential information, are often sent "in the clear" and, therefore, can easily be located and written to the hacker's workstation for future use.
- **Password cracking.** This is actually, on balance, very easy. Most users do not set up passwords or, if they do, use very simple passwords that they can easily remember, like "secret" or "password," or their children's names, birthdays, sports teams, particular anniversaries or family names. While some hackers can quickly identify particular users' passwords, software is now available on the internet that will apply "brute force" to try, automatically and at high speed, every theoretically possible alphanumeric combination of user name and password and, usually aided by a dictionary of common passwords, this can quickly enable a hacker to gain access to a system. Once a hacker locates the list of encrypted passwords on the security server, he or she can use internet-available software tools to decrypt it.
- **"Social engineering."** The easiest and most common method of gaining access to a network is to trick someone into providing confidential information. The hacker, for instance, poses as a network administrator or a fellow employee, with an urgent problem, which can only be resolved by the employee providing confidential information (such as user name or password). Alternatively, the hacker has a false business card, claiming to be a key technical or business support representative, or claims to be a new employee trying to get up to speed in the business. Staff should not divulge their password to anyone, even IT support staff. For emergency access to restricted systems and administrative applications, the

information security manager may want to hold administrator passwords, in sealed envelopes, in a safe. Irregular testing needs to occur so that, should an administrator be dismissed for any reason, the system(s) to which he or she had access can be maintained, and the passwords changed.

■ **Spoofing**. IP spoofing gains unauthorized access to a system by masquerading as a valid internet (IP) address. Web spoofing involves the hacker redirecting traffic from a valid web address to a fraudulent, lookalike website where customer information (and particularly credit card information) is captured for later illegal reuse.

■ **Trojan horses** are programs that, while they might appear to be useful utilities, are designed to damage the host system secretly. Some will also try to open up host systems to outside attack.

Hackers do not exist only outside the organization. They are often employed by the organization that they target. They might also be disgruntled former (or about to be former) employees who want to take revenge on the organization that is letting them go. Internal hackers can be more dangerous than external ones, not least because they start off knowing far more than anyone outside the organization. They might already have access rights that are capable of getting them to places that the organization doesn't want them to visit. Equally, it is possible for an attacker to gain unauthorized access to the organization's premises and, once inside the physical perimeter, to access a relatively unsecured machine through which the entire network can be reached. The fact that an information system is not directly connected to the internet does not mean that it is not liable to be attacked. Such systems have to be subject to the same level of security as those that are connected to the internet, and the risk assessment needs to take all possible risks into account.

System configuration

The first step that any organization should take to deal with the threat of hacking is to eliminate as many of the vulnerabilities that may be native to the Microsoft (and other) packages as are deployed in the workplace. This is done by ensuring that the systems are loaded and configured in line with the Microsoft guidelines (as set out at www.microsoft.com/security) and as amended or strengthened by the recommendations set out on the website of the CERT coordination centre (www.cert.org), the Software Engineering Institute of the Carnegie Mellon University. Their configuration recommendations are independent and, subject to the organization's own risk assessment, their recommendations ought to be adopted as basic good practice in server and workstation configuration. Whatever technical requirements are adopted by the organization, they should be documented and appropriate steps taken to ensure, by means of a regular independent technical check, that they are being maintained.

Access control policy

Control A.11.1.1 of the standard requires the organization to define and clearly document its access control requirements and policy and then to restrict access to what is defined in the policy. Access controls are both physical and logical and, as they should complement each other rather than conflict, they should be considered together. It has to take into account the range of risks from hackers and crackers and, if necessary, specialist advice should be taken as part of the risk assessment process on the latest cracker threats and technological defenses. Access control rules and user rights for individual users and groups of users should be related to business objectives and clearly documented, and users should be aware of them. Failure to implement the policy properly will lead to too many people having access to too much information and at too high a level of confidentiality. This tends to lead to unauthorized access to information, disclosure to third parties of confidential information, etc. Training on the access control policy and access control rules should be part of basic user training. The level of dependency on other, highly individualized components of the ISMS means that each organization has to develop its own unique policy.

The access control policy in the ISMS should, ISO/IEC 17799 says, take a number of factors into account:

- Different business applications have different security requirements. These are determined by identifying all the information that the business systems are carrying and through the individual risk assessments carried out for each critical business system; these risk assessments point at who should, and should not, be allowed access to the system.
- Some information required for particular business applications may be processed by people who do not need access to the application itself (the "need-to-know" principle in action). An example might be in an office workflow system, where the person who inputs a supplier delivery note to a purchase and payments application does not need access to the actual

accounting or payment functions of the system. Such a person would need different access rights from those required by a person who triggers actual vendor payments.

- The information classification system. User access rights should reflect the level of information that users are allowed to see.
- There should be consistency between the access control and information classification policies of different networks within the same organization; inconsistency leads to incoherence, which leads to people taking short cuts (because of too many user names and passwords, and too much variation in responsibility), and this leads quickly to breakdowns in information security.
- Relevant legislation, whether it's HIPAA, GLBA, OPPA or any other state, federal or foreign privacy protection regulation, and any contractual obligations that the organization has to protect particular data should be analyzed and taken into account.
- There should be standard user access profiles for common job categories, as this makes it straightforward to manage and provide training. In situations where people with similar jobs have different access rights, security will break down as individuals unofficially share the most useful access profiles. Authorization to create a new user name should set out the areas of the network to which the user is to have access.
- A distributed, networked environment that recognizes a number of different types of connections should consider all of them, so that, for instance, a user who can access something on the desktop can also do so remotely. The Microsoft Windows roaming profile makes this possible.
- Segregation of duties (control A.10.1.3) should apply here as well: if the organization is large enough, different roles should be responsible for processing access requests, authorizing them and setting them up.
- Access controls, like all ISMS controls, should be periodically reviewed; as a weakness in this control could provide access to sensitive and confidential information or systems, it is as important to monitor this as it is to monitor the activity of those who have access to the organization's bank account.
- Access rights should be removed when an employee is terminated, and the SoA should cross-refer to the policy that is implemented in line with control A.8.3.3.

The policy will set detailed access control rules. In setting these rules, the ISMS must clearly differentiate between rules that are always enforced and those that are optional, conditional or occasion-specific. The rules should preferably be based on the principle that whatever isn't expressly permitted is forbidden; the alternative, that what isn't expressly forbidden is permitted, is much weaker and can, for instance, allow hackers on the organization's staff full license to indulge in whatever they think they can describe as being not forbidden.

Changes in information classifications, in user permissions and in access control rules (and these can happen both automatically through the system and as a result of human intervention, some of which may or may not require other approvals before implementation) should also be considered in drawing up the detailed rules. The overall objective must be to identify and close loopholes in the rules as early as possible. Regular review of access control rules is very important.

User access management

Control A.11.2 of the standard sets out to prevent unauthorized access to information systems. It has four controls, all focused on how user access is set up and how access rights to systems are allocated. It is not appropriate for user access policy to be created and solely managed by either the IT department or the HR department.

It is important to have an overview of the current user authentication technology. At the point that BS 7799 was last reviewed (2002), it was a reasonable assumption that anything outside the network perimeter was dangerous until proven otherwise, but that anyone within the network perimeter (defined by hardware, such as modems and RAS ports) was trusted. The changes being driven by the internet, which were discussed in the Introduction and first chapters, have eroded this assumption and, while network defenses continue to be crucial (and are discussed in Chapter 19) in the age of the porous perimeter, it is now the case that virtually anyone can interact with the connected organization's computers, from business partners accessing the extranet to customers accessing the public e-commerce website. It is therefore no longer the case that anyone who has successfully logged on to the network is a trusted party.

Security technology has evolved to reflect this change and, increasingly, concentrates on application-oriented and endpoint security as distinct from whole-network security, so that each critical resource, application or device on the network has and can enforce appropriate security policies.

For the purposes of this chapter, the related—but different— concepts of user authentication and user identification are fundamental. User authentication is establishing the authenticity of a user in the context of a computer-based interaction. There are three main approaches.

The first is to use a password, or some other information (such as mother's maiden name) that in theory only the user would know. This is the easiest approach and also the easiest to subvert, as a result of which password protection has become inadequate for sensitive information and resources. There are two technology protocols that handle password authentication, TACACS+ and RADIUS. The latter has become an IETF (Internet Engineering Task Force) standard and is increasingly accepted by companies providing internet services; it is used in conjunction with strong authentication (see below). Systems should use one or the other protocol and should process authentication requests using CHAP (Challenge Authentication Protocol) before it falls back to using the less strong PAP (Password Authentication Protocol), set up to use the option of encrypting passwords in transit, before rejecting a user as invalid.

The second approach is to require the user to present proof via something physical, most commonly a dedicated authenticator that generates access codes (usually called a "token"), a smart card, special authentication software or a digital certificate. Tokens that generate a changing numeric authentication code each minute are popular. The security server is able to confirm that the currently valid code is the one shown on the token and the presence of the valid code plus the user's password is usually taken as adequate authentication of the user. This form of two-factor authentication becomes more prevalent as the cost of producing the tokens benefits from economies of scale, even though authenticators can be lost or taken over by an attacker. As smart card technology improves and a single common standard for their use emerges, organizations will have the option of combining two-factor authentication with physical access permissions on the same card.

The third way is to test something that is physically part of the user. This approach, commonly known as biometrics, tests fingerprints or voiceprints or does retinal scans. These systems are considered the ultimate in strong user authentication. High cost and intrusiveness mean that such systems are non-trivial to implement.

The most sensible approach is to combine two or more approaches, such as a password with an authenticator or biometrics. This approach, known as "two-factor authentication," provides a much stronger level of security than any one approach on its own. It is, therefore, also known as "strong" authentication.

User identification relates to the issuing and verification of appropriate access privileges to the authenticated person. Once an individual is authenticated, the user identification that is issued and the user privileges that are allocated to the individual are validated as the individual seeks access to various network resources. Access can be granted to some resources but not to others.

User registration

Control A.11.2.1 of the standard requires the organization to have a formal user registration and deregistration procedure that grants access to all multiuser information services and systems. Wherever possible, the organization should implement a single sign-on access management system, which ensures that a single user name and password enables a user to access all those assets he or she is allowed to access. A user access profile that contains a number of individual system and information access rights can simplify life for the user (only one set of information to remember and therefore fewer written records to compromise) and for the system administrator (easier to control and monitor access rights by an individual and to concentrate on tightening and improving security rather than administering multiple sign-ons). Single sign-on is available with Microsoft systems, and full details of related security issues are available from the Microsoft website. Windows 2000 uses a security protocol called Kerberos to provide users with a single network log-on capability, and it does so by using public key infrastructure to protect the information that is exchanged in the log-on process.

ISO/IEC 17799 recommends that an organization's user registration process should cover the following:

1. Issue unique user identifications (IDs) so that users can be linked to, and made responsible for, their actions. The larger the organization, the more important it will be to have standard protocols that deal with separately identifying people who have the same name or whose user names might otherwise be the same. User names should not be easily guessed, although the larger the organization the easier it will be for an attacker to find out through social engineering the structure of, and actual individual, user names. E-mail addresses (e.g. john.smith@organizationname.com) should identify users differently

from the internally used user name (e.g. jsmith) that will enable the user to access system resources.

2. Group IDs should never be permitted. This is particularly important for the "administrator" and, often, the "guest" user names. Microsoft documentation (available from the Microsoft website) or system administrator manuals (available for each software package, such as Windows XP, or SQL Server, or Server 2003, etc., in all good bookshops) set out how the system administrator user name should be dealt with (retired, and stored under appropriate physical security) and explains how to set up system administrators with individual user names. The ISMS should require all servers to be set up in accordance with the detailed security guidance contained in the relevant Microsoft manual and, where appropriate, should include those specifications in the ISMS itself. Servers that carry sensitive information (such as financial information or substantial personal data subject to data protection legislation) should in addition be configured in line with any specific guidance available from CERT. There are also potential problems with "guest" user names, and these should be properly understood and the appropriate steps taken to deal with them. The information security adviser should not simply accept the system administrator's statement that the servers are set up in accordance with best practice, but should obtain the documents identified here, determine what best practice actually is and ensure that the set-up conforms to it.

3. The user's access rights should be documented and describe what assets and systems the user is allowed to access. System owners should authorize proposed users to use the system, and the access rights document should also be authorized by the individual's line manager, to ensure that it is appropriate. Effective security systems would also ensure that only those persons identified as trusted employees of third parties (see Chapter 7) or who have passed the employer's screening process (see Chapter 9) are granted any access at all. Most usually, HR would originate the access rights document as soon as the background checks on a new employee are satisfactorily completed and should ensure that the requirements of the role as identified in the job description drive the proposed access rights.

4. The access rights granted should reflect the access policy in that they are in line with the definitions therein as to who needs access to what. It should also not compromise segregation of duties, which was discussed in Chapter 12. This is particularly important in regard to access rights

necessary for remote administration of a server or workstation network, as any user who has such access rights will be in a commanding position.

5. Ensure the users get a written statement of their access rights. This can most simply be a copy of the document described in 3) above. Users should also be required to sign a copy of this, to signify that they understand and accept their rights and that they understand that breach of them, and specifically any attempt to access services or assets that they are not authorized to access, may lead to disciplinary action and specific sanctions. This should also be linked to the organization's internet acceptable use policy and its e-mail policy (both discussed in Chapter 17), so that the access rights referred to in this document are also granted subject to the user agreeing to abide by both the internet and e-mail policies.

6. This user access statement should also refer explicitly to password management (control A.11.2.3 of the standard), to specific privileges that have been granted (control A.11.2.2 of the standard), to acceptable password structures (control A.11.3.1 of the standard) and to the requirement for a password-protected screen saver and power off when not in use (control A.11.3.2 of the standard). It should explicitly identify the services to which the user is authorized to have access (control A.11.4.1) and should exclude the use of any software, of whatever provenance, for which the organization does not have a valid license (control A.15.1.2). Any storage of personal information should be in line with the requirements of applicable legislation (control A.15.1.4).

7. Ensure that service providers do not provide access until formal authorization processes are completed. It is better to complete this process before someone joins the company and to do it as quickly as possible, as otherwise there will be pressure to give the person access to systems that might then be compromised.

8. A copy of the signed document should be placed on the employee's (or third party contractor's) individual file. The network administrator who is issuing the user name should also retain a copy, so that he or she is at any time able to evidence that the listed user names on his or her system are all authorized.

9. The access rights of people who change jobs or leave the organization should be immediately removed. There should be an appropriate document that sets this out, which is triggered by HR, signed off by all the people concerned and used to authorize the removal of a user name. All of this is most important in situations when people are informed that

they are to (or are about to) lose their job; it is not unknown for a disgruntled person at this point to take destructive action against the employer. The organization should draw up a clear policy on how it will handle the access rights of people who are to lose their jobs, in any circumstances, and implement it consistently.

10. Redundant user IDs should be removed; the user name register should be periodically checked against the current payroll and HR and third party contractor files to ensure that only currently authorized individuals have user names. In organizations with even limited regular staff turnover, this check should probably be conducted every month, and an initialed copy of the checked user name register filed with the audit records.

11. Redundant user IDs should never be reissued. The person who used it might remember it and might want to attempt unauthorized access to the system; there will be no way of identifying that the attacker was an ex-employee and not the current member of staff.

Privilege management

Control A.11.2.2 of the standard requires the organization to restrict and control the allocation and use of privileges. A privilege is any facility in a multi-user system that enables one user to override system or application controls. Inadequate control of privileges invariably leads to their inappropriate use; equally invariably, this abuse leads to system breaches and is a major contributory factor in system failures. The most critical privileges are those that enable system administrators to do their jobs.

The organization should develop, in its ISMS, rules for the allocation of privileges that start by identifying, for each system (operating system, application, database, etc.), the privileges associated with it and the categories of staff to whom these privileges might need to be allocated. Privileges are usually identified in terms of user categories (e.g. system administrators), and users are allocated privileges by being joined to user groups that have specific privileges. The product manuals, available from all good bookshops, will contain this information. Users who might need these privileges should, in the first instance, have user names for everyday use that have virtually no privileges assigned to them. Privileges should be assigned to a separate user name, so that it is harder for an attacker to view its use and harder for a user inadvertently to exercise one of the privileges. Privileges should be allocated on a "need-to-use" basis and, where possible, event by event, so that users only have the minimum requirement for their functional role and only for as long as needed. There should be an authorization process for the allocation of privileges, which should be part of the documented user authorization process referred to above. The user should not be allowed any special privileges until authorization has been formally granted. Managers should be aware that many staff, particularly technical staff, get an ego trip out of having privileges in excess of those needed for their jobs and will browbeat managers (and try a number of other tactics) in order to get them. These attempts must be resisted; an allocation system that requires privilege allocation to be decided by someone other than a user's direct line manager is, therefore, an effective control against inappropriate privilege allocation.

User password management

Control A.11.2.3 of the standard requires the organization to control password allocation through a formal and managed process. While the ISMS will require specific behaviors of password users (which are required in control A.11.3.1), this control is to do with the organization's side of password management and recognizes that the easiest method of malicious access to an organization's network is through password acquisition:

1. Users should accept in writing that they will keep passwords confidential and will use any group passwords only in accordance with the rules attached to them; this statement should form part of the user access statement identified above in A.11.2.1.
2. Where users are required to choose and maintain their own passwords, they should be issued initially with a secure temporary password, which they are forced to change immediately on first log-on. When users are issued temporary passwords after they forget their own passwords, this should only be done after the user has been positively identified, preferably face to face. This is to stop someone who has obtained a valid user name from also obtaining unauthorized access to the system simply by claiming to have forgotten their password (a form of social engineering).
3. Temporary passwords should be unique to an individual and not guessable, and should be delivered securely to users; they should not be sent in clear across the internet or via untrusted third parties. Some form of secure enveloped document should be used. Users should acknowledge receipt of passwords in writing.

4. The helpdesk function that deals with lost or failed passwords needs effective management, careful training and audit to ensure that any attack on the system by this route can be controlled.
5. Passwords should never be stored in or on computer systems in clear—the post-it note on the computer screen is the classic aide to unauthorized access—and default vendor passwords on every single item of computing hardware or software should be changed on installation. There should be an audit process to ensure that these passwords have been changed.

Review of user access rights

Control A.11.2.4 of the standard wants the ISMS to contain a formal procedure for the regular review of users' access rights, so that effective control over access to data and information services is maintained. Principles of the review procedure might include:

■ review of normal access rights on a predetermined regular basis—ISO/IEC 17799 recommends every six months, or after any changes in the system, structure or the individual's role;
■ review of privileged access rights on a predetermined but more frequent basis—ISO/IEC 17799 recommends every three months;
■ privilege allocations to be checked at regular intervals—perhaps monthly—to ensure that users have not obtained unauthorized privileges, usually through collusion. Any instances where someone has obtained unauthorized privileges should be thoroughly investigated and disciplinary action considered.

This review can be carried out by the information security adviser, in conjunction with the line managers of the individuals concerned, and the outcome of the review should be documented—most simply by an annotation on all the copies of the original privilege allocation document—and reported *en masse* at the subsequent meeting of the information security management forum for formal approval.

User responsibilities—password use

Control A.11.3.1 of the standard recognizes that the cooperation of users is essential for effective information security and requires the organization to ensure that its users follow good security practices in the selection and use of passwords. This is best done by taking two steps. The first is to set out, within the ISMS, a clear set of rules about password selection and use, which are then incorporated into the user access document (as a separate section), which the user signs to signify agreement. The second is to set up the system software in such a way that it enforces key components of these rules.

The password use rules should require users:

- To keep passwords confidential, which includes in no circumstances giving them to a third party, whatever the ostensible reason.
- To avoid keeping any paper or electronic records of passwords (unless this can be security stored—which means encryption and strong, two-factor password protection).
- To change a password whenever there is any possibility that it may have been compromised.
- To select passwords that have a minimum length of six characters (seven or eight would be better), and this requirement can be set in the system software. These passwords should not be based on anything easy to guess such as dates of birth, names, telephone numbers or other person-related information, should not contain words that occur in dictionaries (because these would be vulnerable to automated dictionary attacks) and should not contain consecutive identical characters or all-numeric or all-alphabetical groups.
- To change passwords regularly. The system software can be set to enforce changes, say, every 30 days, with a defined pre-change period during which a warning of the impending requirement is flagged so that someone who will be out of the office at the point that the change is enforced can change it in advance. The system can also be set so that passwords cannot be recycled, and this should be done so that the user is forced always to have new ones. Sequential passwords (e.g. Jamaica 1, Jamaica 2, etc.) should not be possible.
- To change temporary passwords at first log-on.
- Not to store passwords in any automated log-on process.
- Not to share passwords under any conditions—and this includes not using the same password for business and private affairs.

Unattended user equipment

Control A.11.3.2 requires users to ensure that unattended equipment has appropriate protection. The primary focus of this clause is workstations or servers that are logged on and that are left unattended, usually temporarily, by the user. This offers an unauthorized user the opportunity to access resources or assets, using someone else's user name, that he or she may, in fact, not be authorized to access in the first place.

The need for server rooms to remain locked when unattended has already been discussed. All workstations, notebooks and servers should, however, have password-protected screen savers. These are set up by the user and should be set so that the screen saver fires up after a short period—three to five minutes might be the maximum period. Otherwise, users should be trained to trigger the password-protected screen saver when leaving their workstation for any period of time, to log off when they are finished working on a particular application and to ensure that the log-off procedure has completed before any machine is switched off or left unattended. A regular audit of machines to ensure that they have been logged off, and not simply had the screen switched off, is a key part of maintaining this control.

Clear desk and clear screen policy

Control A.11.3.3 of the standard requires the organization to implement a clear desk and clear screen policy to reduce the risks of unauthorized access to, or loss of, or damage to, information. This requirement should be contained in the user access authorization document.

A clear desk policy is one of the easiest to adopt. The first step is to ensure that appropriate facilities are available in the office in which, depending on their security classification (see Chapter 8), computer media (disks, tapes, CDs) and paper and paper files can be stored and locked away, including in lockable pedestals, filing cabinets and cupboards. Sensitive information should be locked away in a fireproof safe (and the security adviser will have to assess the fire resistance of the safe in terms of the sensitivity of the information inside it and its location in order to ensure its survival for long enough to be rescued). Once the facilities are available, senior management simply adopts a "black bag policy." The way this works is that, after 24 hours' due notice that the clear desk policy will be implemented, senior management simply goes around the office after closing time and puts everything that has been left out on desks into a series of plastic bags. The bags are then left with the rubbish that the cleaners will remove for pulping the next morning. The first time this happens, the bags might be left briefly in the morning for people to recover the papers that they need. The second night, there is unlikely to be anything left out on desks to put into the black bags.

Personal computers, computer terminals and printers should be switched off when not in use and should be protected by locks, passwords and the like when they are not in use. Everyone should be required to use a password-protected screen saver, which automatically fires up after only a few minutes (between three and five is reasonable) of inactivity; this ensures that sensitive information is not easily available to the casual observer. While everyone in the office should be trained to switch machines off, the last one out of the office each day should be required to double-check and switch off anything still on.

Incoming/outgoing mail collection points should be protected or supervised, so that letters cannot be stolen or lost, and faxes and telexes should be protected when not in use. Photocopiers should be switched off and locked outside working hours; this makes it difficult for unauthorized copying of sensitive information to occur. All printers and fax machines should be cleared of papers as soon as they are printed; this helps ensure that sensitive documents are not left in printer trays for the wrong person to pick up.

19

Network access control

Networks

The discussion at the beginning of Chapter 18 described briefly how internet developments have been driving information system development. Network access control is extremely important, but needs to be understood in the context of the changing access needs of users and organizations. The objective of this section of the standard is to control access to both internal and external networked services so that users who have access do not compromise the security of those services. This therefore means that there need to be appropriate interfaces between the organization's network and other networks, particularly the internet, that there are appropriate authentication mechanisms for users and equipment and that user access to information services is controlled.

A private network that carries sensitive data between local computers requires proper security measures to protect the privacy and integrity of the traffic. When such a network is connected to other networks, or when telephone access is allowed into that network, the remote terminals, phone lines and other connections become extensions to that private network and must be protected accordingly. In addition, the private network must be protected from outside attacks that could cause loss of information, breakdowns in network integrity or breaches in security.

There is more to the issue of network security than simply considering fixed private networks, whether local area networks (LANs) or wide area networks (WANs). WANs and LANs are usually discrete networks, using fixed private cabling within the organization's facilities to connect their information processing facilities (a LAN) or using privately leased or owned fixed data links to connect LANs in a number of different locations securely. Virtual private networks (VPNs), extranets and wireless networks also have to be considered.

Virtual private networks

Virtual private networks are, in effect, alternative WANs that replace or augment an existing fixed private network. There are two types of VPN: remote access VPNs, which extend the network to telecommuters, home offices and mobile workers, and site-to-site VPNs, which securely connect remote sites to a corporate or central site, using service provider connections or the internet. VPNs utilize specific technologies, such as Internet Protocol Security (IPSec), which takes advantage of digital encryption technology. The creation of a VPN may require specialist technical advice and specialist technology, or may use a relatively easy-to-deploy COTS application. The organization will need to carry out a risk assessment in respect of its VPN, expecting that it should employ the same security and management standards for its VPN as for any fixed network.

Extranets

Extranets support business-to-business (b2b) commerce and collaboration between independent entities, typically via the internet. As markets consolidate and core services are externalized, organizations need to communicate securely with a network of external partners that includes outsourcing companies, demand and supply chain partners, consultants and contractors. Extranets need to be extremely flexible, and must be deployed quickly (in "internet time") without needing to redevelop or re-architect existing applications while leveraging existing infrastructures. They must also be scalable, to allow for future growth to be supported quickly, easily and inexpensively. At the same time, extranets must ensure that confidential information remains confidential and that authenticated users can only access the services they are authorized to access. This needs to be done without requiring the partner, customer or vendor to change its security policies, network infrastructures or any aspect of its existing set-up for the benefit of the extranet.

These needs appear to fly in the face of some of the requirements of ISO/IEC 27001; however, organizations need to respond to market drivers without compromising the confidentiality, integrity or availability of their information. This means that extranets need to be deployed in line with business objectives; there is no such thing as a "one size fits all" extranet. Some extranets are designed for user groups simply to view static information, while others are designed for a more dynamic interaction with the enterprise. The extranet might need to communicate with a mass of customers, or a mass of suppliers, or a small number of partners involved in product development, or some combination of these.

Secure extranets will rely on encryption (see Chapters 18 and 23), strong two-factor or even multi-factor authentication, granular access control and other VPN security features. The extent to which third parties can effectively be bound by contracts (as set out in Chapter 7) is limited by the extent to which their terms can be accepted at the initial log-in stage of accessing the extranet. There are specialist products that can be deployed to create and manage secure extranets, or organizations can create their own simply by implementing the types of security solution discussed in this book. The management process is the same for extranets as it is for other information security issues: carry out a risk assessment and deploy a cost-effective solution that reflects that risk assessment.

NIST's Special Publication 800–47, *Security Guide for Interconnecting Information Technology Systems*, provides guidance on planning, establishing, maintaining and terminating interconnections between independent organizational information systems. It can be accessed at http://www.nist.gov.

Wireless networks

Wireless networks are another issue, in information security terms. Wireless networks are convenient and inexpensive to set up (no category five fiber optic cabling to lay or move), and they enable group working and data sharing to take place easily and simply. They consist of notebooks, workstations, PDAs and other peripherals that access a corporate network using shared radio waves and the Wired Equivalent Privacy (WEP) protocol in the Institute of Electrical and Electronics Engineers (IEEE) 802.11 group of standards for wireless networking. The WEP and the 802.11 group of standards were created to tackle the vulnerability that comes from using shared radio waves to transmit data, in theory making wireless transmissions as safe as using a fixed network by encrypting wireless traffic and using WEP to authenticate nodes. However, WEP is extremely limited as a security technology, and wireless networks have become extremely vulnerable. Flaws continue to be found (by "war drivers" and "war chalkers" and wireless hackers), which means that the standard is continuing to evolve and that specialist security procedures will be necessary for wireless networks. These include advanced encryption key management and, more significantly, placing the wireless network outside the organizational firewall, with no routes to the outside internet other than through a secure VPN. A detailed risk assessment, drawing on specialist advice that reflects the risks of bandwidth theft, security gateway bypassing, identity theft, illegal activity and espionage, should inform the decision on this issue.

These sorts of wireless networks are not, however, the end of the story. Wireless networking includes the increasing array of machines that are designed to access corporate networks other than across fixed links. There is, of course, the cell phone. Cell phones themselves carry increasing amounts of important contact information, and retained voice and text messages make them potential targets for attackers. Cell phones (and laptop mobile connect cards) can also enable notebooks to access networks and, as cell phone technology improves, so will data transfer speeds, with the result that these types of communication will become increasingly popular. They will therefore become more popular with hackers and virus writers as a route into otherwise well-defended networks. Telephones and PDAs are converging, and smart phones are becoming ubiquitous. Digital pens (which can scan and carry substantial amounts of text) are improving and can be easily lost or stolen. Digital ink is developing.

"Bluetooth" is a wireless protocol built into a widening range of products to enable short-range wireless data communication between equipment and with Bluetooth hubs. Voice communication with computers, and voice over IP (VoIP) technology, is becoming more and more effective. All of these technologies have real vulnerabilities and pose real security threats to organizations, from airborne virus infection to data loss and unauthorized network access. These tools will, however, continue proliferating, because they improve the productivity of workers and the interconnectedness of data. Banning these tools will not be an effective solution for organizations. Information security advisers will need to keep themselves abreast of developments and will have to become adept at carrying out risk assessments on new technologies and on finding appropriate security solutions to the vulnerabilities and threats that are thus identified. Specialist advice may be necessary on a regular basis, and organizations may decide that, as a matter of policy, they will not adopt new technologies for a defined initial period during which they hope that their vulnerabilities will be identified and solutions to them found. NIST's paper SP 800–48, *Security for Wireless Networks and Devices*, at www.nist.gov, provides a good technical overview of the security issues.

The essential starting point for tackling the network access part of the ISO/IEC 27001 exercise is a network map that shows clearly all the assets on the network, and all their connections, whether internal or external. It should also show any wireless connections, and any related domains, including certainly any demilitarized zones (DMZs) and extranets. A series of risk assessments is then carried out in respect of each of the external connections, and appropriate controls, selected from those identified by ISO/IEC 17799, which follow in this chapter, are selected to deal with the assessed risk.

Network security

Policy on use of network services

Control A.11.4.1 of the standard requires the organization to design and implement a policy, within its ISMS, that ensures that users have access only to the services that they have been specifically authorized to use. The policy should identify which networks and network services are allowed to be accessed, the authorization procedures necessary prior to any such access and the controls necessary to protect access to network connections and network services—which should extend to how the means of accessing these networks are controlled. This policy should be consistent with the access control policy discussed in A.11.1.1 and should recognize and allow for the future evolution of networking technologies in a way that provides guidance to the organization on how to respond securely to these changing circumstances. This all means that users should see, on their desktops, only icons for those services that they are authorized to access; no information should be provided about other services that are on the network, as attempts to crack into them should not be encouraged.

Firewalls and routers are key components of the network security perimeter.

Firewalls and network perimeter security

Network perimeter security controls access to the network so that only authorized users can access applications, data and services running on the network. Firewalls are generally the first security product that organizations deploy to protect their network perimeters. A firewall provides a barrier to traffic seeking to cross the perimeter and permits only authorized traffic to pass, in line with a predetermined access policy. Firewalls will also usually provide some level of network address translation (NAT) services, denial-of-service (DoS) attack protection, IPSec VPN services and intrusion detection services.

There are a wide number of firewalls available on the market and the organization should thoroughly research the market before making its choice. The Common Criteria (discussed in Chapter 4) may be a useful reference point. In general, vendors that have been in the business for some years and that clearly have resources adequate to maintain the development of their products should be favored. It is important that the chosen anti-malware software (see Chapter 13) should be able to work with the preferred firewall. At the same time, and bearing in mind the speed of change in the security market, current security sites (see Chapter 4) should be consulted to establish which firewall products are proving easiest for hackers to conquer or most inadequate for current performance requirements.

Once the firewall has been chosen, the policies that it is to apply will need to be selected and documented in a way that reflects a specific risk assessment. It is important that these are chosen as the result of an informed risk analysis that is in line with the organization's access control policy, as otherwise it will find itself unable to operate effectively. There are internet resources that the organization needs, and the safest perimeter policy, which is simply to close all ports on the firewall, is not necessarily the most sensible. As usual, specialist technical advice, combined with current information about security vulnerabilities and threats derived from vendor and independent websites, may be necessary for the correct configuring of the firewall.

NIST has released a Special Publication, number 800–41, titled *Guidelines on Firewalls and Firewall Policy*. The document contains guidelines on configuring and administering firewalls as well as covering related issues such as VPNs, web and e-mail servers and intrusion detection. It contains links to other firewall-related resources. The NIST website is at http://www.nist.gov.

The firewall and its correct configuration can be business-critical for any organization, and the vendor's default password must be changed. An ISO/IEC 27001 auditor will therefore want to see evidence that management has reviewed the firewall configuration. The information security forum is best placed to do this. Any subsequent changes to the rules agreed by the forum need to go through the same authorization process, with evidence available to prove this, and not be implemented at the whim of a system administrator.

Routers and switches

In addition, the organizational network infrastructure should be built using routers and switches that, themselves, have adequate security features. The selection of routers and switches should be subject to the same level of care as was the selection of a firewall and, while these are technically simpler devices, they too can provide an attacker with a way in to the network. Routers and switches should be configured in line with the manufacturer's recommendations (including changing the vendor's default password) and have correctly configured and up-to-date access control lists (ACLs). ACLs ensure that only legitimate users can pass through the router or switch. Routers and switches can also have core firewall technology embedded in them, and the choice of which switches and routers to deploy should be made in the light of a risk assessment and a review of independent assessments of vendor products.

Organizations with larger networks should also consider technology solutions that enable them centrally to define, distribute, enforce and audit security policies for a large number of routers, switches and firewalls. Cisco, for instance, provides technology solutions that specifically enable this type of centralized security control. The larger the network, the more important—and cost-effective—such a solution is. In addition, larger organizations should consider (in the light of the risk assessment) deploying intrusion detection systems (IDS) that can monitor and reactively respond to intrusions as they occur, and network vulnerability scanners that proactively identify areas of weakness. These are important because, while firewalls provide an enforced path control for external users, they do not actively analyze the traffic for attacks or search the network for vulnerabilities. In particular, firewalls do not address the threats posed by insiders. IDS packages can be sourced through major vendors of security products and through the security sites on the internet. In considering IDS packages, the total cost of ownership (TCO) will be important, and the organization must be clear on how it will practically deal with the output of the detection system.

Large organizations, or organizations that need to run large networks, or complicated mixes of services, dealing with a complex web of partners, customers and vendors, should consider constructing the network as a whole. This will require the input of a network specialist, and the organization chosen to provide this service should be able to point to similar solutions successfully implemented for similar clients elsewhere. Large networks might be compartmentalized, or structured around a number of separate logical domains, as a method of limiting the extent to which an intruder can affect the entire network.

Network intrusion detection systems (NIDS)

A network intrusion detection system is hardware or software that automates the process of monitoring events in systems or networks to detect intrusions. An intrusion is an attempt to break into or misuse an information system, or bypass its security controls, in order to compromise the confidentiality, integrity and availability of information stored on it.

There are different types of intrusion detection systems. A NIDS, also known as a "network sniffer," monitors packets on the network and attempts to discover if a hacker is attempting to break into the system (or cause a denial-of-service attack). A system integrity verifier (SIV) monitors system files to find when an intruder changes them so as to set up a backdoor. Log file monitors (LFM) monitor log files generated by network services. In a similar manner to NIDS, these systems look for patterns in the log files that suggest an intruder is attacking. There are a number of products that perform these various tasks and that can be quickly and easily identified through a product search. Use of such a product should be as the result of a risk assessment, and its use should be planned alongside any other network monitoring and anti-malware tools that the organization chooses to deploy. Reference should also be made to the NIST publication SP 800-31, *Intrusion Detection Systems*, which can be accessed on the NIST website.

User authentication for external connections

Control A.11.4.2 of the standard requires the organization to ensure that access to the network by remote users is subject to authentication. A risk assessment should be the basis of selecting an appropriate remote access authentication control; clearly, the existence of any dial-up or wireless access to the network offers attackers a potential way into it. There are a number of approaches and technologies that might, depending on the risk assessment, be appropriate.

The most straightforward methods of authenticating remote users were discussed in Chapter 18. RADIUS (Remote Access Dial-In User Service), TACACS+ and Kerberos protocols, combined with CHAP and PAP protocols, are the foundation of secure remote access across the internet. Strong, two-token authentication is also an effective component of remote access authentication, and there are a number of vendors that provide effective services based on these technologies.

Dedicated private lines or network user address checking facilities can be used to provide assurance that the source of the connection is trusted. Equally, dial-back procedures and controls (e.g. by enabling the modem dial-back facility on a remote access service) can provide protection against unauthorized connections although, to be secure, these controls should not be used where network services provide call forwarding (now available on most modern telecommunications services). Call-back processes must only happen after the incoming call has been disconnected, and thorough testing should be carried out to ensure that this control actually works.

Node authentication is an alternative method of authenticating connections to remote computer systems. These might be the computer systems of partners, vendors or other third parties. This clause simply requires that, where a remote computer accesses another computer system, it is authenticated following one of the controls (other than hardware or two-token authentication, which is designed for human users) such as a cryptographic one identified above. This is to ensure that the automatic connection to or from a remote computer does not provide a way of gaining unauthorized access to a business application. A risk assessment should identify the critical nodes and be used to justify the level of control implemented.

Equipment identification in the network

Control A.11.4.3 of the standard requires the organization to deploy automatic equipment identification to authenticate connections from specific locations and portable equipment. This is provided by default on some sys-tems, while on others it is provided by the port address of the terminal's cable.

Automatic equipment identification is a technique that is used where the risk assessment has indicated that it will be important to ensure that a session can only be initiated from a particular location or computer workstation. Organizations might apply this requirement, for instance, to workstations from which bank money transfers can be made or payroll details amended. The workstation can then be subject to physical security measures and an identifier in or attached to it can be used to indicate automatically whether it is permitted to initiate or receive specific transactions. These types of con-trol can also be achieved using strong authentication combined with appro-priate privilege management.

Remote diagnostic and configuration port protection

Control A.11.4.4 of the standard requires the organization to control access to diagnostic and configuration ports securely. Computers and communi-cation systems often have installed a dial-up remote access facility that vendor maintenance engineers can use for access to configure or repair faults in the system. If unprotected, these ports provide an easy means of unau-thorized access to the application and, potentially, to the system. They should therefore be appropriately protected. Physical security might be a first step, with the port disabled until it is required and the port secured by lock and key. When the port is required, the ISMS procedure can allow the maintenance engineer, after appropriate authentication, to access the port for a specific period to carry out the agreed maintenance work. Every such access should be specifically logged.

Segregation in networks

Control A.11.4.5 of the standard requires the organization to introduce con-trols into its network(s) to segregate groups of information services, users and information systems. As organizations extend their information services beyond the traditional boundaries of the fixed LAN or WAN, so they increasingly need to share information processing and networking facilities. These sorts of extensions increase the risk of an attacker finding a way of accessing facilities or information that is confidential and, therefore, some components of networks need protection from other network users. A full risk assessment and cost–benefit analysis (considering also the value of the assets to be secured, and how their interrelationship might need to be safe-guarded—segregation, for instance, might reduce the total impact of a service disruption) should be carried out before making a final decision as to how these issues should be tackled, and specialist external advice may be needed to ensure that the choice of technologies and architecture is appropriate to the organization's needs. The existing organizational policies on access control, access requirements and information classification should be cross-referenced in segregating networks.

The creation of demilitarized zones (DMZs) or extranets reflects exactly these needs. Specific resources are gathered together and placed outside the core organizational firewall, and access is then allowed using one or a num-ber of the protocols and technologies discussed earlier in this chapter. Servers operating on the DMZ, outside the corporate firewall, should them-selves be configured so that they do not help an attacker find a way past the firewall. For instance, unnecessary services running on these servers, such as FTP (File Transfer Protocol), DNS (Domain Name Service) and SMTP (Simple Mail Transfer Protocol), can leave hackers with ways in. DMZ servers should be precisely configured for their desired role, and no addi-tional services should run; the default set-ups should be modified in the light of a risk assessment.

Wireless networks should be considered for segregation; the higher level of risks associated with wireless networks might lead a risk assessment to conclude that wireless resources should be networked together and pro-vided with a single secured link to an otherwise secure network. Such a secure link could be through a firewall or other mechanism.

Network architecture of larger, more complex networks might divide the network into a number of logical network domains, each protected by a defined logical security perimeter. This perimeter is created by installing firewalls between the logical domains and interconnecting them in such a way that they control access and information flow between the domains. The firewalls can be configured to filter traffic in accordance with the risk assessment (one of which should be conducted for each domain) and to block unauthorized access in accordance with the access control policy.

Domains and their relationships should be specifically documented, both on the formal network map and on a schedule that identifies assets and sys-tems and the domains within which they are included. Different parts of a single system (e.g. an ERP system) could be in different domains; this can be secure if the security architecture keeps the different parts logically separated.

Network connection control

Control A.11.4.6 of the standard requires the organization to restrict the connection capability of users on shared networks in accordance with the access control policy specified in A.11.1.1. This issue has effectively already been discussed. The firewall(s) segregating networks should filter traffic between the networks in accordance with pre-defined rules that are based on the access control policy and the risk assessment. Routers should (subject to the risk assessment) be used to control specific transaction flows (e.g. e-mails, file transfers, application access, interactive access, etc.). As with all security policies, the firewall and router rules should be regularly reviewed and updated. The types of application to which ISO/IEC 17799 believes that these restrictions should apply include e-mail, all file transfers, interactive access and any other form of network access, and there might be some benefit in linking access rights to specific times of day (or night) or days of the week, etc.

Network routing control

Control A.11.4.7 of the standard requires the organization to deploy routing controls requiring origin and destination address checking to ensure that computer connections and information flows do not breach the access control policy. This control is particularly important for networks shared with third parties.

Routing controls (gateways) should, says ISO/IEC 17799, be based on positive source and destination checking protocols in the routers. Network address translation (NAT) isolates networks and prevents routes extending or propagating from one network into another. The protocols deployed and configurations chosen should be documented and subject to review.

20

Operating system access control

Control A.11.5 of the standard is intended to prevent unauthorized access to information systems. Its eight sub-clauses all deal largely with technical configuration and implementation issues. Again, the risk assessment drives the selection of controls and, again, they will need to be regularly reviewed. Operating system (O/S) security facilities should (according to ISO/IEC 17799) be capable (where necessary and/or appropriate) of: 1) restricting access to computer resources by identifying and verifying the identity, the terminal or location of each authorized user; 2) recording successful and failed system access attempts; 3) providing appropriate authentication; 4) restricting user connection times; and 5) issuing alarms when system security policies have been breached.

Secure log-on procedures

Control A.11.5.1 of the standard requires the organization to use a secure log-on process in providing access to information services. This clause should be read alongside control A.11.2.3, which deals with user password management, and A.11.3.1, which deals with password use. The implementation of these two controls was discussed in Chapter 18.

A secure log-on process is one that discloses the minimum of information about the system, in order to avoid giving an unauthorized user any assistance. It should be designed to minimize the opportunity for unauthorized access to the system, remembering that poor password control is one of the easiest methods for attackers to gain access. The procedure should, as a minimum, be configured by the system administrator, using the set-up options provided within the Microsoft package in response to the findings of a risk assessment, so that the recommendations of ISO/IEC 17799 can be met:

■ The screen should display no system or application identifiers until the log-on has been successfully completed.

■ The display on the log-on screen should include a general notice warning that the computer should only be accessed by authorized users, with a brief description of the criteria by which they are identified (e.g. employees of organization X).

■ The screen should not provide help messages during the log-on procedure (particularly not warnings about how many incorrect entries are allowed).

■ The system should validate the log-on data only on completion of input and then, if there is an error, the system should not explain which part of the data is incorrect but simply require the user to try again.

■ The log-on procedure should limit the number of unsuccessful attempts allowed to three (and unsuccessful attempts should automatically be recorded) and automatically either enforce a time delay before further attempts are allowed or simultaneously disconnect the data link, send an alarm and reject any further attempts without specific authorization from the system administrator, the user having first been positively identified by the system administrator.

■ The system should limit the maximum time allowed for the log-on attempt and, when the limit is exceeded, the system should terminate log-on; authorized users can correct log-on errors quickly, whereas attackers might need more time to guess the correct details.

■ The screen should display, after a successful log-on, details of the date and time of the previous successful log-on (so that an authorized user can see if the previous log-on was someone else or not) and details of any unsuccessful log-on attempts (so that the user can immediately report this as a security incident).

■ Finally, the password characters should be hidden by symbols and always encrypted before being sent across the network.

User identification and authentication

Control A.11.5.2 of the standard requires the organization to issue all users with a unique identifier or user ID for their personal and sole use so that activities on the network can be traced to the responsible individual. This control applies particularly to all IT staff, none of whom should, for instance, be allowed to use the administrator user name for their normal activity. User IDs should also not give any indication of the level of privileges allocated to the user and, for this reason, all sensible user name policies are based on using one form or another of the individual's actual name.

There was a substantial discussion of authentication and identification procedures and technologies in Chapter 18 and it will not be repeated here.

Password management system

Control A.11.5.3 of the standard requires the organization to have in place a password management system that ensures quality passwords. Again, this clause should be read in conjunction with control A.11.3.1 for situations in which passwords are chosen by the users. As ISO/IEC 17799 states, a good system will enforce the use of individual passwords and will allow users to select and change their own passwords, including a confirmation procedure to flush out any errors. The selection of password characters of a minimum length should be enforced, as should regular password changes (for all of which, see Chapter 18).

In addition, the system should maintain a record of previous passwords and not allow them to be repeated for a defined period (e.g. for 12 months, or forever), should not display passwords on the screen while they are being entered, should store passwords in an encrypted form using a one-way algorithm and separately from application system data and should certainly alter default vendor passwords immediately following installation of software and hardware of any description.

No user names should be permitted to operate without passwords.

Users must have the facility to alter their password at any time that they feel that its confidentiality has been breached. Some organizations do not allow this in their "default" user configuration as they have experience of users changing their passwords x+1 times (where x is the number of passwords checked for repeats and sequences by the system) in a matter of minutes, so as to enable them effectively to retain the same password. Either option presents a pitfall. The pitfall with the first option is as described above. The pitfall with the second is that forcing users to contact an administrator to change their password in advance of the regular, system-enforced change creates an additional obstacle to the process and could lead users to hope that nothing will come of the potential security incident and leave them, therefore, more likely to ignore it than to own up and create more work for themselves and others.

Use of system utilities

Control A.11.5.4 of the standard requires the organization to restrict and tightly control the use of system utilities. System utilities, which are there to help system administrators, might be capable of overriding system and application controls. Their use must therefore be restricted. The information security adviser and the network system administrators should first identify all the system utilities available and the security risks associated with them. The restrictions that ISO/IEC 17799 recommends might be applied, to some or all of the utilities (and, again, a risk assessment will help make appropriate judgments here), are:

- identification, authentication and authorization procedures for system utilities;
- segregation of system utilities from applications software, and not making system utilities available to users who have access to applications where segregation of duties is required;
- limitation of their use to a small number of trusted users;
- ad hoc authorization for system utility use in specific circumstances and/or for a pre-specified period;
- logging and monitoring of all use of system utilities;
- removal from the system or disabling of all unnecessary utilities.

Session time-out

Control A.11.5.5 of the standard requires the organization to shut down inactive sessions, particularly on terminals placed in high-risk locations or serving high-risk systems, after a defined period of inactivity in order to prevent unauthorized access. While password-protected screen savers provide some protection, they do not close down the application or network session. A risk assessment for workstations located in public areas or externally to the physical security perimeter or that are linked to high-risk systems might indicate that this would be inadequate protection against attempts to gain unauthorized access. In these instances, the workstation should be configured so that, after a period of inactivity defined in the risk assessment, it will shut down, clearing the screen and closing application and network sessions. This is now fairly standard security on all web services that allow access to sensitive information such as bank account details.

Limitation of connection time

Control A.11.5.6 of the standard requires the organization to restrict connection times in order to provide additional security for high-risk applications. This control, which can be set up through the configuration routine, should again be the outcome of a risk assessment. Such a control can restrict the period during which unauthorized access can be attempted by allowing access only during supervised office hours or, for very high-risk systems, at predetermined time slots, which might also require re-authentication at predetermined intervals. Connection times can also be restricted for remote users, although this needs to be carefully considered, as many remote users access the network resources at unusual hours, reflecting their individual travel or work patterns.

21

Application access control and teleworking

Application and information access control

The objective of control A.11.6 of the standard is to prevent unauthorized access to information held in information systems. ISO/IEC 17799 goes on to explain that access within application systems should be restricted, using security facilities, and logical access to software and information should be restricted to authorized users. ISO/IEC 17799 states that best practice would see application systems:

- controlling user access to information and application systems in accordance with a clearly defined business access control policy;
- providing protection from unauthorized access to any utility or operating system that is capable of overriding existing controls within systems or applications;
- not compromising the security of other systems with which information or resources are shared;

■ being able to provide only the user, or other authorized individuals, with access.

The implementation of this control requires, first of all, the extension of the existing access control policy to the individual application level and, secondly, the appropriate configuration of the application software to reflect the policy.

There are only two sub-clauses to A.11.6.

Information access restriction

Control A.11.6.1 of the standard requires the organization to restrict access to information and application system functions in accordance with the access control policy that was specified in control A.11.1.1 (see Chapter 18). The business owner of an application (and any related data) must define who will have access to that application and, in terms of any data within it, at what level (i.e. read, write, delete, execute). Users should be given only the minimum level of access that they need to an application or its data, as access to too much can increase the risk of breach of confidentiality and/or loss of integrity. In financial applications, over-authorization can lead to the possibility of fraud. It is particularly important to define access levels in respect of shared databases; each group of users should only be able to access data that are relevant to its own business or activity.

Additional controls that should be considered are:

■ providing access menus on user screens that control (by their limitations) access to application systems and their functions—this is implemented by the system administrator and can be done most simply by providing "standard builds" for desktop software that precisely reflect the business use needs of a specific group of users, and changes to which can only be made by the system administrator on receipt of appropriate authorization;

■ not training in the use of, or restricting knowledge of, application systems and functions that are not required and editing system documentation to support this process;

■ limiting provision of access rights to individuals so that, even if they are able to bypass the system menus, they are unable to access applications that the business doesn't need them to access;

- controlling the access rights of individuals such that they can carry out only the functions they need to, such as read, write, delete or execute, recognizing that, for many applications, individuals only need read access and that the best way of preventing someone from unauthorized deletion or amendment of information is to make it impossible for them to do it;
- ensuring that application system outputs (from systems handling sensitive data, as defined in the organization's information classification system and in line with Chapter 8) are sent only to authorized terminals or locations and that these outputs are periodically reviewed to ensure that redundant information is removed.

Sensitive system isolation

Control A.11.6.2 of the standard requires the organization to provide sensitive systems with a dedicated (isolated) computing environment. The risk assessment will identify those systems that are sufficiently sensitive to need isolation so that the risk of unauthorized access (either physically, logically or simply through oversight) is limited. This is likely to include all the key servers on the network, the firewall and the anti-malware services. The level of sensitivity may be such that an individual (dedicated) computer is required (i.e. not sharing computers, particularly for server applications) or that resources are only shared with trusted applications systems. In Chapter 4, the concept of owners of data assets was discussed; sensitive systems will have owners, and these people must be responsible for drawing up and agreeing with line management and the information security adviser a statement as to the sensitivity of the system (with an explanation of its importance in risk assessment terms) and, where it is to run in a shared environment (e.g. a server room), this person should agree which application systems it will share resources with, and identify and formally accept the risks involved. System documentation for such a system must be secured in the same way as the system.

Mobile computing and teleworking

The objective of control 11.7 of the standard is to ensure information security when mobile or when working remotely. The protection required should, of course, be proportional to the risks identified (through a risk assessment). Many of the issues related to both mobile working and teleworking have been touched on elsewhere in this manual. These include issues around information classification (Chapter 8), equipment security (Chapter 11), virus control (Chapter 13) and access control (Chapter 18). The two sub-clauses deal, respectively, with mobile computing and teleworking.

Mobile computing

Control A.11.7.1 of the standard requires the organization to have in place a formal policy and appropriate controls to protect against the risks of working with mobile computing facilities, particularly in unprotected locations. Any organization that operates a mobile computer network should take specific steps to protect itself. If it also has teleworkers, this policy for mobile computers should be integrated with that for the teleworkers. The first step is to design and adopt, within the ISMS, a mobile computing policy, which must be accepted in writing by those who wish to use mobile facilities before they are allowed to. The sensible organization will also ensure that users receive appropriate training before they are issued with mobile computing equipment (notebooks, PDAs, cell phones).

This policy should consolidate all the procedures discussed elsewhere in this manual in respect of mobile computing and handheld usage (see Chapters 10, 11 and 13–20). It should set out clearly the requirements for physical protection, access controls, cryptography, back-ups and malware protection. It should include clear guidance on how to connect to the organizational network and how mobile tools should be used in public places. "Public places" includes meeting rooms outside the organization's own secure premises and wherever notebooks and handhelds remain tempting targets for thieves, who can have as much impact on the availability of data as a particularly virulent virus. Guidance on where mobile tools may be used, and for which purposes, must also be provided, with due consideration to who may be able to see or hear what is being "processed."

The organization will need to develop an effective method of ensuring that anti-malware protection is completely up to date on mobile computers; this is best done by using an automatic update service that updates all computers the moment that they log on to the organizational network. It is important that the mobile user is not given any authority to override this update and is not able to proceed until the update is complete. This principle should extend to ensuring that the software is fully patched, with all service packs installed; it is not unknown for someone whose primary use of a laptop is for e-mail to avoid actually logging on to the system for months on end, with the consequence that many patches and service packs are not installed.

Where remote users access organizational facilities, strong authentication should be used (see Chapter 18), which makes use of strong protocols. Consideration should be given to authenticating the machine as well as the user to provide for the situation where a notebook has been stolen and the user authentication information compromised. The situations where this will be necessary should be identified through the risk assessment.

Back-up procedures (using the Windows briefcase facility, floppy disks, CD ROMs or web-based data back-up services, for instance) are very important; unlike the requirement that should be in place for computers on a fixed network (no data stored on the C: drive), mobile computers will usually have all their data stored on the C: drive. The requirement for regular individual back-ups, together with a workstation configuration that automatically backs up the "My Documents" folder to the main server when a laptop is logged on to the network (over an appropriate connection), combined with a requirement that any physical back-up media are appropriately protected from theft, loss or degradation (issue protective, lockable boxes), is essential. Physical security (ensuring that unattended notebooks are locked away and/or fitted with security locks and that notebooks with sensitive information are never left unattended) is an equally important component of an effective mobile computing policy. Given the ridiculously high number of laptops and PDAs that are lost, stolen or otherwise go missing every year, organizations need to develop specific reporting and recovery procedures based on a risk assessment that includes any legal or insurance issues that may be relevant to the organization. Users should be physically trained in how to do these and should demonstrate that they know how to before they are released into the world with a notebook or handheld.

The proliferation of wireless networks, wireless networking facilities and public wireless access spots brings a new dimension to mobile computing security. The fact that an individual can access a public wireless network (from, for instance, an airport lounge or a coffee shop) is both extremely convenient and potentially very dangerous. It can be more dangerous than accessing the internet through a fixed link, in that a wireless computer is broadcasting information to the wireless access point—and, therefore, all that information is available to anyone who is interested in it.

The most widely deployed security standard deployed on laptop computers is WEP (Wired Equivalent Privacy). It does not give the privacy of a wired equivalent; it is insecure, and there are a number of websites that provide information on its inadequacies and how to attack WEP, to decrypt current traffic, to inject new unauthorized traffic or, ultimately, to access the laptop itself. The default configuration for laptops is that WEP is switched off. There was a discussion, in Chapter 19, on securing wireless networks. This section is concerned with securing laptops that may use public access points to access corporate networks.

It is essential, before any laptops are issued to mobile users, that the organization carry out a risk assessment, and deploy those technological controls that are most likely to minimize the threat to the organization arising from wireless vulnerabilities.

Increasingly, cell phones and PDAs are falling within the category of information processing devices that this section is designed to address and they should therefore, as previously indicated, also be subject to appropriate controls determined as the result of a risk assessment.

Teleworking

Control A.11.7.2 of the standard requires the organization to develop policies, operational plans and procedures to authorize and control teleworking activities. Where the organization has both teleworkers and mobile workers, the two policies should be integrated. Teleworking has become, increasingly, an extension of mobile working, rather than being simply one or a few workers based outside the organizational perimeter and accessing the network from time to time. The only significant difference between the two is that teleworking involves a fixed base and fixed connection to the organizational network; more information and more extensive facilities tend to exist in the teleworking location. The location itself, usually an employee's home, does not have anything like the physical security that might be available in the workplace and is also vulnerable to domestic thieves.

There are particular controls that should be considered for teleworkers, and these should reflect a risk assessment and be incorporated into a formal policy within the ISMS. The teleworker should be required to sign a suitably modified version of the access agreement discussed in Chapter 18. A NIST publication, *Security for Telecommuting and Broadband Communications*, SP 800-44, available from the NIST website (http://www.nist.gov), is designed to help system administrators and users tackle the information security issues around these areas. There are also issues of health and safety that will need to be considered, but these are outside the scope of this manual.

The risk assessment should consider specific issues in relation to the site. Where the organization has a substantial number of teleworkers (e.g. staff working from home, either permanently or infrequently but regularly) it might consider a standardized form of risk assessment that looks for exceptions to minimum requirements, which can be carried out at a distance and depends on employee information for completion. This input should be subject to random physical checks. If the system is too complex and time-consuming to set up, the benefits to be gained from teleworking will be outweighed by the work it requires to set someone up.

A key issue to consider, for teleworkers, is the physical security of the site. The organization should look at the physical security of the proposed building (usually a house) and also take into account the security of the surrounding area. The teleworking environment within the building should also be considered: is it a separate office or is it in a communal area? The communications requirement should be assessed; this should take into account the information classification, the underlying linking technology and the sensitivity of the system to which it links. Lastly, the threat of unauthorized access to the facilities (including from family and friends) should also be assessed.

There are a number of controls that might be considered and that should be included in the teleworking policy. As with the mobile working policy, teleworkers should not be authorized to commence activity until they are satisfactorily trained. The controls should include provision, by the organization, of suitable and adequate equipment and appropriate furniture that makes storage and proper usage possible. Consideration should be given to printers, files, peripheral drives and safety equipment such as anti-glare screens, wrist rests, etc., as might be available in the workplace. Full-size screens, keyboards and mice might also be appropriate.

The permitted work should be defined, including the hours of work and the classification of information that may be held at, or accessed from, the location. The organizational systems and services that the user is authorized to access should also be described. Appropriate communication equipment should be provided (internal modem, ISDN, ADSL, etc., depending on communication needs, available technology and the cost–benefit analysis), and how secure remote access is ensured must also be decided. Physical security, how the equipment is to be protected against breakage and theft, is as important as the establishment of appropriate insurance cover for it (it should not be left to the employee to organize cover under a household policy, as this will usually not be applicable). There should be rules about what access families and friends can have to the facilities and to the equipment. Critically, this must take into account any other devices that may run on a home network and any wireless devices or wireless networking. Appropriate steps should be taken to provide hardware and software support and maintenance; most usually, this includes an extended service from the organizational helpdesk, whose hours will need to be extended to cover home working and whose skills will need to encompass their peculiar problems.

There are specific issues that will need to be addressed if the teleworker is going to use privately owned equipment. One such issue could be that of ownership of business ideas or intellectual property developed on privately owned equipment either during or after working hours, and this issue should be addressed (depending on the risk assessment) with the help of the organization's professional advisers; appropriate clauses, which should also cover dispute resolution, should be inserted into the teleworker's access agreement. Other issues specific to privately owned equipment include the need for the organization to access the equipment (either to check security or as part of an investigation); software licensing agreements consequent upon the deployment to a private machine of organization-specific software; and requirements about the level of firewall and anti-malware protection. Like the IP issue, these should all be addressed in the light of a risk assessment and with professional advice that informs the teleworker's access agreement.

There should be clear rules about back-up, anti-malware and continuity plans, with appropriate resources provided to make this as easy as possible. It should be borne in mind that the risks to the organization are greater in relation to individual teleworkers than in relation to individual users on the organizational network. Teleworkers should certainly be subject to audit and monitoring just as for any other person attaching to the network, and there should also be a documented process for revoking general or specific teleworking authorities and to ensure that equipment is all returned.

22

Systems acquisition, development and maintenance

Control A.12 of the standard is there to ensure that security is built into information systems as an integral part. "Systems," in this context, include infrastructure, external systems, commercial off-the-shelf (COTS) packages, operating systems, business applications and user-developed systems. How the business process that will support the application or service is designed and implemented will critically affect its security. Therefore, security requirements should be identified at the requirements gathering stage of the project and justified, documented and built into the system from the outset. This is an area in which the organization is likely to need specialist advice, unless it already has the expertise in-house.

Security requirements analysis and specification

Control A.12.1.1 of the standard requires the organization to specify, in the business requirement document for a new system, or that for an enhancement to an existing system, the requirement for controls. Security vulnerabilities should be recognized from the outset (through a risk assessment) and the security requirements (including the need for fall-back arrangements) should be developed alongside the functional requirements. Any procedures that the organization has for system requirements analysis should include reference to security analysis to ensure that it is tackled from the outset, rather than as an add-on. Controls identified and implemented at the outset are much less expensive to implement and maintain and often more effective than ones developed and implemented later.

These specifications should consider automated controls to be included in the system and should also consider the need for any supporting manual controls. Similar considerations should apply when considering third party software applications. As usual, the controls implemented should reflect the business value of the information being protected.

It might be appropriate for the organization to adopt a policy that it will only use third party products that have been independently assessed and certified and that meet minimum security standards. Certainly, there should be a formal process for testing COTS products, and contracts should only be finalized once they can include appropriate requirements for addressing any security issues that have been identified. Where the supplier cannot meet the requirement, alternative controls should be considered such that the organization's risk treatment plan criteria can be met. If a product provides unwanted security features, they should either be disabled or incorporated into the existing framework if there is a way in which this can cost-effectively enhance organizational information security.

Correct processing in applications

Control A.12.2 of the standard aims to prevent errors, loss, unauthorized modification or misuse of information and user data in application systems. These systems tend to be, but are not limited to, those used for batch processing of substantial quantities of data and might include user-developed applications in, for instance, MS Access. As ISO/IEC 17799 says, appropriate controls and audit trails should be designed into applications, including user-developed ones. Additional controls may be required in systems that process, or have a link to systems that process, confidential information as defined by the organization's information classification system. Risk assessments will define the need for these controls. There are four sub-clauses.

Input data validation

Control A.12.2.1 of the standard requires the organization to validate data input to application systems to ensure that the data are correct and appropriate. This is a control that may only be applicable, in whole or in part, to a limited number of organizations. Application systems are vulnerable to the accidental or deliberate input of incorrect or corrupt data and this can lead to system failure, fraud or corruption of existing data. Transaction inputs in particular should be validated, and ISO/IEC 17799 recommends a number of controls (likely to be manual, but also possibly automated, particularly as these can reduce the risk of errors and prevent attacks such as buffer overflow and/or overrun attacks) for consideration, depending on the outcome of a risk assessment. These controls apply to data such as customer names and addresses, credit limits and reference numbers, as well as to parameter tables, such as prices, currency conversion rates and tax rates:

∎ ISO/IEC 17799 says that the organization should (preferably automatically) check for:

— out-of-range values;
— invalid characters;
— missing or incomplete data;
— exceeding upper or lower limits on data volumes;
— unauthorized or inconsistent use of control data.

∎ The content of key fields and data files should be periodically reviewed to confirm their validity and integrity.
∎ Hard-copy input documents should be inspected for unauthorized changes to input data.
∎ There should be a simple procedure for responding to validation errors that is understood by all parties involved.
∎ There should be simple procedures for spot-testing the plausibility of input data.
∎ All people involved in the input process should have clearly defined responsibilities.

■ There might also need to be a log that records the activities of people involved in data input.

Control of internal processing

Control A.12.2.2 of the standard requires the organization to incorporate validation checks into its systems in order to detect corruption (deliberate or accidental) of the data processed. Risk assessments should identify potential problem areas or vulnerabilities in application systems where data within it could be compromised by a faulty program or by a deliberate programming change. Subsequent use of the data will lead to loss of integrity, or opportunities for fraudulent misuse may be exposed. Therefore, there need to be control checks built into applications at key points to ensure that data are, to that point, correct.

ISO/IEC 17799 recommends consideration of the following areas of risk:

■ use and location within applications of add, modify and delete functions to change data;
■ procedures to prevent programs running in the wrong order or after failure of prior processing;
■ protection against buffer overflow/overrun attacks;
■ use of correct programs to recover from failure.

ISO/IEC 17799 then recommends that the following controls (exercised through a checklist) be considered:

■ session or batch controls;
■ balancing controls;
■ validation of system-generated data;
■ integrity and authenticity checks on downloaded or uploaded data;
■ hash totals of records and files;
■ checks that application programs are run as planned and at planned times;
■ checks that programs are run in the correct order and at the correct terminal and that, where problems are identified, activity is suspended;
■ logging the activities involved.

All of these recommendations should be considered; they are particularly important for organizations that process substantial volumes of data and where the risk assessment has identified these as areas requiring intervention.

Even in organizations that process small volumes of data, these specific control objectives should be pursued.

Message integrity

Control A.12.2.3 of the standard requires the organization to use message authentication for applications where there is a security requirement to protect the integrity of the message content. While expert advice on message authentication should be obtained, the principle is that there should be evidence that information within an electronic message is from the identified person and has not been changed. There is a substantial discussion of cryptographic controls in Chapter 23 that is relevant here as well.

There should be a risk assessment that identifies specifically the vulnerabilities and risks in transaction systems (e.g. instructions to transfer money or other assets, contract agreements, etc.) and the controls required. Many financial institutions have their own control and authentication systems for customers to use for sensitive online messages, and the organization should assess the adequacy of these and, if they meet the control requirements, should use them.

Output data validation

Control A.12.2.4 of the standard requires the organization to validate data output from an application system to ensure that the processing of stored information is correct and appropriate to the circumstances. This is because, even with all the input and process validation controls, output data might still be wrong, contain errors or otherwise be corrupt. There should, therefore, be clearly defined responsibilities for everyone involved in the data output process as well as a log of activities and a procedure for responding to validation tests failed. Output validation might, according to ISO/IEC 17799, include plausibility checks and reconciliation control counts to ensure that all data were processed, etc.

23

Cryptographic controls

E-commerce was considered in Chapter 16. This chapter sets out solutions to a number of the problems identified there. Control A.12.3 of the standard has, as its objective, protecting the confidentiality, authenticity and integrity of information. It requires, at A.12.3.1, the organization to develop and follow a policy on the use of cryptographic controls for the protection of information. As ISO/IEC 17799 quite rightly says, any decision as to whether or not a cryptographic solution is appropriate should be part of the wider process of assessing risks and selecting controls. A risk assessment should determine the necessary level of protection to be given to information, and a cost–benefit exercise should be carried out. This risk assessment should also address issues such as unauthorized circulation of encryption keys; it might be appropriate for the organization to retain copies of all employee encryption keys against the danger of their being lost or of a disgruntled employee first encrypting critical information and then destroying the key or removing it and holding the organization to ransom.

If the risk assessment indicates that cryptographic controls are appropriate, the organization needs to develop a policy statement within its ISMS that sets out how it intends to deal with this issue. The basic principles that the organization is going to apply need to be implemented across the whole organization. The policy statement should include a description of the management approach and general principles under which information should be protected (refer to Chapter 8). These should include:

- The circumstances under which business information should be protected, why this might be necessary (i.e. the risks that are being addressed) in relation to the sensitivity of particular types of information and the means by which they are being transported (whether wireless, mobile device, removable media, etc.), and how the appropriate level of cryptographic protection is determined (assuming that the individual operator has any discretion in the issue).
- The required level of protection (and this should be reflected through a documented risk assessment), taking into account the type, strength and quality of the encryption algorithm that is being deployed.
- How encryption keys should be managed and how to deal with lost, compromised or damaged keys, responsibilities, standards, etc.
- Roles and responsibilities in regard to implementation of the policy and generating and managing keys.
- Where more than one cryptographic standard is to be deployed, the policy should identify which standard applies to which process and information classification so that there is no room for error or uncertainty.
- The policy should be communicated to all users before any use of these controls commences.
- Consideration must be given to any legislation or regulation that may cover the use of encryption, such as the Encryption Export Control Regulations, which is briefly discussed in Chapter 27.

Encryption

Encryption enables the organization to protect the confidentiality of sensitive or critical information. There are two types of encryption: symmetric encryption, which uses the same key (or code) to encrypt and decrypt data, and asymmetric encryption, which uses one key to encrypt information and a completely different (but mathematically related) key to decrypt it.

Symmetric encryption

Data Encryption Standard (DES) is a widely used symmetric encryption standard. It is used for long communications and is relatively speedy to use. It is, however, quite an old system and this has led to triple DES, in which the same data are encrypted three times, employing different keys, which exponentially increases the strength of the encryption. Only the creator and receiver have the DES key (or keys); the key(s) are usually exchanged using either a shared master key or a pre-existing key exchange protocol.

Asymmetric, or public key, encryption

Under this methodology, an organization has two keys, one private and one public. Anyone can use the public key to encrypt a message for the organization, knowing that only the possessor of the private key will be able to decrypt it. Equally, anything that decrypts properly using the public key must have been encrypted using the complementary private key. A critical issue in public key cryptography is to attest the validity of the key pair and, in particular, that the named public key really is the organization's public key. This is done with a digital certificate (sometimes called a server ID). A digital certificate is an encrypted file that attests to the authenticity of the owner; it is created by a trusted third party known as a certificate authority (CA). A certificate authority will review the credentials of any organization that wants a digital certificate before issuing it. This review will include the Dun & Bradstreet number or Articles of Incorporation and a thorough background check to ensure that the organization is who it claims to be. Applications can usually be done online, via the CA's website, and the verification process will typically take between one and three days. The digital certificate is proven to be authentic because it decrypts correctly using the public key of the CA. The CA may be a secure server on the network (the single trust model) or an external organization recognized by many (the multi-party trust model). The keys used are either 40-bit or 128-bit.

Public key infrastructure (PKI)

Vendors of public key technology are working to create an industry standard implementation that standardizes certificate types as well as the principles used for recognizing and managing a CA, the trusted party that issues certificates to identified and known third parties. Critical issues in the development of PKI include directory services for locating certificates for particular individuals, and means of effectively communicating revocation of certificates, particularly when an organization ceases to trade and its certificate and technology are acquired by a less scrupulous operator than the one that originally obtained the certificate.

The organization should, again, use a risk assessment to determine whether or not encryption is a key component of its ISMS. The two areas for which encryption should be considered are the protection of sensitive information on notebook computers and the protection of information being sent across public networks. Only the most sensitive of information (depending on its classification) traveling on public networks should need to be encrypted, and such a policy should only be adopted if all components of it can be fully implemented. Dangers include employees losing keys (which would render useless, and potentially irretrievable, anything encrypted with it).

If the outcome of the risk assessment is that encryption is an appropriate protection, then specialist advice should be sought in selecting an appropriate technology and in considering any legal implications that there might be in using encryption, or cryptographic technology. A well-known supplier of certificate authority services is Verisign (http://www.verisign.com). Most large, specialist security organizations could provide specialist advice on cryptography. This advice should reflect the latest situation in terms of any government restrictions on the use of cryptographic technology and the countries in which it can, and cannot, be used.

Digital signatures

Digital signatures can be applied to protect the authenticity and integrity of electronic information. Digital signatures can be applied to any form of electronic document, such as electronic payments, funds transfers, contracts and agreements. Symmetric cryptography systems do not support the enhanced proof of data integrity that is required for a digital signature. The public key methodology is ideal for this; a digital signature is used to assure both sender and receiver that a sensitive document originated as represented and that it was not tampered with since origination.

This is done by using a one-way hash function to transform a document into a unique, fixed-length character string (or digest), which is included with the transmitted and encrypted document. Any changes that are made to the original document will change the digest and, when the receiver runs the hash function on the received file, it will not duplicate the digest. Digital signatures are therefore strong proof that a file is genuine and in its original form and, therefore, digital signatures have a role to play in non-repudiation.

However, organizations should also take legal advice on the status of digital signatures within the jurisdiction that they will want to uphold the underlying agreement. Not all countries have the same level of recognition of digital signatures and, therefore, additional agreements may be necessary between organizations that set out clearly the basis on which they will use and recognize digital signatures. This means that organizations should consider the cost–benefit equation in respect of using digital signatures and should not embark on this course lightly.

Clearly, the confidentiality of the private key has to be protected, and the organization needs to address this specifically so that it can ensure that only authorized personnel have access to it and that records are maintained of its use. The public key should logically be protected by using one of the recognized certificate authorities.

Non-repudiation services

Non-repudiation services can resolve disputes about the occurrence or the non-occurrence of an event or action. While someone could, for instance, copy an e-mail to him- or herself or retain a copy in his or her outbox, to provide some proof of both origin and dispatch, this is not foolproof. A proof of receipt e-mail (which can be set up in the sending person's instance of Outlook) from the receiver's e-mail server is also not ironclad.

The discussion, above, of public key infrastructure dealt with the services offered by certificate authorities. Such trusted organizations can provide evidence of origin, submission and receipt that are ironclad. They do this by applying digital certificates to e-documents. Proof of origin, for instance, is provided by the CA attaching its digital signature, encrypted with its private key, to the communication that is to be authenticated, and this attests to the authenticity of both the document and its creator. Proof of receipt is provided by a digitally signed document sent via the CA stating that it has been received.

Once the organization has chosen, and been accepted by, a CA, there should be a contract in place with the CA that specifies the service to be provided, all in accordance with the ISMS requirements set out in Chapter 7.

These contracts should cover issues of liability, reliability of services and response times for the provision of services.

Key management

Control A.12.3.2 of the standard requires the organization to set out, in its ISMS, an encryption key management system that is based on an agreed set of standards, procedures and methods that support the use of cryptographic techniques. As ISO/IEC 17799 points out, any compromise or loss of a cryptographic key can lead to compromise of confidentiality, integrity or availability of information. Clearly, therefore, the organization needs to put in place a management system that reflects the risk assessment and is appropriate for the cryptographic technique that it uses. There are, as explained above, two types of encryption, and the organization may use one or both of them.

A symmetric encryption technique will require the organization to keep secret its key, as anyone who obtains the key will be able to decrypt any information encrypted with it. The private key for an asymmetric system must also be kept secret, for the same reason, although the public key is obviously intended to be accessed by the public. All keys, both secret and public, should be protected against unauthorized modification or destruction. Physical protection (see Chapter 10) should be considered for any equipment used to generate or store cryptographic keys.

The ISMS should set out how these keys are to be managed. Technical input into this section of the ISMS should be provided by the information security adviser or the supplier of the cryptographic tools selected by the organization. ISO/IEC 17799 sets out a number of issues that it recommends should be considered for inclusion in a procedure for private or secret key management. The questions that should be answered as part of a risk assessment process are:

- How are keys to be generated for different cryptographic systems and different applications?
- How are public key certificates to be generated and obtained?
- How should keys be distributed to intended users and how should they be activated?
- How should keys be stored, and how should authorized users access them?

- How should keys be changed or updated and when? (For preference, keys should have defined activation and deactivation dates so that the risk of compromise is reduced.)
- How should compromised keys be handled?
- How should keys be revoked, withdrawn or deactivated and when? (For example, when a key user leaves the organization.)
- How should keys that have been lost or corrupted be recovered (so that encrypted information can be retrieved)?
- How should keys be archived (because information encrypted with them may need again to be decrypted with them)?
- How should keys be destroyed, if at all, and when and on what authorization?
- How should key-related activity be logged, monitored and audited?
- How should legal requests for access to cryptographically encoded material be handled? (The unencrypted version of currently encrypted information might, for instance, be required as evidence in a court case!)

Public keys also have to be protected. Unless a public key certificate is used, there is always the danger that someone might forge a digital signature by replacing an organization's public key. The only really reliable way to produce such a public key certificate is to use a recognized certification authority.

24

Security in development and support processes

This chapter deals with two sets of controls: security of system files (A.12.4) and security in development and support processes (A.12.5). The objective of the former is to ensure that IT projects and support activities are conducted in a secure manner (and without exposing sensitive data in a test environment), while the objective of the latter is to maintain the security of application system software and information. There is no deep, structural relationship between these two controls.

System files

Control of operational software

Control A.12.4.1 of the standard requires the organization to apply controls to the implementation of software in operational systems. This is an obvious need; organizations are vulnerable where unauthorized software is installed or updated and the result could be loss of data or loss of integrity. Major new software packages should only be rolled out after they have been extensively tested against predetermined criteria, which should be identified by means of a risk assessment. It is usually sensible to have planned fall-backs in place, including extensive copies of data, for roll-outs that affect the most critical of the organization's functions. Beware "big bang" roll-outs where a whole new system is rolled out and goes live without having been extensively tested and stress-tested.

This book is written primarily for systems based on the Microsoft software suite and, therefore, the best practice contained within ISO/IEC 17799 regarding the deployment of software developed in-house will not be discussed here, other than to observe that it would be worth referring to ISO/IEC 17799 if operational programs are to be developed or deployed.

Vendor-supplied software, such as that found on many organizational systems, should be maintained at the level supported by its supplier. This means that the organization should track upgrades and, as soon as it is satisfied that the upgrade is secure, should implement it. Patches and hot fixes should be applied as they become available, unless there is significant reason not to do so. This can be established by reference to a vendor's website and to any of the regular information sources identified in Chapter 4. Suppliers should only be given physical or logical access to the software installed on the organization's systems with prior approval from the line manager and, possibly, the information security manager as well. The supplier's activities should be monitored. The organization must also decide who is to be responsible for ensuring that systems are updated, and this responsibility should be documented in line with the principles laid down in Chapter 4.

The organization should also ensure that all new software products (including upgrades) are obtained against an authorized and clearly identified business need and that adequate copies of the software licenses are obtained for the actual number of users (ensuring that the right distinction is made between "concurrent user" and "per seat" licensing regimes).

Protection of system test data

Control A.12.4.2 of the standard requires the organization to protect and control test data. As ISO/IEC 17799 makes clear, this is a control that applies primarily to the development of operational programs. However, even the roll-out of "off-the-shelf" software packages should only be done after extensive testing that they are correctly configured, and this might involve using test data. If personal data are to be used, then their use will be subject to personal privacy legislation. Such data should be depersonalized. If real operational data are to be used (and this is the most realistic form of testing) then there are potential vulnerabilities that ISO/IEC 17799 recommends should be recognized in a risk assessment and protected by the introduction of appropriate controls. These should include an authorization process, a process for ensuring that operational data are deleted from the test system after use, and an audit trail of all related activity.

Access control to program source code

Control A.12.4.3 of the standard requires the organization to maintain a strict control over access to program source code and associated items, usually kept in program source libraries. ISO/IEC 17799 sets out very clearly the steps that an organization ought to take to protect its program source library. It is not directly relevant to a system that runs COTS or pre-packaged software and, therefore, is receiving no further discussion here. The statement of applicability can afford to make this, or a similar comment, against this control in the documentation. Where program source codes and associated items do exist, access to them should be controlled in line with ISO/IEC 17799:2005, 12.4.3.

Development and support processes

Change control procedures

Control A.12.5.1 of the standard requires the organization to control strictly the implementation of changes by the use of formal change control procedures to minimize the potential of corrupting information systems. All changes to systems, even properly authorized ones, can damage the system, with resulting loss of integrity, availability and confidentiality. Application and operational change procedures should be integrated, for the sake of simplicity. There are a number of items that ISO/IEC 17799 recommends ought to be considered for inclusion in this procedure, which might use a standard form with space for ticking boxes or inserting additional information as necessary. Where an organization already has a formal project management procedure (e.g. based around PRINCE 2), the requirements below are likely already to be included:

■ There should be a central record of approved authorization levels, which is kept up to date for leavers and joiners, or changes to authority levels.

■ Proposals for changes to systems should only be submitted through a centralized scheme by authorized users of the systems, and there should be an audit trail of change requests, indicating what decision was made for each, and why.

■ Existing controls and procedures should be regularly reviewed to ensure that they will not be compromised by the proposed changes.

■ All computer software, hardware, information assets and database entries that may need to be changed as a result of the change should be identified.

■ There should be formal approval of the change before work begins, and this approval should probably be from a line manager, to evidence that there is a business need for it, and from the information security adviser, to evidence that all the security issues have been risk-assessed and resolved. There may also need to be technical approval to evidence that the change, or the new software, will run on the existing system and with the other software deployed on the network. Significant changes should be authorized by an entity such as the information security management forum or the IT governance committee.

■ Code changes to sensitive applications should be checked by a second person—this could be required on something as simple as a set of changes to accounting or project codes as well as on more complex applications.

■ The implementation should be carried out in a way and at a time that minimizes business disruption and does not disturb the business processes.

■ System documentation and user procedures should be updated as soon as the change has been implemented, and the completion of this step should be identified on the approval form.

■ There should be some form of version control for all updates (using the vendor numbering system for vendor software updates), and this should be logged on a central register.

■ An easy way back to the pre-change status quo (perhaps through the most recent back-ups, or through the existing disaster recovery procedure) should be identified prior to any change being implemented, and a process should be defined to identify and correct any errors, or lost work that may have resulted from a failed change.

Technical review of applications after operating system changes

Control A.12.5.2 of the standard requires the organization to review and test (business-critical) application systems when changes occur. As stated in the section above on change control procedures, technical approval for changes might also be necessary. ISO/IEC 17799 recognizes that this is to ensure that there will be no adverse impacts on system security or operation. Testing of the systems may be necessary to ensure that this is the case. The budget and maintenance plan may need to be amended to take these changes into account, and business continuity plans may also need to be amended.

Restrictions on changes to software packages

Control A.12.5.3 of the standard requires the organization to discourage modifications to COTS software packages and, where these appear absolutely necessary, to control them strictly. It is usually better, and generally more cost-effective, for the organization to change its operating procedures to accommodate the software package than to seek to change the software package to suit its procedures. Software packages are increasingly complex and the skills to modify them are generally native to the vendor. Where, for some business-critical reason, the organization is unable to find any solution other than to try to change a software package, ISO/IEC 17799 recommends that a risk assessment should first be carried out that identifies, amongst other things:

■ what the risk may be of compromising vendor-designed and in-built controls and integrity processes;
■ whether or not the consent of the vendor must be obtained;
■ the possibility of the desired change appearing from the vendor at some point as a standard program update (in which case, membership of a product vendor group and pressure on the vendor may be the best course of action);
■ the problems that there might be around future upgrades and maintenance if the changes go ahead and the vendor will not support the changes.

Where changes do go ahead (after initiating the change management process discussed above), retain a copy of the original, unchanged software; fully test and document the changes, and ensure that they can be reapplied after all future upgrades. Better still, adapt to the software!

Information leakage

Control A.12.5.4 of the standard requires the organization to control and check its purchases, use and modification of software to protect against possible information leakage through covert channels or Trojan code. Almost all vendor software contains covert channels, which are introduced at the time of production; a lot of them are harmless but some are not. Organizations should take current advice on the likelihood of there being covert channels in the software that they are running and the possible vulnerabilities that these might create. On the basis of this advice (and one of the benefits of using common vendor-produced software is that most such covert channels should be identified quite quickly after its release), organizations should decide what action, if any, they want to take in respect of covert channels. Research to identify covert channels in purchased software is likely to be both expensive and time-consuming. It is much better simply to adopt a policy of only buying software from reputable manufacturers, distributed by reputable distributors, that arrives with any seals or other authentication (from, for example, an independent evaluator working to ISO 15408, the standard for IT security technology evaluation) intact and then only allowing reliable staff near it.

Depending on the risk assessment, it may be necessary to implement countermeasures such as scanning outbound media to identify hidden information, masking or encrypting outbound activity to make it difficult for a third party to interpret the information, and regularly monitoring staff activity and the use of system resources to identify suspicious behavior that might identify information leakage.

Trojans are a slightly different matter. There was an initial discussion of them in Chapter 13, which discussed malware and protection against it. Trojans are best protected against by running appropriate anti-malware software programs that have been evaluated as effective against all known Trojans running loose in the wild.

Outsourced software development

Control A.12.5.5 of the standard requires the organization to apply controls that will make outsourced software development secure. Where the organization cannot help itself by using vendor-developed software and must have its own developed, there are a number of controls that ISO/IEC 17799 recommends it should introduce to try to protect itself during a process over which it has little direct control.

The issues that it must consider, only some of which can be incorporated into a contract, and others that will require expert supervision that the organization might not have in-house, are as follows:

- licensing, code ownership and intellectual property rights (and see Chapter 27);
- certification (possibly by a third party) of the quality and accuracy of the work done;
- escrow arrangements (particularly for the source code) in the event of the developer's financial failure;
- rights of access for audit of the quality and accuracy of the work;
- contractual requirements for code quality;
- pre-installation testing for Trojan and other malicious code;
- delivery dates, change management control and budgetary control.

Vulnerability management

Vulnerabilities are exploited by threats. All software has vulnerabilities and, as soon as a new one is identified and announced, there is a race between the criminal community and the software company to respond. The software company needs to patch the vulnerability before the criminals can exploit it. Bugtraq (www.securityfocus.com/archive/1) and CVE (www.cve.mitre.org) are the best places for the criminals to get updates about vulnerabilities. Vulnerabilities are how criminals (hackers, virus writers, malware writers, spammers, spies and others) can get into corporate systems, steal corporate data and disrupt the organization.

Control A.12.6 of the standard is designed to ensure that organizations take adequate steps to prevent damage that could arise from the exploitation of published vulnerabilities. As was discussed in previous chapters, we live and work now in an era where the elapsed time between publication of details about a newly identified vulnerability and the appearance of the first virus or hack to exploit it has reduced to a matter of hours—what are called "zero day" exploits. In this environment, organizations cannot afford to go without a policy and process for the timely, systematic, comprehensive and reliable updating of their systems with all patches and hot fixes issued by the manufacturers.

Of course, the prerequisites for such a process are the asset inventory (discussed in Chapter 8), a timely and reliable information alert system, and the deployment of vulnerability scanning software that has regular updates from Bugtraq and CVE and that can be set to run on a regular basis. It is essential that, when vulnerabilities are detected, the recommended patches are installed as quickly as possible. If there is any question about the order in which vulnerabilities should be addressed, the SANS top 20 can answer it. The asset inventory needs to be complete and current, and needs to include adequate software information: vendor name and contact details; software serial number and version number; details of upgrades, fixes and hot fixes currently installed; and the person responsible for the item.

A four-stage vulnerability management system should be developed. It should ensure that vulnerabilities are identified, that a decision is made as to how to react to that vulnerability, that there is careful testing prior to patching and that actions are tracked so that success (or otherwise) can be monitored. This system should link to any vulnerability scanning software (chosen in the light of a risk assessment):

■ Prioritize high-risk (see Chapter 6) systems.
■ Define roles and responsibilities with respect to vulnerability management, including monitoring and identifying (for all of the software and hardware) the vulnerabilities and release of patches, risk assessment, identifying the urgency with which the patch needs to be deployed, carrying out the actual update (refer to control A.12.5.1) and dealing with any coordination. There should be absolute clarity about accountability, and individual responsibilities should be clearly written into job descriptions.
■ Identify, for each of the software and other technology items, the relevant source of information about vulnerability identification and patch release (usually the vendor website, or through use of an appropriately configured automatic update facility), and this information should be regularly reviewed and, where necessary, updated.
■ Ensure that there are set steps, within a predetermined time line (such time line to be developed in the light of a process-level risk assessment), for identifying the risks of proceeding and of not proceeding with any given patch, for deciding what steps should be taken and for implementing that decision—which should usually be to install the patch unless there are good reasons not to.

- Allow, under certain emergency circumstances, the patch to be installed following the incident response process (see Chapter 25) rather than the change management one; any such decision should be properly tracked and all the records updated appropriately.
- Ensure that, where necessary (the risk assessment process drives this) and prior to implementation, patches are tested and evaluated to ensure that there are no side effects on other systems. This needs to be done in a proper test environment, which is running a duplicate of the systems for which the patch is being tested.
- Allow, in circumstances where a patch for an identified vulnerability is not yet available or the side effects of implementing it are not acceptable, the organization to adopt alternative controls, such as turning off services that are affected by it, modifying firewalls or other access controls, increasing user awareness to detect and respond to attacks or increased monitoring of activity to identify an attack on the vulnerability.
- Ensure that there is always an audit log of activity in relation to vulnerability management.
- Provide for regular monitoring and review of the vulnerability management process, not just through the internal audit function to ensure that it is working according to specification but also by the information security adviser to ensure that the specification remains adequate in the light of the organization's evolving risk assessment and risk treatment plan, in the changing security environment.

25

Monitoring and information security incident management

ISO/IEC 17799:2005 consolidated all the different monitoring and logging activities into a new control objective (A.10.10, Monitoring) and did the same with all the information security incident reporting and management issues (new clause A.13) and, in doing so, ensured that the importance of these two areas (which are linked) was highlighted.

Monitoring

Control A.10.10 of the standard has, as its objective, the detection of unauthorized activities. Monitoring will detect deviations from the controls adopted, including the access control policy, preventing repetitive abuse; monitorable events should be recorded to provide future evidence in dealing with security events. Such an approach allows the organization to check the effectiveness of its controls. The clause has six sub-clauses.

Audit logging

Control A.10.10.1 of the standard requires the organization to produce, and keep for an agreed period, audit logs, which record exceptions and other security-related events, to assist in future investigations and access control monitoring. Audit trails are essential when investigating what has gone wrong. They help establish events leading up to an incident as well as in determining indisputably the accountability for the event.

An event logging policy should therefore be determined by an appropriate management level, probably proposed by the information security adviser and agreed by the management information security forum. Extensive and detailed logs (which many systems, including Microsoft ones, can produce) may provide more information than is useful, as it can be difficult to analyze a mass of data when looking for possible misuse. The policy should, therefore, reflect how this is to be tailored to the needs of the organization and should reflect both best practice guidance contained on the Microsoft security website (www.microsoft.com/security) and that available through CERT (www.cert.org) and NIST (www.nist.org).

As a minimum, audit logs should contain user IDs, dates and times of log-on and log-off, terminal identity or location, details of attempted and successful and/or rejected access attempts to systems, data or applications, changes to system configurations, use of privileges, system utilities and applications, detail of files and networks accessed and any alarms triggered and details of either activation or deactivation of protection systems such as anti-malware software. Logs should be kept for a specified period, in case they are needed for an investigation. While this period may depend on the volume of data, it is likely that a minimum period of one year would be appropriate. Access to the logs should obviously be protected, both logically and physically, from unauthorized access designed to cover up unauthorized activity. It is not self-evident that these logs should be kept by IT staff; it is more appropriate for them to be collected and retained by the organization's internal audit function. It should certainly not be possible for IT administrators to erase or deactivate logs of their own activity, and the organization should take specific steps to ensure that administrator access rights and privileges are constructed so as to exclude this capability.

Monitoring system use

Control A.10.10.2 of the standard requires the organization to establish procedures for monitoring the use of information processing facilities and to review regularly the results of this monitoring. This is necessary to ensure that users are only performing the activities they are authorized for and is part of the "prevention is better than cure" approach to information security. Ensure that this monitoring is carried out in line with relevant state and federal legislation and, just as sensibly, that provision was made in the internet acceptable use policy (see Chapter 17) for staff agreement for this to happen. ISO/IEC 17799 recommends that a risk assessment should be used to determine the appropriate level of monitoring for individual facilities and event logging should be automated. The items that should be monitored include details of authorized access, including details such as user IDs, dates and times of key events and their natures, the files accessed and the programs or utilities used. All privileged operations (see Chapter 18) should be monitored, including the use of supervisor accounts, systems start-up and stop and the attachment or detachment of input or output devices. All unauthorized access attempts should be logged, as should access policy violations and any notifications to network gateways/firewalls and any alerts from intrusion detection systems. System alerts or failures such as console or workstation alerts or messages, system log exceptions and network management alarms should also be tracked. The audit functions in Windows should be used to carry out this monitoring and configured to reflect the risk assessment and in the light of advice on configuration both from independent experts and in documentation drawn from organizations such as CERT (www.cert.org).

The result of the monitoring should be reviewed regularly, and the frequency of the monitoring should depend on the risks identified. The factors that will affect it include the criticality of the applications, the classification of the information involved, past experience of system abuse and the extent of system interconnection (particularly to the internet).

Protection of log information

At control A.10.10.3, the standard requires all the carefully collected log information to be protected against unauthorized tampering and access of any sort. It will be critical, in any court case, that the organization be able to prove that its log information is reliable, and this can only be achieved if it is appropriately protected from the outset. Similarly, if log information can be altered or deleted, the organization may not get the warning of malicious activity that it relies on to trigger security steps. Protection involves ensuring that the log files cannot be edited or deleted, that any alterations to message types are recorded and that log file storage capacity is never exceeded, as this might trigger either overwriting of past events or a failure to record new events.

One of the biggest issues with audit logs is that they contain a massive amount of information, most of which is completely innocent because it records all the employees doing what they are supposed to be doing. It may be necessary, therefore (depending on cost–benefit and risk assessments) to have a process for copying specific types of information to a second log, which because it would be smaller would be more easily searchable. Even in this case, the original log needs to be retained for as long as is specified in the organization's data retention policy and may require a technological solution such as a data vault.

Administrator and operator logs

Control A.10.10.4 of the standard requires system administrator and operational staff to maintain a log of their activities. In most organizations, this requirement applies to those staff responsible for the network system resources. ISO/IEC 17799 recommends that their logs, which are usually kept in the server room and are in paper format (preferably not loose-leaf, as this makes it easy for pages to "get lost"), should include:

- system or event start and finish times and who was involved;
- event information (files handled, processes involved);
- system errors (what, date, time) and corrective action taken;
- back-up timing, details of exchange of back-up tapes, handling of any other critical media;
- the name of the person making the log entry.

These records should be checked by the organization's internal audit function against the ISMS to ensure that procedures are being properly followed. Such checks can identify errors that one might not consider possible, such as the insurance company that backed up its main client-data holding server on to a head cleaning cassette for in excess of three weeks. The problem was quickly rectified once identified but, if it hadn't been, it could, under certain circumstances, have had massive consequences.

An intrusion detection system could be deployed (or an existing one configured) to monitor the system and network administration activities of system and network administrators. Obviously, it would need to be deployed and monitored by someone other than the administrators and it certainly has a cost of ownership and operation that should be assessed as part of the risk assessment that decides whether or not this is a cost-effective control.

Fault logging

Control A.10.10.5 of the standard requires faults to be logged and analyzed and corrective action to be taken. These faults should be logged, and the most effective and practical way to handle this, for networks of any size (but there may need to be a cost–benefit analysis for the organization to ensure that this is appropriate), is to install some form of helpdesk software. These packages log details of all user reports, and track action taken to deal with and close them out.

The ISMS should have clear procedures for how faults should be dealt with, setting out who is to take what action in respect of which faults and the time period within which the issue is to be resolved. The same sort of detailed operating standards would appear in a third party contract that specified the level of service that the third party was to provide.

Fault logs should be reviewed on a regular basis to ensure that faults have been satisfactorily resolved. The regularity will depend on the size of the network and the number of faults reported. In some organizations it might be appropriate to review the log on a daily basis, while in others weekly might be enough. Independent checks should be made to ensure that the resolution was satisfactory for the user and that the recorded details are correct. This review should also ensure that any corrective action has not compromised other controls and that any steps were fully authorized.

In the longer term, the analysis of such logs can be used to identify trends that indicate skill or competence shortfalls in staff or fault trends in particular equipment.

Clock synchronization

Control A.10.10.6 of the standard requires the organization to synchronize its computer clocks for accurate recording. This is important because it ensures the accuracy—across all the organization's systems—of audit logs, which may be needed for incident investigation. Microsoft systems can operate real-time clocks, and the time should be set, on all computers within the domain, to a standard laid down in the ISMS, such as Universal Coordinated Time (UCT) or a local standard time, such as PST or GMT. As electronic clocks can drift, there should be a procedure for checking on a regular basis and correcting any variations. Radio receivers that can provide a computer with the atomic clock signal might be considered as a labor-saving approach, as these can maintain temporal accuracy to the second. A risk assessment might be necessary to ensure that these do not also provide unguarded routes into the network.

Of course, it is also important that the ISMS lay down a standard date/time format and that this is implemented rigorously across the network. Local variations, such as daylight saving or cross-time-line networks, should also be taken into account, and internal audit should, on a regular basis, carry out spot checks to ensure that the policy is systematically applied.

A failure at this level could hamper event investigation, invalidate disciplinary action and fatally undermine court actions.

Information security events

Section 13 of the standard is new; it deals with information security incident management and makes an important distinction between an event and an incident. An event is not necessarily an incident, whereas an incident will always be an event. In other words, there are a number of events that, either because they are expected or unexpected, might not compromise the integrity, availability or confidentiality of the organization's information. Events are reported; incidents are managed—which means that there has to be a decision, for each event, as to whether or not it is an incident. The control objective is to ensure that events that relate to or might compromise information security, or weaknesses associated with the information systems, are communicated in a way that ensures timely corrective action. The key management perspective is that, however good the ISMS, there will be information security events. They may be accidental, or they may be deliberate; a deliberate breach may be malicious or simply for the entertainment of a hacker. What matters is that the organization has in place a tested and thorough method for responding to the inevitable. Only in this way can the organization ensure the availability and integrity of its data.

Reporting information security events

Control A.13.1.1 of the standard requires the organization to establish a procedure that ensures that information security events are reported to management as quickly as possible. This procedure should be integrated with the incident response and escalation procedure so that an effective overall process is established. The event reporting procedure should start by referring to every employee's (and third party's) responsibility in respect of information security within the organization, as identified in their contracts of employment or other service contract. The organization should, from the outset, develop a "no blame" reporting culture. This will encourage staff to report security events no matter the cause or who might be at fault. This is important, because the organization should want to ensure that appropriate staff are aware of events that might point to vulnerabilities that are widespread or critical and that need to be formally addressed. The vulnerability might be a result of weaknesses in training, or management, or system design, or anything—but, if they are kept hidden, they cannot be tackled.

Security events fall, broadly, into four categories: 1) security breach (e.g. non-compliance with policies or guidelines, uncontrolled system changes, access violations, breaches of physical security arrangements); 2) threat (e.g. a member of staff identified as a hacker); 3) weakness (e.g. inadequate firewall control or spam filtering); and 4) malfunction (e.g. loss of service, equipment or facilities, system malfunctions or overloads, human errors, malfunctions of software or hardware). An organization might provide a covert duress alarm in high-risk environments (e.g. bank counters), the use of which indicates that the staff member is operating under duress. The procedure should set out clearly what the required response to such an alarm call is, and should ensure that anyone working in the exposed, "high-risk" environment has appropriate training.

As information security is a fast-changing environment, in which new threats emerge daily, it would be dangerous for a reporting procedure to be limited to specifically defined events. Every employee or contractor should be trained to be on the lookout for suspicious events that, in their opinion, might affect information security, and to report them as soon as possible. The reporting procedure can provide non-exclusive examples of events that might fall into each category.

In general, the reporting procedure should be quick and have redundancy built in. It should also allow for perceived emergency issues to receive more immediate attention. There should be some form of escalation procedure. While ISO/IEC 17799 recommends that there should be a single point of contact for reporting all security events, we believe that this is usually inadequate. All incidents should be reported to at least two people, who should both be required to take appropriate action.

The procedure might, therefore, require all incidents to be reported to the immediate line manager (or for third party contractors the contractually identified organizational contact) or, in his or her absence, his or her deputy. It should simultaneously be reported directly to the information security adviser, who should have a widely advertised mobile telephone number reserved specifically for receiving these reports. Both of these people should be required to take immediate, appropriate action (within the limits of their training and proven competence) to deal with the issue and to communicate with one another as soon as possible thereafter to coordinate their actions. This structure would allow a line manager to pull someone off a particular task while the information security adviser arranges to isolate an apparently infected workstation or take more significant action in the event of a larger-scale attack.

Reporting should be by e-mail (unless for a suspected malware incident) and either by telephone or in person. The benefit of e-mail is that it provides evidence, later, of precisely when the event was reported and, from the employee's point of view, it proves that the report was made immediately. If, however, the employee's workstation is malfunctioning, reporting this fact electronically may not necessarily be wise! The organization's information security adviser has to decide how this circumstance is to be dealt with and incorporate, in the light of his or her risk assessment, appropriate instructions into the reporting procedure.

The time within which a response to an event is required should be clearly stated in the policy, in respect of each type of event. The procedure should require that the person who notified the event is told of the outcome within this period or, if there is to be a later investigation, within a specified period after its completion. There should be an escalation procedure, so that the employee knows who else to report the event to if there is not an appropriate response within the defined period. Every organization will want to tackle escalation differently and in line with other escalation procedures and its existing culture. This is appropriate; the faster that the ISMS can be integrated into existing behaviors, the faster it will be effective.

The event reporting procedure should also set out what steps are to be taken in response to the event and the time-frames within which they should be taken. The information security adviser should be asked to draft the event response procedure, creating an event report document that will be used to describe the event (and which contains a checklist that ensures all the critical information—date, time, what happened, screen messages, who did what, key strokes, etc.—about the event is collected), as well as who reported it and when, and that sets out the action required to deal with it and the time-frame within which it needs to be taken. It should be clear to all employees (and third parties) that they are not to take any action on their own to deal with the event, and the procedure should remind everyone of the disciplinary process that will apply in the event of breaches of the ISMS.

The procedure should differentiate between standard responses (such as invoking a standard control specified in the ISMS in response to a related breach) and flexible, or discretionary, responses (dealing with an event, or a variation on an event, that has not previously occurred). It is important that this distinction is made, and that the procedure does not try to set out standardized responses to weaknesses or threats that it has not experienced before. The danger of such an approach is that the response will be inadequate or inappropriate. It is better to employ an information security adviser who has the skills and competence to evolve a new and appropriate response to a new threat; this characteristic was discussed in Chapter 4.

Certainly, the procedure should require that, for serious incidents, the information security adviser reports it to his or her superiors within a specified time period. On major issues (that, for instance, require the business continuity plan to be invoked or the computer infrastructure to be shut down) senior management and, almost certainly, the chief executive of the organization should be consulted.

Of course, as the organization accumulates experience of security events and improves its procedures as a result of controlling its response to them, so a bank of material that the organization can use in future training is built up.

Reporting software malfunctions

This control (A.13.1.1) of the standard includes a requirement to report software malfunctions. Apparent software malfunctions are concerns for two reasons. The first is that they affect the ability of one (and potentially more than one) user to use the organization's information processing facilities. The second is that the apparent software malfunction might be some form of infection that could not only destroy data, and thereafter the integrity of information, on the user's workstation but also, if not properly controlled, spread to other workstations on the organizational network.

The event reporting procedure should, therefore, incorporate the following steps:

1. Users should, for a start, have been trained that any unexpected or unusual behavior on the workstation is possibly a software malfunction.
2. Users should be required to note the symptoms and, if possible, any messages appearing on the screen.
3. Users should, if possible, immediately disconnect the workstation from the network and stop using it. The contacts identified in the event reporting procedure should immediately be notified.
4. The information security adviser should supervise the recovery of the workstation, and the work should be done by adequately trained and experienced staff. The workstation should not be re-powered while connected to the organizational network, and any diskettes in it should not be transferred to other computers until the incident has been completed and the diskettes cleared of carrying some form of malware.

Clearly, this type of incident cannot be reported using e-mail, as the procedure requires the workstation to be disconnected as quickly as possible from the network to avoid a possible problem spreading across the network. An alternative reporting methodology needs to be available. This can be by telephone; the person reporting the incident should be working with the same event reporting form as the person who experienced it; the objective is to ensure that as much as possible is gathered of that information essential to deal with the event.

Reporting security weaknesses

Control A.13.1.2 of the standard requires users of the organization's information systems to note and report any observed or suspected security weaknesses in systems or services. Where weaknesses are reported directly to a service provider (which may be how the service contract is set up) they should also be reported internally. The service provider's response should be monitored and the effectiveness of its action to repair the weakness should be noted. This information has value in monitoring the overall contractual performance of the service provider; there is also the possibility that, if a weakness is not dealt with quickly, the organization might be exposed, and therefore it is essential that progress in dealing with it is monitored.

The response to a reported weakness should, just as for security breaches, differentiate between those for which there is a standard response and those for which a non-standard but appropriate response will have to be determined. Most weaknesses will require a specific step, or series of steps, to be taken to deal with them. For non-standard weaknesses, the event reporting form should be signed off and dated by the security adviser once the required steps have been taken and the tests that demonstrate their effectiveness completed. For standard events, a sample can be signed off once the information security adviser is confident, on the basis of systematic sampling, that the events are being appropriately dealt with. Over time, and on the basis of satisfactory sampling, the level and frequency of sampling can be decreased. The forms should, clearly, all be numbered and filed as part of the ISMS records.

Weaknesses should be reported through the same event reporting procedure as deals with events. In other words, the organization should have just one, comprehensive event reporting system that deals with the entire range of possible security events. It is easier for staff to learn to use a single consolidated system than to give them a number of distinctions to make as to the type of event and therefore which system to use before they can make a report. This system should be referenced in employee and third party contracts, as described in Chapters 7 and 9.

The event reporting procedure should clearly state that those uncovering a potential weakness should not, themselves, attempt to prove it. Not only might their own skills be inadequate to do this in a controlled manner, but such an action could (and should) also be treated, by the organization, as a potential misuse of the system and therefore likely to lead to disciplinary action.

Management of information security incidents and improvements

This new control objective was introduced to ensure that the organization has a consistently effective approach to dealing with information security events and weaknesses, particularly those that are identified as "incidents." It also contributes to demonstrating that the requirements of the standard's clauses 7.2 (Corrective action) and 7.3 (Preventative action) have been met, and the procedures discussed below should, therefore, be considered alongside the monitoring, audit and review requirements discussed in Chapter 27. There are three sub-clauses.

Responsibilities and procedures

Control A.13.2.1 requires the organization to establish management responsibilities and appropriate procedures to ensure a "quick, effective and orderly response" to information security events. This forms part of the overall requirement for clear delineation of responsibility and clearly thought-through procedures for dealing with events before they become critical.

The first step is for the information security adviser to decide whether or not the event is an incident and, therefore, what the appropriate response to it might be. Events that are likely to be classified as incidents, and therefore subject to the incident response procedure, include:

- Malware infections (there does need to be a distinction between those carriers that are caught and neutralized at the gateway and those that are successful in infecting a machine).
- Excessive spam.
- Information system failures.
- Denial or loss of service, whether through hacker attacks or through provider action/inaction (a user may not always be able to distinguish between the two and, although the symptoms have different causes, it is worth treating them together). Recovery will involve specific action by the information security and IT staff and may require the use of back-ups, UPSs, and back-up sites and systems.
- Business information errors resulting from errors in input data (incomplete or inaccurate).
- Breaches of confidentiality or integrity.
- Misuse of information systems.

The incident response procedure (which should be a seamless continuation of the information security event reporting procedure and which should dovetail into the non-conformity reporting and review procedures discussed in Chapter 27) should set out how to deal with each of these types of incidents and should include contingency plans that help the organization continue functioning while the incident is being dealt with. It should reflect the organization's risk treatment plan, and the criteria by which incidents are dealt with should be formally approved by the management information security forum. The board may need to sign off on those response criteria that involved a significant period or breadth of outage, or to which there may be significant costs. Contingency plans should, to the greatest extent possible, be tested prior to their being needed. Users should be trained in their use and involved in a regular contingency plan testing program. Findings from this testing program should be incorporated into the next version of each procedure, and all the documentation that describes the planned tests and their outcomes should form part of the ISMS records. The incident management (contingency planning) process should, therefore, encompass:

■ immediately limiting or restricting any further impact of the incident;
■ identification of the incident, and of its seriousness, with any analysis necessary to ascertain its cause(s), including the vulnerabilities it exploited;
■ tactics (which are in line with organizational priorities and affordable) for containing the incident, so that damage does not spread;
■ corrective action, which should only be carried out after appropriate planning (remember the PDCA model) and which should also aim to prevent recurrence;
■ communication, certainly with those affected and with those involved in the corrective action; and
■ reporting the incident internally, almost certainly to the management information security forum (or whatever alternative oversight mechanism the organization has put in place).

The incident identification and corrective action stages of the process should include collection of any evidence that might later be necessary for analyzing how the problem occurred, for deployment as forensic evidence in court (criminal or civil) that might follow or in relation to any regulatory breach that might have occurred, and for support in any compensation negotiations with software or service suppliers. The information security adviser needs to be aware of how to gather and secure evidence that might have a forensic value and, if not, arrangements should be made for a suitably qualified professional to attend an incident management planning and recovery meeting (but see below).

Overall, action to recover from security incidents and to correct system failures should be under formal control:

- Only identified and authorized personnel should have access to affected live systems during the incident management period.
- All emergency actions should be documented in as much detail as is possible at the time—which may require someone to be deputed to work alongside the information security adviser with the sole responsibility of recording decisions and actions as they happen (or, if it can be done only after the event, as soon as possible, while memories are still fresh).
- The escalation procedure needs to be clear, and management should be informed about events in line with a previously agreed set of criteria, so that the most serious events are notified to the board, less serious ones to the management information security forum only, etc. Line managers and appropriate functional managers should receive the reports that the ISMS requires them to receive.
- The overriding objective must be to get business systems back into working order as quickly as possible and to confirm that their integrity has been re-established and that all the necessary controls are working again. As soon as possible after an incident, the information security adviser needs to be in a position to confirm that the integrity of the systems has been restored. This confirmation should be timed, dated and signed, and filed with the incident records in the ISMS documentation.
- Provision must be made for working beyond organizational and national boundaries, as some event security incidents transcend single organizations or countries.

Learning from incidents

This is a major contributor to conforming with clause 7.3, Preventative action, part of the continual improvement process. Control A.13.2.2 of the standard requires the organization to list, quantify and monitor the types, volumes and costs of incidents and malfunctions. This can easily be done by including in the incident response form sections that enable the base information to be gathered at the point of occurrence. It is sensible to use a standardized description for the majority of weaknesses and incidents, but it will not be practically possible to design a standard list until the organization has 12 months or more of practical experience of what sort of incidents occur frequently enough in its own environment for a standard set of terms to be adopted. At the outset, it will be enough to analyze incidents between the categories identified in the standard: incidents, weaknesses and malfunctions.

The information from the incident response forms should be collated on a regular basis and, every six months or at least annually, the information security forum should review the information. The information security management forum should want to see an analysis (monthly, quarterly or annually, depending on a risk assessment) of security incidents so that any trends can be identified, and resources reallocated to minimize appropriately the impact of any future threats. This review should also identify reoccurring or high-impact incidents, or a sequence of low-level incidents, which when considered together might be the symptoms of a much larger or more significant single problem, any of which may point at the need for enhanced measures to limit the frequency, damage or cost of future occurrences. The half-yearly report should also be one of the documents taken into account whenever the security policy and the ISMS themselves are reviewed. Minutes of the forum meeting should set out what decisions, if any, were made in respect of the incidents review.

Collection of evidence

Control A.13.2.3 of the standard requires the organization to ensure that any evidence that it presents in an action (whether civil or criminal) against an individual or an organization conforms to the rules for evidence laid down in either the relevant law or in the rules of the court in the jurisdiction in which the action will be held. This requirement includes compliance with any published standard or code of practice for the production of admissible evidence, such that there is a reasonable prospect that the evidence produced will be both admissible and of an adequate quality.

This requirement is fairly obvious; the organization's lawyers are likely to provide this input at the point that a case is being prepared. At one level, therefore, no further action is needed at this point. At another level, of course, initially sensible systems will make this process that much easier. Such sensible systems will be based on retaining copies of all documents, ensuring that changes take place within a proper change management environment and ensuring that policies and procedures are understood and observed.

It is also important to ensure that the procedure for dealing with security events and incidents includes a section on the gathering and preparation of evidence and that all personnel likely to have roles in investigating such incidents are trained in this aspect. It is not always clear, at the commencement of the investigation of a security incident, whether or not legal action may follow. It is possible, therefore, that without proper procedures vital evidence may initially be lost.

As ISO/IEC 17799 sets out (in clause 13.2.3), the steps that should be included in the investigation procedure are the collection of originals of all relevant documents, including details as to who found it, where and when, with witness details if available, and that these records should then be securely retained so that they can only be accessed by authorized persons and so that there is no tampering with them. Copies of computer media (information on hard disks and on removable media such as CD ROMs and USB sticks) should also be retained, together with copies of access logs and details of any witnesses. Where copies are made of any computer media, there should be a detailed log of the actions taken (what, how, time, etc.), and these actions should be witnessed; one copy of this log and the computer media should be securely stored.

It may even be worth creating an event investigation kit, which would include a digital camera (set so that date and time are printed on the image), resealable and tamper-proof bags, digital recorders, etc. Such a kit should be secured, when not in use, so that it cannot itself be tampered with.

26

Business continuity management

Control A.14 of the standard deals with continuity, with ensuring that the organization is able to survive major disasters, can counteract major disruptions to its activities and can protect critical business processes from the effects of major failures or disasters and ensure their timely resumption. This used to be one of the 10 "key controls" of the original version of BS 7799 and, even though ISO/IEC 17799:2005 weights it more toward information security, it is still critical today. Far too many businesses fail because they didn't have in place properly thought-through and adequately tested disaster recovery procedures. Some 80 percent of organizations that suffer a disaster simply don't recover from it, but rather struggle through and then go out of business within a year or two.

While the five sub-clauses of control A.14 of the standard are more interested in how information security should be included in a business continuity plan, our view is that the reader usually needs to address the whole issue simultaneously. Business continuity can be addressed by contracting with one of the many specialist business continuity vendors to help develop such a process (in which case, you will need to ensure that the information security aspects have been adequately addressed and that specific information protection and recovery components are built into and integral with all other components of the plan), or it can be developed in-house, possibly using an external specialist vendor for testing the plan and for a specialized review of it.

Business continuity management process

Control A.14.1.1 of the standard requires the organization to have in place a managed process for developing and maintaining business continuity throughout the organization, and that addresses the information security requirements of continuity. The information security adviser could take the lead in setting up this process, which should be agreed by the information security management forum. ISO/IEC 17799 recommends that the process should:

■ Ensure that the risks faced by the organization, in terms of their likelihood and potential impact, are understood, and that critical business processes are identified by means of risk assessments and their protection prioritized.

■ Identify all the assets involved in critical business processes (by means of an extension to the asset inventory discussed elsewhere).

■ Understand the range of impacts that interruptions may have on the organization and recognize that small incidents (power failures, virus attacks) may be as significant in terms of data availability, integrity and confidentiality as larger, more dynamic events (fires, bombs, floods).

■ Ensure that adequate financial, organizational, technical and environmental resources are available to address the identified requirements.

■ Ensure the safety of staff and the protection of information systems and organizational assets.

■ Consider the purchase of insurance that covers the risks identified and ensure that premiums are kept up to date.

■ Formulate and agree with line managers, and everyone likely to be affected, a business continuity strategy that is consistent with the organization's documented objectives and strategy. This needs to be no more than a single page that states clearly the overall approach to continuity, the prioritization of processes and the extent of training and review.

- Formulate and document detailed business continuity plans that are consistent with the strategy.
- Ensure that plans are regularly tested, lessons learned and plans updated.
- Ensure that the management of business continuity is as embedded into the organization's processes and culture as is information security generally, and that specific responsibilities for business continuity, and its information security aspects, have been allocated at an adequately high level in the organization.

A number of the steps in this process are discussed in more detail below. The point of this clause is that all these activities need to be integrated into a whole process, so that loopholes do not develop and the planning is coherent and complete.

Business continuity and risk assessment

Control A.14.1.2 of the standard requires the organization to develop its strategy and plans for business continuity (and for information security events that could interrupt critical business processes) on the basis of appropriate risk (probability and impact) assessments. These really require the initial identification of all the events that might interrupt business continuity. There are both major and minor potential interruptions and both should be considered. The major external ones include bombs, terrorist activity, riots, fire and flood. The immediate external environment should also be considered and the possible risks assessed. There are particular locations where some such risks are obvious—the danger, for instance, of a vehicle coming off the road at a sharp bend and going through the wall of the business premises right there—and others where they are not—such as the possibility of the staff member taking the day's takings to the bank being mugged. Every possible external, physical danger, event or occurrence should be listed in a brainstorming session. Then there are the possible system dangers. Malware, hacker activity and power failures are all possible dangers.

Once an exhaustive list has been compiled, a risk assessment should be carried out for each of them and for each of the critical systems and processes (not just the IT ones) within the business and should involve the owners of the processes. The risk assessments should be carried out using the process and documentation that was developed for the ISMS (and discussed in Chapter 6) and should determine the probability and likely impact on the organization of each of these possible interruptions. Impacts should include periods of time potentially out of action, and costs to the business in terms of repairing the loss and in terms of lost business, as well as the other possible damage that such interruptions might cause. Specific consideration should be given to the information aspects and impacts of these interruptions.

Not the least of the risks is the potential of injury or death of customers, suppliers or employees while involved (or not) in organizational activity. There are the potential impacts of unavailability of suppliers, partners or staff (a public transport strike, or a ban on aircraft flights, might have extremely disruptive effects on the organization). The risk assessment should "identify, quantify and prioritize risks against criteria and organizational objectives"; this means, for instance, that the risk assessment should identify the time within which the system has to be back, up and running, if damage is to be limited; it is likely that, for a number of systems, there will be a range of options where, for instance, if the system is up after five minutes the damage will be 5 percent of the total cost of loss, whereas if it is up only after 30 minutes (or three hours, or three days) the damage will be 30 percent of the total.

This type of analysis (which may require expert external guidance and for which there is more information on the website) helps the initial prioritization to be reviewed and contributes to the development of the business continuity strategy. Once the strategy has been developed, it should be signed off by the board, and then work to develop an implementation plan can commence.

Developing and implementing continuity plans

Control A.14.1.3 of the standard requires the organization to develop plans for maintaining and/or restoring business operations—and ensuring availability of information systems at the required level—in a timely manner (i.e. within a specified timescale, which is arrived at as a result of the impact analysis) following an interruption to, or failure of, a critical business process. Individual plans should be written for each of the identified processes and should be written in line with the prioritization that was arrived at following completion of the impact analysis. This, usefully, will give the organization early recovery plans based on its biggest risks and its business objectives, rather than on the interests and skills of an individual manager. All the staff and resources that might be necessary to make a particular emergency plan work should be considered. Plans should be drafted by process or asset owners, in accordance with the planning process, and then submitted to the information security adviser for review.

ISO/IEC 17799 recommends that the business continuity planning process should ensure that:

- There is a clear description of the circumstances in which the procedure is to be carried out.
- There is a clear description of what constitutes the maximum acceptable level of loss of information or services, and this criterion should drive all activity.
- All responsibilities and detailed emergency procedures for all identified interruptions are themselves identified and agreed internally.
- Emergency procedures are implemented quickly enough to allow recovery and restoration of the service within the specified timescale, and these need to allow for any internal or external business dependencies and for external contracts that may be in place. The services or resources— staffing, other resources, external contracts, fall-back arrangements—necessary to return the business, or the information systems, to an acceptable level should all be identified, as should the methods for accessing them.
- Agreed procedures and processes are documented, and those involved in implementing the procedures must be involved in their creation. These plans, which must address organizational vulnerabilities, will themselves be highly sensitive documents and therefore need appropriate protection. Copies of them need to be securely stored in a remote location, beyond the damage perimeter of the site to which they refer. One effective method of doing this is to provide members of the emergency response team with CD ROMs (and adequately powered laptops) that contain the plans.
- Staff are trained in the emergency (both recovery and parallel operational) procedures, as well as in the overall crisis management situation. This training should be in the workplace and should involve carrying out the various actions specified in the emergency procedures until they are adequately memorized.
- Plans are tested and updated—see the discussion on control A.14.1.5 below.
- The owner of the process or system is responsible for updating and maintaining the recovery plan and for ensuring that the central copies, and those stored remotely, are up to date.

Business continuity planning framework

Control A.14.1.4 of the standard requires the organization to maintain a single framework of business continuity plans to ensure that all plans are consistent and that they all address information security requirements adequately, and to identify priorities for testing, maintenance and reassessment. When there are changes to plans (as a result of personnel changes that lead to changes in owners of plans, or people affected by them, or environment, or systems, for instance) or to the assets that they cover (the diamonds come out of the wall safe and go to the bank for safekeeping) or to the environment within which they operate, then these effects could impact other continuity plans. It is therefore necessary to have a framework, particularly within a large organization, to ensure that all the impacts of any changes are carried through all the plans. This framework should be integrated with the organization's overall change management framework.

The basis of this framework can be as simple as a matrix (an extension of the asset inventory) that identifies links between assets, processes, owners and continuity risks, so that, for instance, it is easy to see at a glance all the assets or processes that would be affected by fire, or flood, or to see all the processes owned by particular individuals and the impact on the overall plan of failures in individual plans or failures in the dependencies of individual plans. It should also enable the information security manager (or, in some organizations, the risk manager) to identify critical dependencies, where more than one plan is dependent on a single person or resource whose own failure, therefore, will have significant ramifications for the entire organization.

Each process owner should be responsible for drafting and agreeing with the information security adviser a continuity plan for his or her process. This should include an emergency plan, a fall-back plan and a resumption plan, together with criteria that identify when each is to be invoked and the individuals responsible for each. The owner should also be responsible for maintaining his or her plan. Contractors should be responsible for fall-back arrangements for contracted technical services, although the organization's process owner should be responsible for the emergency plans.

The framework, which should be owned by the information security adviser, should provide for coordination of plans across an organization, setting planning and continuity priorities, and cover individual domain plans, testing and continuous maintenance. It should also, as ISO/IEC 17799 identifies, include:

∎ An escalation procedure, which identifies how to assess the situation, who is to be involved in the decision that an incident is to be escalated and who is told what, when and the criteria that will trigger escalation. This should allow for the possibility that nominated individuals could be absent when a continuity incident occurs and therefore alternatives should be identified. This procedure should ensure that the appropriate level of management is informed within specified timescales of continuity incidents. This clearly means that contact information for all the nominated managers must be available; some managers may also have to provide emergency contact details for holiday or other periods of absence.

∎ An internal mobilization and briefing procedure to ensure that everyone within the organization who has a role to play in dealing with the incident is alerted and appropriately briefed within a specified timescale. This involves the creation of a "calling tree," which identifies how managers should cascade information through the organization by talking to their direct reports who are then responsible for talking to theirs. Key individuals at all levels of the calling tree should have access to the whole tree, so that the cascade briefing can still happen even if some key individuals are not available to play their roles. This calling tree should be documented, contact details should be kept up to date by the HR department, and it should be accessible to staff (particularly any who have critical roles in a disaster) even when the network is out of action.

∎ An external mobilization and briefing procedure should include all third party organizations that may have a role to play in dealing with the disaster, and should include relevant and appropriate press contacts. There should be an appropriately trained media team, capable of handling all media enquiries in relation to this event. It may also be necessary to include contact details for key customers, partners and suppliers, all of whom may need reassurance or other information in the case of disaster. All the public authorities (e.g. ambulance services, fire services, etc.) who may need to be notified or involved in the case of serious interruption or injury or loss of life also need to be included in this calling tree.

∎ The information security adviser should ensure that all individual continuity plans are presented in the same format. This makes it simpler and easier for people to follow in an emergency and for people not familiar with specific plans to understand them quickly. This format should show clearly the conditions under which the plan will be activated, how the situation should be assessed, who else might need to be involved and what type of actions might be required. It should show clearly who is responsible for activating the plan. The size of the potential risk and the impact of time should also be considered.

■ There should be a full range of emergency procedures, including how to deal with attacks on systems, fire, flood or other physical impact on the premises of the organization. There should be emergency evacuation procedures as well as appropriate accident procedures. These should set out precisely what has to be done by whom and should be clearly linked into the calling trees described above.

■ Fall-back procedures should also be planned in advance. For each of the critical systems identified in the business impact analysis, there should be a plan that enables the service to move to and operate from alternative premises within the specified timescale, and that ensures that affected business processes are returned to operation within this timescale. The level of investment in alternative facilities and fall-back services should be driven by the risk analysis and impact assessment; clearly, processes and services that are essential for the survival of the organization need to be made operational extremely quickly. This fall-back planning should also identify minimum staff levels required to operate the fall-back services, and set out how these staff are to get to the fall-back site. Fall-back sites should be subject to their own risk assessment and should provide a level of security appropriate to the classification of the information to be processed there.

■ Each plan should detail any necessary temporary operational procedures that will apply until resumption is complete. These will range from handling incoming telephone calls or customer/staff enquiries through to alternative goods delivery sites.

■ Each plan should contain resumption procedures, setting out how the service is brought back to normal operation. This might include setting down details of suppliers of particular equipment, how it is to be configured and what its dependencies and dependants are. "Normal" needs to be clearly defined (number of transactions, level of configuration, etc.), so that it is possible to establish when it has been achieved.

■ There should be a process for testing plans and for ensuring that lessons learned from tests are built into new versions of the plans. There needs to be a schedule setting out when, and how, the plans are to be tested. This should range from frequent tests for critical components of the plans that have an everyday importance (e.g. fire alarms, UPS tests, etc.) to much less frequent tests for those components of plans that the risk assessment says are much less likely to be required (e.g. fire sprinkler systems). Common components of a number of plans (e.g. emergency evacuation procedures) should also be tested regularly.

■ Staff and key personnel at contractors should all receive training in the continuity plans that will affect them and, in particular, should receive training in recognizing the circumstances in which the plan may need to be invoked and to be aware of what changes in circumstances might affect the smooth operation of the plan when it is invoked and then ensuring that the plan is revised to take these changed circumstances into account. The process by which this training is to take place should be documented and there might even be an internal website where those who have responsibilities under the continuity plans are able to share experience and learning.

■ The responsibilities of all individuals who may have to take specific action as identified in one of the continuity plans need to be specifically documented and added to the person's job description. Alternatives should be identified to deal with holidays and other absences, including unplanned and involuntary ones. The staff exit process should include a step that reviews whether or not there is a continuity plan role and en-sures that the plan and any related calling tree are appropriately updated. Similarly, the new starter process should allow for a continuity plan role to be identified at this stage, and for the plan and calling tree documents to be updated.

■ The critical assets, and their whereabouts (together with any information necessary to access them), need to be documented for each of the components of each plan. Any special operating skill or knowledge that may be required to operate any of these assets also needs to be identified together with provision for its availability.

Testing, maintaining and reassessing business continuity plans

Control A.14.1.5 of the standard requires the organization to test business continuity plans regularly and to carry out regular reviews to ensure that they remain up to date and effective, and that they address the requirements for information security. Untested continuity plans are only slightly more useful than having none at all. The reality is that, when a disaster strikes, people do not have time to search out the last copy of their continuity plan, check to see whether or not it is up to date, work out what they are supposed to do and then do it.

A useful continuity plan is one that clicks into action smoothly and effectively when it is needed. This will only happen if everyone with a role to play in the plan has rehearsed the role one or more times and if the plan is then regularly tested by simulating the circumstances within which it has to work and seeing what happens. It is relatively easy to check whether or not the UPS runs, just as it is easy to confirm that the alarm bell works. There should be regular scheduled tests of such basic infrastructure.

The complex situations are the ones that have more than one variable, and continuity plans, and the simulation of triggering circumstances, need, therefore, to be as realistic as possible. For instance, simply switching off the power to the server room to check that the UPS enables planned close-down of the server systems is not an effective test of the ability of the systems to survive a power failure.

A generalized power failure will affect lighting and air-conditioning systems as well as the power supply to the servers. One needs to be sure that the air-conditioning will start up again after a power failure or else the servers will overheat; and if the power failure happened after hours on a Friday night, the impact on the business of the resulting system crash could be severe, and certainly expensive. A live simulation of such an event would reveal this risk, and would lead to revisions of the continuity plan such that the air-conditioning was set up to restart properly and that an electronic temperature gauge inside the server room was linked to an alert service that could deliver a human intervention before the overheating became extreme.

Continuity plans often fail on being tested, usually because of wrong assumptions about people, hardware, software, the order in which things happen, interdependencies, changes in equipment or personnel, or oversights. Testing is therefore an essential component of the planning process. It is also an essential part of the maintenance process, as the organization needs to be sure that changes to equipment and personnel have been taken into account in revised plans.

There needs to be a detailed testing schedule, which sets out clearly which components of the continuity plan are to be tested when, and who has the responsibility for doing so. Common components of a number of plans, and basic emergency procedures and warning systems, should be tested much more regularly than those that are more complex and less likely to be needed. The risk assessment determines which plans fall into which categories.

Continuity plan tests should be monitored; the expected results of the test should be documented at the time that the testing plan is drawn up, and the actual results should be recorded and compared with the expected ones. Differences should be analyzed and appropriate changes made either to the plan or to the expected results in future. Further testing may then be necessary to ensure that changes to the plan do now produce the expected results.

ISO/IEC 17799 recommends a variety of scenarios to use in testing continuity plans:

- Table-top testing of various scenarios—an imaginary "walk-through" of a continuity plan in a specific set of circumstances, using imaginary events and predicting what is likely to happen on the ground.
- Simulations, which is one of the most important testing approaches, as it also serves to train the people concerned and helps identify other issues that could be critical but that have not been identified through the walk-through test.
- Technical recovery testing is designed to ensure that systems can be recovered efficiently, and this should start with ensuring that the system, or individual elements of it, can be restored from back-up and should then move on to test the restoration of individual servers and then groups of servers and then the whole server room. Weaknesses in any of these areas could be significant, and the processes and staff skill sets are critical. The availability of back-up personnel and third party services, particularly out of hours, should be tested at this time.
- Testing recovery into an alternative site (depending on the recovery strategy of the organization). A prepared alternative site is essential for most organizations, as otherwise fire, flood, or any other major natural disaster may force the organization out of existence. It is important to test the ability to resume service and operations from an alternative site, getting back-up processes working and dealing with all the staff issues that there might be in such an event.
- Supplier facilities and services should be tested to ensure that they will meet their contract commitment. It is particularly important to test those components of their contract that relate to emergency or out-of-hours support as well as to stress-test the services to find out the point at which they might fail.
- Complete rehearsals of dealing with major disasters should be carried out at least annually and perhaps twice a year. These are best handled by using an outside, specialist organization to stage and manage the

rehearsal, which should test all the components of the plan and all parts of the organization. The learning points from such a rehearsal are likely to be numerous and, therefore, the post-test review should be comprehensive and should involve feedback from all the people involved in it.

■ Post-event trauma counseling may be a sensible component for the disaster recovery plan. It should perhaps be available after major rehearsals as well.

Change management is an essential component of maintaining business continuity plans. The organization's change management procedures should be extended to accommodate the needs of the continuity framework. This extension should simply be a requirement that, for all changes in hardware, software and business processes, a check should be made as to the changes necessary in the related continuity plan and these should be carried out. Where the changes are significant (e.g. a complete change of server technology) then it may also be necessary to alter the testing schedule to ensure as early as possible that the revised continuity plan operates as required.

The way in which personnel changes should be fed into the plan was discussed earlier in this chapter. Individual continuity plans, as well as the organization's overall continuity strategy, should be formally reviewed at least once a year and the information security adviser should be able, at this review, to demonstrate that all changes (since the last review) in personnel, addresses, telephone numbers, locations, facilities, resources, legislation, contractors, suppliers, key customers, business processes and, of course, risk and overall business strategy have been taken into account and appropriate changes made.

In the absence of explicit guidance on the development of business continuity plans, it is appropriate to point the reader toward PAS 56, a publicly available specification for business continuity plans, which can be accessed through www.27001.com, which also has links to other useful business continuity planning resources.

27

Compliance

Control A.15 of the standard is intended to ensure that the organization avoids breaches of any criminal or civil law, as well as any statutory, regulatory or contractual obligations, and of any security requirements. It deals with legal requirements, security policy compliance and technical checking and with system audit. It is the last clause of the standard and it has 10 sub-clauses.

The outline of relevant legislation in this, the legal requirements section of this book, is not intended to be authoritative. Current legal advice must be taken from qualified, specialist legal counsel if an organization wants or needs to rely on any matter discussed here. Equally, it should be noted that this section is dealing with current compliance issues for organizations based or operating in or supplying the United States. While there is a brief summary of relevant laws in the EU and the UK, it should be noted that laws are likely to be different in other countries and, therefore, organizations seeking certification that are based elsewhere should take specialist local advice. Organizations based in the United States with operations elsewhere in the world will need to deal with the US requirements as well as those of the countries in which they operate and, again, specialist legal advice should be taken.

Web trading (even for US-domiciled corporations) could potentially take place in a multitude of countries, and the law in this area is constantly changing and developing. Any organization that is trading across the web without limits on who may access its website should take specialist advice to ensure that contractual and trading terms are watertight and that issues of jurisdiction and which law (that of the country in which the server is based, or the organization is based, or the customer is based, or to which delivery is made) will apply to any transaction have been resolved, and to ensure that there is an appropriate acceptance and/or waiver of liability on the entrance to the website.

Identification of applicable legislation

Control A.15.1.1 of the standard requires the organization to define explicitly and document the statutory, regulatory and contractual requirements for each of its information systems, and this documentation should be kept up to date to reflect any relevant changes in the legal environment. The specific controls and individual responsibilities to meet these requirements should be similarly documented and kept up to date. The ISMS should already contain a complete list of all the data assets and processes in the organization, together with ownership details (see Chapter 8). This matrix should be extended so that it identifies, for each of the processes, the compliance requirements. This then enables the necessary controls and individual responsibilities to be identified and added to this matrix.

Of course, in an integrated management system there would be an integrated approach to tracking legal and compliance developments in all the components of the system. Information security, health and safety, environment, quality, human resources, commercial and other issues would all be systematically tracked and appropriate steps taken toward compliance inside the organization.

The legislation that any organization might need to identify could include, but is not necessarily limited to, what we have outlined below.

US legislation

Relevant US legislation and regulation include the Gramm–Leach–Bliley Act (GLBA), dealing with consumer financial data; the Fair Credit Reporting Act

(FRCA), designed to protect people from identify theft; the Health Insurance Portability and Accountability Act (HIPAA), which requires healthcare organizations to protect—and keep up to date—their patients' healthcare records; the SEC's Regulation FD, which bars selective disclosure of material non-public information; the SEC's rule 17 a-4, which requires broker dealers to retain trading records (therefore including e-mails, etc.) for six years; section 404 of Sarbanes–Oxley (the overall importance of which is much greater than this single issue), which requires companies to safeguard (amongst other assets) their information, including e-mails, attachments, etc.; the Californian Senate Bill 1386, which requires notification of breaches of personal data security; and the California Online Privacy Protection Act of 2004 (OPPA), which requires websites serving Californians (irrespective of their geographic or jurisdictional location) to comply with strict privacy guidelines.

HIPAA

HIPAA, passed in 1996, applies to health plans, healthcare clearinghouses and healthcare providers, which are known in the Act as "covered entities." The Act requires healthcare organizations to protect—and keep up to date—their patients' healthcare records (which includes patient account handling, billing and medical records), in order to streamline health industry inefficiencies, reduce paperwork, make the detection and prosecution of fraud easier, and enable workers to change jobs more easily, even if they have pre-existing medical conditions. The information security requirements of the Act are contained in Health Insurance Reform: Security Standards; Final Rule (45 CFR Parts 160, 162 and 164; 20 February 2003). This requires covered entities to "ensure the confidentiality, integrity, and availability of all electronic protected health information they create, receive, maintain, or transmit" (s 164.306(a)(1)); to "protect against any reasonably anticipated threats or hazards to security or integrity of such information" (s 164.306(a)(2)); and to "protect against any reasonably anticipated uses or disclosures of such information that are not permitted" (s 164.306(a)(3)). The compliance date, for all covered entities with the exception of small health plans (which had an extra year), was 20 April 2005.

The Administrative Simplification (AS) Provisions state the specific rules that institutions must implement in order to comply with HIPAA; these include rules for EDI, electronic signatures and standards of privacy. They are intended to be technology-independent, and each institution is expected to deploy the technology it considers appropriate.

GLBA

GLBA, passed in 1999, applies to financial institutions and their service providers. The Financial Information Privacy Protection Act (to give it its full title) covers all US-regulated financial services corporations, and charges their boards with protecting their customers' personal information against any "reasonably foreseeable" threats to its security, confidentiality or integrity. GLBA also applies to a wide range of "non-bank" managers, and the Federal Trade Commission (FTC), which is responsible for enforcing the act, requires compliance with both the letter and the spirit of the Act. GLBA requires management to develop, draft, approve and implement an appropriate information security program as part of their normal accountabilities. The information security requirements of the Act are contained in the Standards for Safeguarding Customer Information: Final Rule (16 CFR Part 314, 23 May 2002) (the rules issued by the other banking agencies are substantively identical). The rules relate to "nonpublic personal information", which consists of "personally identifiable financial information" and includes any information collected through a "cookie." The purpose of GLBA is defined as setting standards for "developing, implementing, and maintaining reasonable administrative, technical and physical safeguards to protect the security, confidentiality and integrity of customer information" (s 314.1(a)).

The GLBA Final Rule is explicit in requiring financial institutions to "identify reasonably foreseeable internal and external risks to the security, confidentiality, and integrity of customer information that could result in the unauthorized disclosure, misuse, alteration, destruction or other compromise of such information"; to consider risks in each area of operations, particularly "information systems, including network and software design, as well as information processing, storage, transmission and disposal" (s 314.4(a)(2)); and to be responsible for "detecting, preventing and responding to attacks, intrusions, or other systems failures" (s 314.4(a)(3)).

The interplay between regulatory regimes is exemplified in the statement that GLBA does not "modify, limit or supersede operation of the FRCA," and does "not pre-empt any state law that provides greater protections." The growing body of state regulations that interact with GLBA include California's Senate Bill 1386 and the Online Privacy Protection Act (OPPA) and, for a growing number of companies, the EU Safe Harbor provisions are also relevant.

The Fair Credit Reporting Act (FRCA)

The FRCA was passed in 1999. It is designed to "promote accuracy and ensure the privacy of the information used in credit reports," applies specifically to consumer reporting agencies (such as credit bureaus) and is enforced by the FTC. It is underpinned by a range of state laws.

The Californian Senate Bill 1386 of 2003

SB 1386 requires any "state agency or entity" holding personal information about customers living in California to divulge (which means press releases, communications to entire classes of customers, etc.) any breaches of security for any databases that hold that personal information (unless the data are encrypted). SB 1386 is being used as the template for similar privacy legislation in other states; the "unauthorized acquisition of computerized data that compromises the security, confidentiality, or integrity of personal information maintained by the person or business" triggers reputational damage for the data holder.

The California Online Privacy Protection Act of 2004 (OPPA)

OPPA requires websites serving Californians (irrespective of a website's geographic or jurisdictional location, or that of the organization owning or operating the website) to comply with strict Californian privacy guidelines, including the conspicuous posting of privacy guidelines that themselves must meet strict requirements. This law goes further than the requirements of GLBA and was amongst the first of a number of similar laws already enacted or still being considered at state level. Penalties and reputational damage follow for organizations that are not compliant and against which a complaint is made, whether officially or by an aggrieved consumer.

Anti-spam legislation

Closely allied to the issues of privacy and data protection is the global challenge of spam. Spam, or unsolicited commercial e-mail, is a threat to the availability of networks and information, because of the extent to which it can clog up the arteries of the internet; it can also—when it is carrying an appropriate payload—be a threat to the confidentiality and integrity of that information. In both these contexts, spam is an information security issue and should be addressed as part of the organization's overall information security strategy.

CAN-SPAM Act

The CAN-SPAM Act (Controlling the Assault of Non-Solicited Pornography and Marketing Act) of 2003 set national standards for the sending of commercial e-mail and requires the FTC to enforce its provisions. This act permits e-mail marketers to send unsolicited commercial e-mail as long as it contains an opt-out mechanism, a functioning return e-mail address, a valid subject line indicating it is an advertisement, and the legitimate physical address of the mailer. The bill includes many other provisions, such as the formation of a national do-not-spam list, and the prohibition of certain e-mail address collection methods. The "do-not-spam" list idea was not a good one.

Many states have also enacted anti-spam laws, some of which prohibit sending unsolicited commercial e-mail to state residents unless they have specifically opted in to receive it.

In January 2005 it was reported that, a year after the CAN-SPAM Act entered into force, some 97 percent of US-originated e-mail was still non-compliant.

Enforcement of legislation has been, in most jurisdictions, both weak and inconsistent. This is partly because enforcement is technologically difficult and partly because so much spam originates in jurisdictions beyond the control of any individual state. However, where authorities and affected organizations determine to take action, they do get results, as actions by various ISPs and by Microsoft, the jailing of a number of spammers, and the April 2005 bankruptcy of the internet's third-biggest spammer all demonstrate.

The real anti-spam action, though, is really being taken by individual organizations. The most effective defenses against spam are at the ISP level, the individual organization's internet gateway, and the individual user's anti-spam filters. These technological defenses—which lead to the creation of "black" and "white" lists of e-mail marketers—are the key barriers now faced by any organization attempting legitimately to use e-mail marketing as part of its marketing mix. And e-mail marketing works, but it only works for reputable companies if they comply with the law and apply best practice. Target customers have to trust you if they are going to put you on their e-mail marketing "white list." These are all good reasons for the ISMS to deal effectively with e-mail marketing in both inbound and outbound terms.

Federal Information Security Management Act (FISMA)

The E-Government Act, signed into law by the president in December 2002, recognized the importance of information security to the economic and national security interests of the United States. Title III of the E-Government Act, entitled the Federal Information Security Management Act (FISMA), requires each federal agency to develop, document and implement an agency-wide program to provide information security for the information and information systems that support the operations and assets of the agency, including those provided or managed by any other agency, contractor or source.

FISMA, along with the Paperwork Reduction Act of 1995 and the Information Technology Management Reform Act of 1996, explicitly emphasizes a risk-based policy for cost-effective security. In support of and reinforcing this legislation, the Office of Management and Budget (OMB) requires executive agencies within the federal government to:

■ plan for security;
■ ensure that appropriate officials are assigned security responsibility;
■ periodically review the security controls in their information systems; and
■ authorize system processing prior to operations and, periodically, thereafter.

FISMA Implementation Project

The FISMA Implementation Project was established in January 2003 to produce several key security standards and guidelines required by the Act. These publications include FIPS 199, FIPS 200 and NIST Special Publications 800-59 and 800-60. Additional security guidance documents are being developed in support of the project, while not specifically identified in FISMA. These include NIST Special Publications 800-37, 800-53 and 800-53A. These, together with other security standards and guidelines produced by the Computer Security Division, can be obtained by visiting the division's Publications page at http://csrc.nist.gov/publications/nistpubs.

PCI Standard

The Payment Card Industry Standard is an example of the type of security requirements that corporations might have to adopt as a result of contractual commitments. The credit card companies Visa and MasterCard collaborated on the development of a security standard that they required all their merchants to accept, implement and provide evidence of successful compliance with. The PCI requirements map to ISO/IEC 17799, and the KnowledgeBank have more information on how this mapping works.

EU regulation

The two most important EU instruments, from the perspective of this clause of the standard, are the EU Data Protection Directive of 1995 (note that, although the United State was declared a "safe harbor" for the purposes of EU data protection regimes in 2000, only a relatively small number of US companies fall within the "safe harbor") and the EU Privacy Directive of 2003. These directives give the context for local legislation in each of the countries of the EU, and for any changes that may occur in future.

The Safe Harbor framework

This allows US corporations that are regulated by the FTC and have operations in the EU to receive European data. They can comply with the EU Data Protection Directive by adopting the seven Safe Harbor Principles (these compliance standards are certified through the Department of Commerce and enforced by the FTC), which are set out on the Department of Commerce and FTC websites, and submitting themselves to Commerce Department certification. Only a small percentage of corporations have met a requirement that enables them to obtain EU member state (one-year, renewable) permission to transfer data out of the EU.

UK legislation

In the UK, Intellectual Property Rights (IPR), through the Copyright, Designs and Patents Act 1988 (CDPA), is one of the most obvious legal issues for most information processing systems, but there is a web of other, relevant legislation. One of the most important of these is the Data Protection Act 1998 (DPA) and, in addition to this, there is the Human Rights Act 1998 (HRA), the Regulation of Investigatory Powers Act 2000 (RIPA), the Computer Misuse Act 1990, the Electronic Communications Act 2000 and the Privacy and Electronic Communications Regulations 2003. The Freedom of Information Act (FOIA) was passed in 2000 and, while primarily applicable to public bodies, it has the potential to force confidential commercial information about (for instance) public sector contracts into the public arena.

In the UK there is a complex array of anti-money laundering laws including the Terrorism Act 2000, the Proceeds of Crime Act 2002 and the Money Laundering Regulations 2003. Detailed client verification records will need to be maintained and kept secure.

Intellectual property rights (IPR)

Control A.15.1.2 of the standard requires the organization to implement appropriate procedures to ensure compliance with legal restrictions on the use of material to which IPR might apply and on the use of proprietary software products.

Organizations deal with all sorts of third party material, some of which may contain IPR, in the form of copyright, design rights or trademarks. These are complex areas of the law; the lay reader could begin an appreciation of the complexities of the subject by reference to the FAQs available from the United States Copyright Office (www.copyright.gov) and the US Patent and Trademark Office (www.uspto.gov). Specialist legal advice should also be taken in drafting an appropriate set of procedures to deal with these issues, in each organization's specific operational context.

Copyright infringement can lead to legal action, even involving criminal proceedings, if there has been a clear breach of copyright legislation. Organizations should, therefore, adopt appropriate controls to avoid this happening. There are, broadly speaking, two controls that might be adopted. The first is educational, ensuring that everyone in the organization understands the issues and takes action to avoid copyright infringement. Such an approach would require everyone to understand where the boundary between legal and illegal copying lies and what the requirements are, for instance, for identifying sources of information contained in new publications.

The second would be simply to ban anyone in the organization from using any material that wasn't developed within the organization. This, while keeping the slate very clean, might be unnecessarily limiting, and the organization has to decide, in the light of a risk assessment, what its best course will be.

Software copyright

A most important issue in dealing with copyright is for the organization to ensure that it is not infringing the copyright of the suppliers of the software that it is using. Any software that is running on the organization's network is potentially subject to copyright restrictions and it is essential that the organization ensures that it has the correct type and number of licenses for this software.

There are two types of user license. The first is known as a "per seat" license; the second is for "concurrent users." Per seat requires there to be a license for every installation, or instance, of the software; typically, Microsoft Office licenses, for instance, are supplied on this basis. Concurrent user allows for a maximum number of simultaneous users and is more normal for shared software, such as some database applications. This enables the client software to be installed on as many machines as is wished, but typically the server software is set so that it will not allow more than the licensed number of users to work simultaneously. Different software packages are licensed on different bases, and the organization needs to be clear how each of its software packages is licensed and that it has paid for the correct number of licenses.

There is also a wide range of "freeware" available on the internet, which is software that can be downloaded subject to specific license terms. This includes plug-ins, such as Real Player, Macromedia Flash, etc. As these usually cannot be downloaded without the user accepting the license conditions, there are not usually any license-tracking issues here, although the organization ought to maintain a register of all such licenses, to ensure that their terms are being complied with.

Organizations need to maintain a register of software licenses, which lists all the licenses that they own, as well as the purchase dates and, where appropriate, the disposal dates. The register should be updated whenever an upgrade is installed; a migration from (say) MS NT4 to MS Windows XP should be clearly noted in the register. Equally, whenever a new PC is purchased, or added to the network, the register should be updated to reflect any additional software purchased or installed, and this requirement should be built into the change management documentation. The licenses that are identified in the register should all be stored with the register and available for an auditor to confirm their existence.

The organization should include, in the access agreement signed by each member of staff before he or she is allowed to access any organizational computer, a statement that only licensed and formally approved software may be used on the organization's computers and that any use of illegally obtained or unlicensed software will lead to disciplinary action. The organization will have to decide how to handle the wide range of freeware that is available across the internet. A risk assessment is the appropriate way to do this; maintaining a ban on the installation of freely downloadable software may not be cost-effective. This risk assessment needs to consider that allowing anyone to download whatever they want may result in non-business-related programs appearing on the network and taking up valuable time, bandwidth and storage capacity. If these programs are then circulated internally by e-mail they could potentially cause a system crash as a result of system overload. This would be a security incident, as data required by the organization to pursue its objectives might become unavailable.

On a regular basis, the network administrator should carry out an audit of the software that is actually installed on the network PCs. This should be conducted at least annually, but experience shows that (particularly in fast-changing or growing networks) this could usefully be done as often as every quarter. These audits can be carried out by centralized network administration software and, while this will deal with permanently connected PCs, it will be necessary to ensure that all notebooks are scanned on a regular basis as well. Records should be kept of these audits, demonstrating that all machines have been audited and showing what action, if any, has been taken to remove illegal software (or acquire additional licenses where necessary) and to deal with offenders.

Finally, organizations need to have an appropriate policy in place to deal with disposal of copyright material, which needs to be done in accordance with the licenses.

Safeguarding of organizational records

Control A.15.1.3 of the standard requires the organization to protect its important records from loss, destruction or falsification. As ISO/IEC 17799 explains, some records must be retained to meet statutory or regulatory requirements, while others may be needed to provide adequate defense against potential civil or criminal action or to prove the financial status of the organization to the range of potential interested parties, including shareholders, tax authorities and auditors, and to meet contractual liabilities. Records do not need to (and should not) be kept forever—this can make it difficult to find what is required as and when it is required.

Therefore, time limits should be set for the retention of individual categories of information. After this time, records should be destroyed—in line with the procedure adopted by the organization to ensure that any confidential information within those records is not inadvertently made public. Some time limits will be set by statute or regulation, and the organization should establish, with its legal advisers, what the current categories of documents and retention requirements are. The requirements of the IRS and all federal and state statutes on corporate document retention should be identified and met. Other categories and retention periods should be set as a result of a risk assessment. Due consideration should be given to the possible degradation of media over time, and any manufacturer's recommendations for storage should, obviously, be followed. There may be implications, in change programs, for data stored on—or only accessible through—media that are being replaced; adequate resources may need to be retained to access this information throughout its designated retention period, and the need for this should be assessed at the outset of any IT change plan.

Where paper archive facilities are to be used, it is important to consider not only the physical security of the premises but also how watertight they are and what their fire defenses are like. Consideration should also be given to what the back-up plan would be in the case of the archive facilities themselves being the subject of destruction. Storage should be carefully planned and carried out; individual cartons or boxes should be clearly marked as to their contents, the owners of the contents, the date of storage and the planned date of destruction. There needs to be an indexing system that enables the storage box for individual documents to be quickly identified and documents retrieved. The retrieval and document return process also needs to be tightly controlled, to ensure that a neat archive system does not break down through use, with documents becoming increasingly difficult to find. Ideally, the organization should appoint someone to be responsible for the maintenance of the archive, and there should be both clearly documented procedures, within the ISMS, about how to use the archive and also a regular audit to ensure that the records are being maintained in accordance with the procedure.

These same principles (retention schedule, data inventory, appropriate protective controls and clear allocation of responsibility) should be applied to information stored digitally or on microfiche and, where organizations have more than one medium for storage, there should be a master index and guidelines for how each type of data should be treated. Where digital data storage vaults are to be deployed, the organization will need to ensure that the technology enables it to meet its data storage responsibilities cost-effectively.

ISO 15489-1 provides further information about managing organizational records and, as it has been referenced by ISO/IEC 27001, it would be worth any organization that has substantial record retention issues at least to be familiar with the guidance of this standard.

Data protection and privacy of personal information

Control A.15.1.4 of the standard requires the organization to develop and implement a data protection and privacy policy, applying controls to protect personal information in accordance with relevant legislation. Within the United States, this primarily means compliance with the applicable parts of legislation such as HIPAA, GLBA, FRCA, OPPA and so on, all of which were outlined at the beginning of this chapter.

Usually, the organization will appoint someone to have direct responsibility for ensuring that the organization complies with the relevant personal privacy legislation. The organization's staff should all be aware of the requirements of the legislation and their personal role in ensuring that the legal requirements are met. The user access statement signed by all staff and other people before they are granted access to organizational information facilities should include the requirement that any proposals to keep personal information in any structured file should be cleared with this executive and maintained in compliance with the organization's procedures.

In particular, organizations should be cognizant of the fact that transferring personal data to countries that are outside the United States does not remove the requirement that the data be collected and maintained in line with the law. This issue is particularly important for organizations "offshoring" any part of their customer support operations, or consolidating in a single location services previously delivered from multiple jurisdictions.

Prevention of misuse of information processing facilities

Control A.15.1.5 of the standard requires management to deter users within the organization from using information processing facilities for unauthorized purposes; in effect, management must specifically authorize the use of information processing facilities and apply controls that prevent the misuse of these facilities.

Specifically, consideration must be given to the non-business use of organizational information processing facilities. It is a premise of a certified ISMS that these facilities should be authorized for business use only and that the organization should employ appropriate monitoring techniques to ensure that this is complied with. While the user access statement, discussed elsewhere, serves the purpose of ensuring that users are made aware of, and sign to agree to, the rules surrounding their use of the organization's information processing facilities, it is also sensible for all computer screens to display appropriate warning messages at log-on. There should be an initial, general statement that the system is a private one, belonging to the named organization, and that unauthorized access is not permitted and action will be taken against transgressors. Any user should be forced to accept this statement as part of the log-on process (see Chapter 20) before proceeding and then, once logged on, should receive a message that sets out specifically which resources he or she is allowed to use.

Regulation of cryptographic controls

Control A.15.1.6 of the standard requires the organization to put in place controls to ensure compliance with any national agreements, laws, regulations or other requirements regarding the access to or use of cryptographic controls. This is because different countries have taken different steps to prevent the misuse of cryptography, including controls over the import and/or export of hardware and software that has cryptographic capabilities, or that could have such capabilities added, and requirements as to ways in which authorities should be able to access information encrypted by particular hardware or software.

Specialist legal advice should be taken to ensure that the organization is complying with the law as it currently stands and, where encrypted information or cryptographic equipment or controls are to be moved to another country, advice about that country should also be taken. As was said in Chapter 23, which dealt with cryptographic controls, it is worth considering, by means of a risk assessment, the costs and benefits of implementing such a security approach.

Compliance with security policies and standards

Control A.15.2 of the standard requires the organization to ensure that its systems comply with its policies and standards and that the security of its information systems is regularly reviewed against the policies and technical standards laid down for them. It has two sub-clauses, one concerned with policy compliance and the other with technical compliance checking.

Compliance with security policy and standards

Control A.15.2.1 of the standard requires the organization's managers to ensure that all security procedures within their areas of responsibility are carried out correctly; the organization also must ensure that all areas within the organization are subject to regular review to ensure that there is compliance with its documented security policies, procedures and standards. Clause 6.4 of ISO/IEC 27001, Internal ISMS audits, sets out the broader requirement, and there should be a written procedure, and an audit plan, that describes how the audit process should be carried out. This will be essentially similar to an ISO 9000 audit plan.

The first requirement is dealt with by including the responsibility for ensuring that security policies are complied with in the job description of all line managers. The real issue is for the organization to ensure that this is actually happening. The only effective way of doing this, as all ISO 9000 organizations know, is through a process of internal quality audits, using appropriately trained staff or external consultants or other services providers. The authors recommend using the organization's own staff for this role as internal auditing provides them with a good developmental opportunity—not only in the direct training in audit skills but in gaining an understanding of how different functions of the organization interact and how their processes work. Auditors' communication skills become highly developed, and their profiles are raised as a consequence of interviewing staff at all levels of the organization.

One or more members of each department throughout the organization should be encouraged to volunteer for basic internal auditor training (which is usually offered by the company that will undertake the ISO/IEC 27001 audit) and should then receive internally whatever additional training they will need. They will not need a significant level of technical skill or competence. They should be able to undertake this audit activity in addition to their normal work, and this responsibility should be added to their existing job descriptions.

Staff cannot carry out audits of their own departments or of areas that are the responsibility of their own line manager; they can carry out audits of other areas within the organization. The organization will need to have in place a method for ensuring that it trains up enough auditors to cover staff turnover, holidays and other absence, planned or unplanned. The information security adviser should plan the audit schedule at least a year ahead, and in conjunction with the existing internal quality department, so as to ensure that all areas are covered at least annually, that activities are coordinated and that there are no clashes or disruptions. A risk assessment might identify some areas as being in need of more frequent audit (the areas where the organization has most risk) and this should also be factored in.

Audits should be documented, with non-conformances identified in writing. Managers are expected to determine the cause of non-compliance, determine appropriate actions to ensure the non-compliance doesn't reoccur, implement the decision and review its effectiveness. These action plans for rectification, together with dates and responsibilities, should be documented, and the information security adviser (or internal quality function) should have a system for ensuring that all due dates are achieved or otherwise followed up as appropriate. All non-conformances, together with action plans and status (i.e. showing which are closed and which not) should be reported to the regular meetings of the management oversight committee (see Chapter 4), together with an analysis of trends or assessment of larger threats that might not be immediately apparent at the individual incident level. These internally identified non-conformances and the results of corrective action should be available to external auditors when they carry out their review of the ISMS.

Sensibly, the non-conformances raised by any external auditor should be integrated into the organization system and receive numbers (usually in addition to the numbers given by the external auditor) that tie them into the existing system for purposes of monitoring and analysis.

Technical compliance checking

Control A.15.2.2 of the standard requires the organization regularly to perform independent checks of its information systems to ensure that they comply with the documented security requirements and that the required hardware and software controls have been correctly implemented and maintained. This applies to network protection hardware and software (firewalls, routers) as well as to network resources (servers, user settings, access policies, etc.). There should be a plan for these checks (which should be repeatable and documented) and they should be carried out as often as a risk assessment indicates is necessary. These checks should be carried out by someone who has the necessary technical skills and certainly not by the organization's own technical staff.

Specialist assistance is required and it can be obtained from any one of the major security organizations. Some checking will have to be done manually, by a trained engineer; other checking can be done using automated software tools whose reports can later be analyzed by a trained engineer. This type of checking includes intrusion or penetration testing of network defenses. ISO/IEC 17799 cautions that penetration testing should be carried out carefully, as it could lead to a system compromise. In practice, penetration testing should not be scheduled until the organization considers that it has implemented the controls identified by its risk assessment and SoA, and planning for the tests should include ensuring that suitable back-up and business continuity arrangements are in place beforehand.

A number of organizations should be approached, with a schedule of the technical checking that will be required, and competitive prices obtained. References should be thoroughly investigated. The contract in place with any organization retained to do this sort of security checking should, of course, conform to the standards discussed in Chapter 7, and there should be particular consideration of how the contractor will be required to report vulnerabilities, so as to ensure that all that are detected are reported.

All non-conformances established under this process should be reported under the non-conformance procedure discussed earlier in this chapter and should be subject to the same level of monitoring, analysis and follow-up as any others.

Information systems audit considerations

Control A.15.3 of the standard requires the organization to maximize the effectiveness of (and to minimize interference from) the audit process by applying effective audit controls and protecting its system audit tools.

Information systems audit controls

Control A.15.3.1 of the standard sets out clearly the requirements for effective management of the audit process, starting with the need for careful and advance planning of audit activity, with the objective of minimizing disruption to business activity while maximizing effectiveness. This is particularly important for the audit of operational systems.

ISO/IEC 17799 suggests that audit requirements should be determined following a risk assessment and should then be agreed with appropriate management. The scope of the individual audits should be predetermined and agreed and all the resources necessary for performing the audits made available in advance. This is particularly important for external technical compliance checks. All audit activities should be monitored and logs retained to provide a trail if necessary, and all audit tasks and responsibilities should be documented within the ISMS and the job descriptions of the individual auditors. Of course, as discussed elsewhere, the person carrying out an audit should be independent of the area being audited.

One issue raised in ISO/IEC 17799 relates to how access to files other than read-only should be allowed; we believe that, while this guidance should be considered, any organization should carry out its own risk assessment as to how it will tackle this specific issue.

Protection of information system audit tools

Control A.15.3.2 of the standard requires the organization to restrict access to its system audit tools to prevent possible misuse or compromise. This applies in particular to software tools used for system checking and to audit files (including log files, etc.). These should be kept in a secure area and only authorized persons (the information security adviser or the internal audit manager) should have access to them. The ISMS procedure dealing with this should identify precisely which documents or other tools should be treated like this and how they should be secured.

The use of software audit tools should be specifically authorized and a record kept of all instances of their use; otherwise a member of staff might use them illicitly to find vulnerabilities in the organization's systems for later exploitation. Risk assessment documentation should be treated as a tool that needs to be kept secure.

ISO/IEC 17799 identifies the possibility that third party auditors might, in the course of their work, be given passwords that will need to be changed immediately their work is completed. Any decision to give passwords to third parties in these circumstances should be appropriately authorized, and there should be a process that ensures (with verification) that they have been changed on completion of the audit.

28

The ISO/IEC 27001 audit

While some, particularly larger, organizations will debate the value of actual ISO/IEC 27001 certification (arguing that what matters is the implementation of an effective ISMS rather than a badge), the purpose of this book is to help those organizations that see the value in certification to be successful in achieving it. The first three chapters explained, clearly, all the benefits that accrue from a successful certification and these will not be rehearsed here.

A certification audit will use negative reporting (i.e. it will identify inadequacies, rather than adequacies) to assess an ISMS to ensure that its documented procedures and processes, the actual activities of the organization and the records of implementation meet the requirements of ISO/IEC 27001:2005 and the declared scope of the system. The outcome of the audit will be a written audit report (usually available at completion of the audit) and a number of non-conformances and observations together with necessary corrective actions and agreed time-frames.

Selection of auditors

Chapter 3 touched on some of the issues that should be taken into account in selecting an ISO/IEC 27001 certification body (also known as a registrar, because it will register that your system complies with the standard). Of course, any organization seeking certification will want to be sure that there is a cultural fit between itself and its supplier of certification services, and there will certainly be all the normal issues of ensuring that there is alignment between the desires of the buyer and the offering, including pricing and service, of the vendor. It is completely appropriate to treat the selection of a certification body with the same professionalism as the selection of any other supplier.

There are two key issues that do need to be taken into account when making this selection: the first is relevant to organizations that already have one or more externally certified management systems in place; and the second applies specifically to organizations tackling ISO/IEC 27001.

It is essential that your ISMS is fully integrated into your organization; it will not work effectively if it is a separate management system and exists outside of and parallel to any other management systems. Logically, this means that the framework, processes and controls of the ISMS must, to the greatest extent possible, be integrated with, for instance, your ISO 9000 quality system; you want one document control system, one set of processes for each part of the organization, etc. Clearly, therefore, assessment of your management systems must also be integrated: you want only one audit, which deals with all the aspects of your management system. It is simply too disruptive of the organization, too costly and too destructive of good business practice to do anything else. You should take this into account when selecting your ISO/IEC 27001 certification body, and ensure that whoever you choose can and does offer an integrated assessment service.

The second issue that you should take into account when selecting your supplier of certification services is their approach to certification itself. An ISMS is fundamentally designed to reflect the organization's assessment of risks in and around information security. In other words, each ISMS will be different. It is important, therefore, that each external assessment of an ISMS takes that difference into account so that the client gets an assessment that **adds value** to its business, rather than one that is merely a mechanical comparison of the ISMS against the requirements of ISO/IEC 27001.

Once a certification body has been selected and terms agreed (using the same basis of contracting as is applied to any other third party supplier, as discussed in Chapter 7), the organization can turn to the actual process of certification. This process will be completely familiar to any organization that has already undergone certification to ISO 9000 or any other management system standard. The certification body will want to go through an initial two-stage process. The first stage will be a pre-certification visit, which enables the auditors who will carry out the actual formal initial visit to become acquainted with the organization, to carry out a document review, to assure themselves that the ISMS is sufficiently well developed to be capable of withstanding a formal audit and to obtain enough information about the organization and the intended scope of the certification to plan their audit effectively. This visit is usually relatively short and, depending on the size of the organization, may require only one or two days to carry out.

Initial visit

The formal audit, known as the initial visit, will take place over a number of days. The audit process involves testing the organization's documented processes (the ISMS) against the requirements of the standard, to confirm that the organization has set out to comply with the standard, and then testing actual compliance by the organization with its ISMS. The audit will follow a preordained plan, and the auditors will have communicated with whoever is their liaison point (usually the head of the quality function) about whom they will wish to interview and in what order they will want to do it. Some negotiation is possible here, but usually over timing and availability rather than subject matter.

The audit will start and finish with a management meeting. The auditors, just like financial ones, will need a separate room for the duration of the audit and appropriate arrangements made for refreshments. Most audits will involve at least two auditors, who may have different areas of expertise. There will be a lead or principal auditor, who will be responsible for the overall progress of the audit. The organization being audited should ensure that its liaison is on hand to support the auditors throughout the process; this might include guiding auditors around the premises, introducing them to those staff next on their list to interview and dealing with queries and issues arising.

At the end of each day, there will usually be a brief, wrap-up meeting at which (usually) any areas of non-conformance with either the standard or the ISMS are identified. This part of the process will, again, be completely familiar to any organization that has gone through an ISO 9000 certification. Non-conformances can be either minor or major; minor ones should be seen as improvement opportunities and major ones could very easily mean the organization is not (at this stage) capable of successful certification. Often, upon identification of a major non-conformance, the auditors will suggest that the audit process be suspended and started afresh once the organization has had time enough to repair this major issue. This can be expensive and time-consuming and have a negative effect on morale and the commitment within the organization to achieving certification.

There are two components to carrying out successful certification audits. The first is the level of preparedness of the organization's ISMS and the second is the way in which the employees of the organization are themselves prepared for the audit.

Preparation for audit

No audit can take place until sufficient time has passed for the organization to demonstrate compliance with both the full PDCA cycle and with clause 7, the requirement for continual improvement. In other words, auditors will be looking for evidence that the ISMS is continuing to improve, not merely that it has been implemented. This means that a period of time will have to elapse between completion of the implementation and commencement of audit. How long will depend on the complexity of the organization and its ISMS but one should assume that there will need to be at least one cycle of internal audits for all of the key processes and arrangements.

The level of preparedness for an audit should then be assessed by carrying out a comprehensive review. The detailed work should be carried out by the information security adviser and by the quality function, and this should all be reviewed by the management information security forum. A comprehensive review could use this manual, starting with Chapter 4, and question the extent to which adequate steps have been taken to implement the various recommendations, particularly the requirement to evidence the PDCA process.

The statement of applicability needs particularly detailed review. It should be possible to identify the extent to which each of the controls identified as necessary has been implemented and, where implementation has been only partial, to determine what steps (and how long they will take) will be necessary to complete its implementation. In particular, all instances in which the organization has chosen not to implement a recommended control should be reviewed in detail, to ensure that this decision was appropriate. Similarly, all instances in which a control has been implemented to a greater or lesser extent than indicated as necessary by a proper risk assessment should be reviewed and either the risk assessment or the level of implementation corrected.

Once a comprehensive review has been completed, and the management steering group is satisfied that the ISMS is complete, complies with the standard and has been adequately implemented (and at least one cycle of internal audits of key areas of the ISMS as identified by the risk assessment also needs to have been completed), then the organization can safely move on to the pre-certification visit by its external auditors.

Preparation of staff within the organization, prior to the audit, as to what they might expect and how to handle auditors, is also a valuable step. Staff should be taught that auditors should be treated with complete honesty and direct answers should always be given, even if this requires admitting to a lack of knowledge or other error. Equally, staff should be trained to answer the question asked by the auditor and not to provide more, or less, information than is required. Auditors will usually ask for an explanation as to how a particular component of the ISMS works and will then want to be shown. This is normal and is how the audit is conducted.

The outcome of the initial visit should, if the organization has diligently followed all the recommendations contained in this manual, be certification of the ISMS to ISO/IEC 27001 and the issue of a certificate setting this out. The certificate should be appropriately displayed, and the organization should start preparing for its first surveillance visit, which will take place about six months later. Any minor non-conformances should be capable of being closed out by mail, and any certificate issued will be dependent on this happening within an agreed timescale.

The certificate will refer to the issue status of the statement of applicability at the time of assessment. Therefore, when supplying a copy of the certificate to clients, stakeholders or other parties, the organization should be prepared to provide a copy of the statement of applicability (whether controlled or otherwise) at the stated issue level. If the statement of applicability has been reissued or amended since the certificate was awarded, the organization will need to be assessed to the new version prior to an updated certificate being issued. How the cost of this process is handled should be part of the contract negotiation in selecting, and subsequently appointing, an appropriate third party accredited certification body.

Useful websites

ISO/IEC 27001:2005 Portal
www.27001.com

IT Governance Ltd (the company)
www.itgovernance.co.uk

Blogspot
http://alancalder.blogspot.com

Governance

(US) Corporate Governance
www.corpgov.net

Internet Watch Foundation
www.iwf.org.uk

National Association of Corporate Directors
www.nacdonline.org

(UK) Office of Government Commerce
www.ogc.gov.uk

Project Management Institute
www.pmi.org

Information security

Anti-phishing Working Group
www.antiphishing.org

Carnegie Mellon Software Engineering Institute Computer Emergency Response Team (CERT) Coordination Center
www.cert.org

Computer Security Institute
www.gocsi.com

Computer Security Resource Clearinghouse (US National Institute of Standards and Technology)
http://csrc.nist.gov

Federal Computer Incident Response Centre
www.fedcirc.gov

Forum of Incident Response and Security Teams
www.first.org

General Accounting Office
www.gao.gov

Information Systems Audit and Control Association
www.isaca.org

Information Systems Security Association
www.issa.org

Institute for Internal Auditors
www.theiia.org

Internet Security Alliance
www.isalliance.org

National Infrastructure Protection Centre
www.nipc.gov

The SANS Institute
www.sans.org

Accounting, finance and economics

Federal Electronic Commerce Program Office
www.egov.gov

General Accounting Office
www.gao.gov

International Federation of Accountants
www.ifac.org

International Organization of Securities Organizations
www.iosco.org

Organization for Economic Development and Cooperation
www.oecd.org

Securities and Exchange Commission
www.sec.gov

Securities Industry Association
www.sia.com

Further reading

The following list of books may be of interest to the business manager who wants a more detailed understanding of specific security issues. This reading list is not designed for an experienced information security adviser, nor is it intended to be a source of detailed technical information. Anyone who requires such information should visit the "computing" shelves of any good bookstore, where there will be an extensive range of detailed, current technical books on anything and everything that may be of interest.

Readers should bear in mind that the nature of security threats and the appropriate responses (particularly those provided by technology) are changing all the time and that any reading list, such as this one, rapidly becomes outdated. The website associated with this book, www.27001.com, is a good starting point when looking for information about current issues.

Allen, Julia (2001) *The CERT Guide to System and Network Security Practices*, Addison-Wesley

Beaver, Kevin (2004) *Hacking for Dummies*, Wiley Publishing

Calder, Alan (2005) *A Business Guide to Information Security*, Kogan Page

Cobb, Chey (2003) *Network Security for Dummies*, Wiley Publishing

Egan, Mark and Mather, Tim (2004) *The Executive Guide to Information Security: Threats, challenges and solutions*, Addison-Wesley Professional

Feinstein, Ken (2004) *Fight Spam, Viruses, Pop-Ups and Spyware*, Osborne/McGraw-Hill

Fulmer, Kenneth (2005) *Business Continuity Planning: A step-by-step guide*, Rothstein Associates

Gallo, Michael and Hancock, Bill (2002) *Networking Explained*, 2nd edn, Digital Press

Hiles, Andrew N (2004) *Enterprise Risk Assessment and Business Impact Analysis: Best practices*, Rothstein Associates

Jolly, Adam (2004) *Handbook of Intellectual Property Management*, Kogan Page

Komar, Brian, Beekelarr, Ronald and Wettern, Joern (2003) *Firewalls for Dummies*, Wiley Publishing

Kovacich, Gerald L (2003) *The Information Systems Security Officer's Guide: Establishing and managing an information protection program*, 2nd edn, Butterworth-Heinemann

Lewis, Barry D and Davis, Peter T (2004) *Wireless Networks for Dummies*, Wiley Publishing

Mitnick, Kevin D and Simon, William L (2005) *The Art of Intrusion: The real stories behind the exploits of hackers, intruders and deceivers*, Hungry Minds

Mitnick, Kevin D, Simon, William L and Wozniak, Steve (2003) *The Art of Deception: Controlling the human element of security*, J Wiley

Paquet, Catherine and Saxe, Warren (2004) *Business Case for Network Security: Advocacy, governance and ROI*, Cisco Press

Patterson, Tom and Blue, Scott Gleeson (2004) *Mapping Security: The corporate security sourcebook for today's global economy*, Addison-Wesley Professional

Peltier, Thomas R (2004) *Information Security Policies and Procedures: A practitioner's reference*, 2nd edn, Auerbach

Peltier, Thomas R (2005) *Information Security Risk Analysis*, 2nd edn, Auerbach

Poole-Robb, Stuart and Bailey, Alan (2003) *Risky Business: Corruption, fraud, terrorism and other threats to global business*, Kogan Page

Schneier, Bruce (2004) *Secrets and Lies: Digital security in a networked world*, Wiley Computer Publishing

Schneier, Bruce and McClure, Nancy (2002) *Security Savvy: A visual guide*, J Wiley

Solomon, Michael G and Chapple, Mike (2005) *Information Security Illuminated* (Jones and Bartlett Illuminated), Jones and Bartlett Publishers

Tipton, Harold S (2003) *Information Security Management Handbook*, 5th edn, Auerbach

Zacker, Craig (2001) *Networking: The complete reference*, Osborne/McGraw-Hill

Index

Further reading from Kogan Page

Dirty Dealing: The Untold Truth about Global Money Laundering, International Crime and Terrorism, Peter Lilley, 2006

A Handbook of Intellectual Property Management: Protecting, Developing and Exploiting Your IP Assets, Adam Jolly and Jeremy Philpott, 2004

IT Governance: A Manager's Guide to Data Security and BS 7799/ ISO 17799, Alan Calder and Steve Watkins, 2005

Managing Business Risk: A Practical Guide to Protecting Your Business, 3rd edn, Jonathan Reuvid, 2006

Risky Business: Corruption, Fraud, Terrorism and Other Threats to Global Business, revised edn, Stuart Poole-Robb and Alan Bailey, 2003

The Secure Online Business Handbook: A Practical Guide to Risk Management and Business Continuity, 4th edn, Jonathan Reuvid, 2006

ALSO AVAILABLE FROM KOGAN PAGE

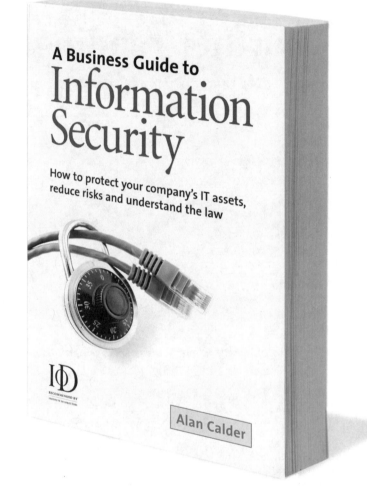

0 7494 4395 2   Paperback   2005

ALSO AVAILABLE FROM KOGAN PAGE

"Unravels the myths, allays our fears, eliminates doubts and helps us to adopt a risk-oriented approach."
Gan Subramaniam, Head of Information Security, Homeloan Management Limited, UK Contributing Editor, Information Systems Control, ISACA, USA

"Alan Calder has written a compelling book. He asks CEOs and other business leaders to make information security and the protection of valuable digital assets an important priority. After reading this book you will be ready to face the challenge."
Kofi Dwinfour, President, EIMG LLC

"An invaluable, if somewhat scary, read... it offers support for how to protect oneself and one's business from corruption, pilferage, abuse or malfeasance."
David Hill, Managing Director, Echelon Learning Ltd

"An ideal starting point for the non-legal manager who wants a broad picture of current compliance requirements."
Mark Turner, Partner, Herbert Smith, UK

"A very enjoyable and informative read."
Wipul Jayawickrama, Infoshield, Australia